W9-CNI-708

Manierre Dawson

AMERICAN PIONEER OF ABSTRACT ART

With essays by
Dr. Henry Adams and
Dr. Randy J. Ploog

October 1–30, 1999

HOLLIS TAGGART GALLERIES

48 East 73rd Street, New York City 10021

Library of Congress Card Catalogue Number: 99-073680

Front cover: *Prognostic* (center panel detail), 1910
Back cover: *Morning Figure* (detail), 1959
Half title: Manierre Dawson, c. 1910
Frontispiece: *Venus and Adonis*, 1912

Copyright © 1999
Hollis Taggart Galleries
48 East 73rd Street, New York, NY 10021
Tel 212 628 4000   Fax 212 717 4119
www.HollisTaggart.com

Reproduction of contents is prohibited.

Publication Coordination: Connie Freeman
Editing: Stephanie Salomon
Design: Russell Hassell, New York
Printing: Capital Offset, Concord, New Hampshire

Photo Credits:
Pls. 1–5, 7–13, 20–26, 28, 30, 33, 35, 39, 41, 42, 45–51, 53–55, 58, 59, 61–63, 65–73, 75: Larry Amato, Creative Photography, Jacksonville, Florida; pl. 6: John Tennant, courtesy of Hirshhorn Museum and Sculpture Garden, Smithsonian Institution; pls. 16 (left), 27, 29, 31, 32, 36–38, 40, 43, 57: Helga Photo Studio, New York; pl. 17: Michael Tropea Photography, Chicago; pl. 44: Lee Stalsworth, courtesy of Hirshhorn Museum and Sculpture Garden, Smithsonian Institution; pl. 60: Furla Photography & Video, Glenview, Illinois; pls. 64 and 74: Gary Andrashko, courtesy of Illinois State Museum.

LENDERS TO THE EXHIBITION

Hirshhorn Museum and Sculpture Garden, Smithsonian Institution

Illinois State Museum

Milwaukee Art Museum

National Museum of American Art, Smithsonian Institution

Norton Museum of Art

Curtis Galleries, Minneapolis, MN

David and Mary Winton Green

Mr. and Mrs. Meyer Potamkin

Anonymous Lenders

Manierre Dawson in his Ludington, Michigan studio (1966). Courtesy of the Peter Lockwood Collection, Arlington, Texas.

CONTENTS

FOREWORD

It has been our personal mission at Hollis Taggart Galleries to contribute to the scholarship and research in American art with the projects we undertake. We believe we have been successfully accomplishing this with many of our past historical exhibitions, and feel particularly proud now, to present the groundbreaking exhibition, *Manierre Dawson: American Pioneer of Abstract Art.*

Manierre Dawson is one of the most fascinating enigmas of American Modernism. Working as an architect in Chicago, the young Dawson, enlivened and inspired by the new tenets on the nature of art, sought to develop a personal artistic vocabulary based upon his own spiritual philosophies. His contributions to the artistic vanguard begin as early as 1910, likely predating the work of Wassily Kandinsky and Arthur Dove, with his extraordinary series of abstract paintings. Theoretically, this makes him the first non-objective painter in American art history. This startling revelation is our statement here, the essence of the exhibition and why we were committed to this project, why we believe it is so important. The pure originality of this painter is intriguing, and it seems fitting that his work be re-evaluated and his place within art history be carefully re-examined. Unfortunately, Dawson's merit and his significant contribution to the American avant-garde movement have been clouded and his story compromised—a situation we hope will be rectified with this exhibition and extensive research.

This retrospective exhibition and accompanying catalogue provide the most comprehensive examination of this artist to date. With the presentation of some of his earliest works, including his masterpiece, the triptych entitled *Prognostic*, and never before exhibited sculpture, combined with the scholarly catalogue essays and the reprinting of the artist's journal, we have sought to give Dawson's work the intense scrutiny it has long deserved and bring recognition to this pioneer of Modernism.

In an attempt to truly champion our cause, we enlisted the assistance of two prominent art historians, Dr. Henry Adams, Curator of American Art at the Cleveland Museum, and Dr. Randy Ploog, Associate Director of the Institute for the Arts and Humanistic Studies at Pennsylvania State University, whose own research has centered on this artist for over a decade. Dr. Adams' essay takes a provocative approach to Dawson's work and poses intriguing thoughts as to how Manierre Dawson fits into the large overview of the evolution of Modernism in America. Similarly, Dr. Ploog's contribution is also invaluable. In the biographical essay in the catalogue he chronicles the artist's life, adding much new information, and also expertly interprets individual works with detailed entries.

With a project of this magnitude, many individuals warrant our gratitude. First and foremost we would like to thank Dr. Lewis Obi and Myra Bairstow, who share our passion for Dawson, and have in essence been co-curators of this exhibition. They have been more than generous, helping us with their personal research gained over many years and their insightful opinions of the artist and his work. They, along with Tim Foley and his preliminary work with the Tilden-Foley gallery, have been indispensable in bringing Dawson's story to the forefront. We would also like to thank Peter Lockwood, Dawson's grandson who graciously allowed us to reprint his grandfather's diary, which has added further to the depth of this investigation, as well as other family members who wish to remain unnamed. For Martin Diamond's assistance in tracking down some elusive details, we are most grateful. Many thanks go to the staff at the gallery as well. Everyone displayed their customary high level of professionalism with all of the many tasks that were required. Special thanks go to Connie Freeman, the project coordinator, and to Gregg Deering, Molly Eppard, Stacey Epstein, Andrew Keim, Debra Pesci and Cynthia Seibels. For her skillful editing of the extensive text of this catalogue, we acknowledge Stephanie Salomon. And for his creativity, continued good humor and beautiful design of this elegant catalogue, we thank Russell Hassell.

Finally, we sincerely thank all of those lenders, both institutions and private collectors who are named in this catalogue or who wish to remain anonymous. Their generous participation has allowed a wide audience the pleasure of viewing these works first hand. We hope that you enjoy the exhibition and the catalogue. Whether it is your introduction to this amazing American Modernist, or whether it gives you an opportunity to revisit Dawson's work and learn more about the artist, we hope you will be as intrigued as we have been with this quiet genius who anticipated so much that was to follow.

Hollis Taggart
Vivian Bullaudy

MANIERRE DAWSON, 1887–1969

HENRY ADAMS

Those pictures chased business out of my head. Tell your reckless brother.
—Carl Sandburg to Manierre Dawson's brother Mitchell, February 21, 1922

The First Abstract Painter

In the early 1960s an elderly fruit farmer from Ludington, Michigan, with the slightly peculiar name Manierre Dawson, came forward with a group of paintings that he maintained had anticipated many of the most significant developments of modern art. The most provocative of these was a group of abstract compositions, said to have been painted in 1910, which, according to Dawson, pre-dated the earliest known previous abstractions, those by Arthur Dove in Westport, Connecticut, and Wassily Kandinsky in Munich. This would make them the first pure abstractions produced by any artist in the world—surely an accomplishment of major significance within the history of modern painting. But a number of other works were unusual and startling as well: a somewhat naive painting of an ash heap that he allegedly had painted three years before the first exhibition of the Ashcan school in 1908; a group of "Cubist" paintings from 1911–14 that strikingly parallel Picasso's work of that time period; and a very curious group of three-dimensional works, often made of materials such as wallboard, laminated wood, and cast concrete, that seemed to reprise much of the history of modern sculpture. Along with the works themselves, Dawson produced letters, exhibition lists, and diaries that supported his claims. This documentation indicated that he had made his first sale to Gertrude Stein, first exhibited in the Armory Show, and showed his work in Milwaukee and elsewhere early in the second decade of the century. Despite his presence on the peripheries of the modernist venture, however, somehow his work had been overlooked—evidently because it was so visually startling, so far in advance of its time, that for decades viewers were simply bewildered by Dawson's achievements. It seemed that he had been just too far ahead of the game to be understood.

By the 1960s, while Dawson's work still could not be described as easy to understand, the nature of what he was attempting was easier to grasp. By that time, however, abstract art had already appeared, and its history had been written without the inclusion of Dawson's achievements. How should one look at an outsider like Manierre Dawson, who had seemingly invented much of modern art but who had had virtually no influence on its development or history?

One would have thought that this unusual body of material might have inspired strong reactions pro or con—that perhaps some advocate would have seized on its seminal importance, while some cynic would have denounced it as a hoax and fraud. But in fact, what actually happened is rather different, no doubt because the art world, rather like a snake, has difficulty digesting anything that is too large. Before his death, Dawson sold paintings to the novelist James Michener, and to Ralph Norton, the founder of the Norton Museum of Art, in West Palm Beach, Florida. He also found an excellent New York dealer, Robert Schoelkopf, to represent his work. Dawson's paintings can now be found in many of America's major museums, including the Museum of Modern Art, New York; the Whitney Museum of American Art; the Brooklyn Museum of Art; the Milwaukee Art Museum; the Art Institute of Chicago; and the National Museum of American Art. Over the years, several institutions, including the Ringling Museum of Art in Sarasota, Florida, the Museum of Contemporary Art in Chicago, and the Whitney Museum in New York, have staged small exhibitions of Dawson's work, and his paintings have made their way into several surveys of American modern art.[1]

Yet despite this sort of recognition, curators, collectors, and art historians seem to feel uncomfortable in coming to an assessment of exactly how Dawson's work was innovative or important. Consequently, while he has quietly become fixed in the history of modern art, he has been put in the wrong place. Recent major studies of the early development of abstract painting do not even mention Dawson.[2] Instead, he has been grouped with early American modernists such as Max Weber (who introduced Americans to Cubism) or William Yarrow (who explored Synchromism).[3] Yet Dawson's work was essentially distinct from that of these figures, who built their achievements from the foundation of existing European styles. Even the most original and influential of American modernist movements, the Synchromism of Morgan Russell and Stanton Macdonald-Wright, was basically synthetic in its approach, retaining the flavor of a student's report from Paris. Dawson on the other hand, at least in his abstract paintings of 1910 (which were produced just before his first trip to Europe), was doing something fundamentally different—inventing something new and previously unimagined. In short, Dawson does not belong in the same category as the American modernists of his generation—he deserves a new rubric. Moreover, while he has sometimes been dismissed as a "minor modernist," surely an artist who has an excellent claim to having produced the world's first abstract painting can hardly be considered a "minor figure" in the usual sense.[4]

The Dawson Documents

As this brief introduction suggests, the telling of Dawson's story presents a difficult challenge, since to interpret it, it is necessary to examine its meaning at different levels. What Dawson made in his art must be set against previous and subsequent accomplishments by other modern painters. To assess the authenticity of his achievements, what he allegedly did must be tested, to the extent possible, against other forms of evidence. To attempt these tasks at once would create confusion, so I will focus first on unfolding Dawson's story and describing the development of his art—sometimes probing into his apparent sources and motives. The question of his truthfulness I will largely hold off to the end—although surely the internal coherence of his account, and the internal logic of his artistic development, provides one of the most significant factors in determining his honesty. Moreover, the very narration of events from Dawson's journal raises questions of context and circumstance that need to be addressed at the start, and lead rather rapidly into a swirl of other questions.

Dawson assembled several documents that provide a trail through his life and work. At the time of his death, he had arranged to keep his work together—some 250 paintings and sculptures. Many of the paintings are dated on the front, and many also carry dates and inscriptions on the back. Along with the works themselves, Dawson left a notebook in which he listed the paintings and sculptures by year, apparently putting the majority of them in their precise chronological sequence. Since this notebook contains little sketches, it offers evidence not only about extant works but sometimes also about those that were sold and can no longer be located. Dawson seems to have been still working on this project until just before he died, and consequently, some paintings or sculptures are difficult to match with titles and some appear to be unlisted. Nevertheless, it is a valuable tool for dating his output and analyzing its stylistic development.

Along with this body of artistic work, Dawson produced an intriguing written document, an intermittent journal that, while it is marked by gaps and is sometimes cursory or cryptic, provides a wealth of evidence about what he was doing and what was thinking about. Finally, Dawson kept a collection of letters, clippings, and catalogues that document his activities. These include letters from Walter Pach, the art impresario; Dudley Crafts Watson, the director of the Milwaukee Art Society; Jerome Blum, a Post-Impressionist painter; and W. C. Wing, the director of the Ludington State Bank. Although these letters mostly date from 1913 or later, they complement perfectly the statements in Dawson's journal, and sometimes contain references to events that happened earlier. (According to Dawson, as described in his journal, an earlier group of documents, including letters from Arthur Davies and Maurice Prendergast, was lost when his father's house was sold and demolished.)

Although his own records offer the most detailed evidence, other sources also shed light on Dawson's work. The first step in exploring these achievements is to weave these disparate materials into a coherent story.

Dawson's Early Life

A product of the nineteenth century, though he lived well into the twentieth, Manierre Dawson was born in windy, sprawling Chicago on December 22, 1887. His unusual first name was taken from his maternal grandfather, Edward Manierre, who had served both as a Chicago alderman and as city treasurer. Hardly more than twenty years before, Chicago had been a desolate marsh on the edge of Lake Michigan, but with the development of railroads, these formerly almost worthless lowlands became prime real estate. Indeed, Chicago soon supplanted the older cities that had been laid out on hills, such as Cincinnati, which for years had been the cultural center of the Midwest. During Dawson's childhood, Chicago amazed the world with its rapid growth.

The artist's father, George Dawson, although born on a farm, earned a law degree, studied in Europe, and learned to speak six languages. For over twenty years he served as a partner in the legal firm of Petrick and Dawson, except for a three-year interruption when he acted as attorney for the Sanitary District of Chicago, and played a major role in developing a forty-mile-long ship canal. In the course of this enterprise he made many contacts with engineers and architects. George Dawson seems to have been a serious man, of generally sober taste, but liked to relax through music. He could sight-read music and often sang to the piano accompaniment of his wife, who had studied music for two years in Vienna. The family also subscribed to both the symphony and opera. Not surprisingly, Manierre Dawson also came to love music, and during the peak of his productivity as a painter noted that attending concerts was the one evening diversion he allowed himself, other than working on his art. Dawson's journal contains numerous reflections on the parallels between painting and music, and music surely served as his principal model for an art form that was abstract and mathematically logical, yet also effective as a form of emotional communication.

Though they lived quietly, the Dawsons had many slightly oblique connections with cultural luminaries. They were good friends of the brother of the famous trial attorney Clarence Darrow. Their acquaintance Kate Kellogg was the sister of the artist Alice Kellogg Tyler, who in turn was an old romantic interest of the well-connected painter Arthur Davies, one of the organizers of the 1913 Armory Show.[5] Dawson worked briefly with Albert Chase McArthur, a protégé of the distinguished architect Frank Lloyd Wright, and, as noted, his father had many contacts with Chicago architectural firms. Dawson's younger brother Mitchell wrote poetry, contributed to Jane Heap's *Little Review*, and got to know the noted poet Carl Sandburg, who in later years sometimes made visits to Dawson's Michigan fruit farm. So, while not exactly at the center of things, the Dawsons were not culturally isolated.

We know very little about Dawson's childhood, although a little book he assembled at the age of seven, containing sketches of unusual animals with their full Latin appellations, shows a precocious maturity of intellectual curiosity and organizational enterprise for a child. He received his only formal artistic training from Miss Katherine Dimock, who taught at Chicago's South Division High School, from which he graduated in the spring of 1905. Around this time a family tragedy occurred that must have had some psychological impact. In 1903, George Dawson had purchased a farm in Ludington, Michigan. Since it was sited on rolling, hilling land, the boys came to call it "The Humps." While the family was staying there in the summer of 1904—the summer before Manierre's last year of high school—Manierre's older brother, George, Jr., drowned while sailing his canoe across Bass Lake. The loss devastated his father. He seems to have transferred his most intense parental aspirations to Manierre—though it was a younger son, Mitchell, who eventually satisfied him best by becoming a lawyer and entering his father's firm.[6]

On graduating from high school, Manierre was eager to devote himself to painting, but his father judged this to be impractical, and Dawson entered the Armour Institute of Technology. There he dutifully completed the four-year program in civil engineering, receiving his bachelor of science degree in the spring of 1909. Shortly afterward, through one of his father's connections, he was hired to work in the drafting room of Holabird and Roche, Chicago's largest architectural firm. Though hired as an engineer, during his first day of work he was assigned to produce some architectural drawings, a task that he did well. From that time on, Dawson's work for Holabird and Roche regularly moved back and forth between architectural and engineering projects.

FIG. 1 *Ash Heap*, 1905 (pl. 2)

The Early Paintings

From the beginning, Dawson made unusual, provocative paintings, though his ideas often ran ahead of his technical skills. His earliest surviving works, which seem to date from his early teens, are a set of dark renderings of the night sky, painted on small wooden shingles, which presumably were inspired by the work of James Abbott McNeill Whistler, who was popular in Chicago. What is surprising about these paintings is their degree of abstraction. Most people who looked at them at the time probably would have felt that they were not recognizable scenes, and were on the edge of pure nonsense.

By 1905, at the age of nineteen, Dawson had begun producing larger, more colorful canvases, which often might pass for the work of a professional artist. One of these portrays the log house at the family farm in Michigan. Another is a remarkably beautiful pink and green landscape, as glimpsed through the silhouetted shapes of tree trunks and dark leaves. Though the works are more closely observed than the night sky series, in both paintings Dawson's realism is slightly deflected by bright, decorative color, and an Impressionist or Post-Impressionist interest in boldly patterned brushstrokes. Both pieces reveal that Dawson was aware of, and was consciously or unconsciously synthesizing, ideas from various art forms and movements of the time, including Impressionist and Post-Impressionist landscape painting, Japanese prints, and the Arts and Crafts movement. The canvas showing a landscape seen through branches and leaves, for example, might well have been inspired by one of the plates in Arthur Dow's book *Composition*, of 1893, a widely used teaching manual of the period.

In this same year, Dawson also produced a thoroughly surprising rendering of a tin can, four lemons, and some old suspenders forlornly discarded on the ash heap of an urban lot (fig. 1, pl. 2). So far as is known, this little painting was Dawson's only venture into urban realism. What is truly surprising is that Dawson's composition pre-dates by three years the first exhibition of the so-called Ashcan school (the first organized American group of urban realists), which opened at the Macbeth Gallery in New York in February 1908. Possibly, Dawson had seen paintings by artists of Robert Henri's circle, although the style of his painting is rather crude and distinctly different from their work.[7] But, like this one, there are paintings from throughout Dawson's career that astonishingly parallel the discoveries of other artists in utterly distant places. He might also have derived his interest in urban realism from some other source, perhaps from the urban fiction of novelists such as Theodore Dreiser and Upton Sinclair (though Sinclair's most famous book, *The Jungle*, which was set in the meat-packing plants of Chicago, was not published until the next year).

At this stage, Dawson's artistic growth was still not narrowly focused. Indeed, in the works of 1906 and 1907 we can sense an alternation between opposing sides of his personality—the mathematical and rational, and the mystical or even weird. On the one hand, in 1906 he produced several elegant still-life paintings with crisp outlines that look like the drawings of an engineer, though their vantage points are distinctly odd. (Dawson liked tipped viewpoints and high horizons, similar to those found in Japanese prints.) Both the unusual vantage points and the clean flat color give these paintings a surprisingly modern look, vaguely reminiscent of Matisse. On the other hand, just a year later, Dawson produced a very different group of fantastic works that do not seem rational at all. They are filled with dark foreboding, and portray such subjects as children and ghosts, Indians in an encampment, Adam and Eve, and an elderly couple seated at the base of a flight of steps, with children playing on a terrace above them. While their technical crudity is jarring, these canvases show a peculiar and original insight into the "big questions" of life, such as the contrast between material and immaterial, life and death, childhood and old age, male and female, savage and civilized. Dawson himself confessed in his journal that these paintings were "somewhat cartoon-like" but noted that they were "painted in all seriousness."

This moment roughly marks the point at which Dawson's "juvenalia" comes to an end. At the age of twenty, rather abruptly, Dawson emerges as a mature artist. Three figure paintings of 1908 and 1909 show his nascent sophistication: *The Dreamer* (1908, fig. 2, pl. 7), *Scarp* (1909, pl. 8), and *Germinal* (1909, fig. 3, pl. 9). The earliest of the three, *The Dreamer,* depicts naked figures dancing, standing, and sitting in a stark blue landscape with a purple tree. At first glance it appears to relate to French modernist painting. The blueness brings to mind Picasso's Blue Period, while the idyllic subject and style of figure handling recalls Matisse's *Joy of Life* of 1905 (Barnes Foundation). But Dawson could hardly have known of such work at this time, which suggests that he was simply drawing on traditions of stylized figures in Arcadian settings that he and the French artists shared.

In fact, if we look at *The Dreamer* beside *Scarp* and *Germinal,* their common source becomes apparent: Dawson was basing his work on that of Arthur Davies, who produced similar compositions of naked figures in pastoral settings, in various stages of pose and repose.

FIG. 2 *The Dreamer,* 1908 (pl. 7)

Dawson knew of Davies' work through a family friend, Kate Kellogg. In his journal of May 1, 1910, he notes that he had seen "some small dream-like sketches" by Davies that the artist had left with the Kellogg family. (The word "dream-like" suggests that these were not early canvases, but specimens of the artist's most recent work).

Scarp and *Germinal* are particularly close to the work of Davies, both in their form and their symbolic approach. Dawson clearly conceived the two as a pair, since they are on canvases of the same size, and portray complementary themes. In *Scarp,* figures slide down an embankment into an abyss, whereas in *Germinal* they emerge from underground and move toward the light. Significantly, both paintings express themes that would find a parallel in music or dance, and both attempt to find a visual analogue for an emotion—in the one case, downward-turning and depressed, and in the other upward-reaching and uplifting.

In addition to resembling the work of Davies, these paintings evoke another family of prototypes—the intensely stylized geometric ornament popular in Chicago buildings. In the hands of the more modern architects, like Frank Lloyd Wright, such designs often achieved a high degree of abstraction. In 1903, for example, Wright made designs for the leaded windows, doors, and lamps of the Susan Lawrence Dana house, which are boldly geometric in their character. These

FIG. 3 *Germinal*, 1909 (pl. 9)

provide an exciting contrast to the more realistic presentation of the sumac in the frieze-like mural that encircles the room. Indeed, some writers have proposed that Wright's process of geometric simplification echoes European Cubism (although Wright did not explore spatial ambiguity in the same way that the Cubists did). Dawson's paintings *Scarp* and *Germinal* bear a striking resemblance to this type of design—their heavy black outlines, for example, call to mind the lead lines of a stained-glass window.

For Dawson, what was most significant about these two paintings was that they were free inventions, made without reference to any reality other than his imagination. In his journal he described them as "arbitrarily constructed paintings of arranged figures" in which he was "blocking things out without rhyme or reason other than to make the picture look *right*." He also wrote, "Early attempts were always an effort to copy most accurately what nature gives, particularly the gorgeous variety of sky effects. Now, however, there seem to be transcendent forms, shapes, relations that require the development of invented themes that can only be found in fancy, the inner mind." This latter passage is notable because it shows that even while still painting realistically, Dawson was beginning to consider the possibility of "transcendent forms"—that is, of a form of painting that was not copied from nature, but invented from abstract principles.[8]

Sometime around 1910–11, either Manierre Dawson in America or Wassily Kandinsky in Europe—depending on your conviction in this matter—first set foot upon the continent of modern abstract or "non-objective" art.

—Harry Rand, *Art in America*, 1997

The Early Abstractions and *Prognostic*

Scarp and *Germinal* are remarkable paintings for a young, self-taught artist. Several years later, when Dawson had moved beyond it in style, his friend Dudley Crafts Watson still singled out *Germinal* as one of the handful of canvases he most wanted for a showing of Dawson's work at the Milwaukee Art Center. But none of these paintings quite prepares us for what Dawson produced in the first two months of 1910, a series of seven pure abstractions, of which the most startling and ambitious is a triptych with the resonant title *Prognostic* (pl. 16). This is a remarkable explosion of abstract shapes—parabolas that form undulating peaks, complex curves that become cloud-like shapes, and a background scaffolding of vertical and horizontal lines. In this triptych Dawson produced something that, to an amazing degree, looks similar to many of Kandinsky's abstractions (although, strangely, it has greater connections to Kandinsky's work of the 1920s than to his early abstract paintings). We also find comparable visual rhythms in the first abstractions of Dawson's American contemporary, Arthur Dove. What should we make of these visual parallels with works that Dawson could not possibly have seen?

Dawson's reputation as a painter may be said to rest largely on this small group of works. Perhaps the central question to ask of Dawson's career is what the artist intended in these compositions, and whether he did indeed produce the world's first purely abstract paintings. Most scholars would agree that the development of abstraction is one of the most significant, if not *the* most significant development of modern art. If so,

Dawson's achievement marks one of the great turning points of twentieth-century painting.

Along with Dawson's youth (he was only twenty-two when he produced *Prognostic*), the early date of *Prognostic* is quite astonishing, as becomes apparent when we consider how it fits into the evolution of abstract art. Dawson has two chief rivals for the title of "first abstract painter," Arthur Dove and Wassily Kandinsky. Most art historians concur that Kandinsky and Dove both made "abstract" paintings around 1910, but are elusive about specifics. In fact, while Kandinsky, in particular, owes his place in art history to his alleged discovery of "abstraction," art historians generally rather quickly slide by the moment when this must have occurred. Precise months or days, corroborating evidence, or other particulars of this sort are remarkably vague. The dawn of abstract art seems to be something that either will happen, or that has happened, but never something that actually is happening and can be closely examined.

Dove's status as a pioneer of abstract painting is based on a group of six small oil paintings that he called *Abstraction Numbers 1 Through 6*. These paintings were never exhibited in Dove's lifetime, and it is possible that the artist considered them as sketches or studies rather than as finished works. Dove later stated that they were painted in 1910. Most scholars believe that they were executed not very long after an exhibition titled *Younger American Painters*, organized by Alfred Stieglitz in New York in March 1910, in which Dove participated. Circumstantial evidence suggests that Dove's abstractions were made in Westport, Connecticut, where Dove moved on July 4 of that same year. The imagery of the painting seems to relate to Dove's move from the city to the country, and the greenness of the paintings suggests late spring or summer. In 1911, the following year, Dove produced a more ambitious series of ten pastels, titled *The Ten Commandments*.[9]

Therefore, Dove appears to have made his first notably abstract paintings after July 4 of 1910. This would make his work a few months later than that of Dawson, who had apparently completed his first seven abstract paintings before June 17, when he left Chicago for Europe. Indeed, the evidence suggests that he finished them a month or so before that date, since his journal entries indicate that in the weeks before his departure he had no time to paint.

The case of Kandinsky raises slightly different questions. Unlike Dove, Kandinsky did not burst into the field of abstraction with a single group of paintings. Instead, over a period of several years, he moved in a somewhat erratic progression toward images that become more and more difficult to read in a representational manner. To a surprising extent, however, even Kandinsky's most seemingly "abstract" designs contain references to landscape or the human figure—scenes of horses and riders, canon, the archangel Gabriel, churches on rocky hillsides, and so forth. The best candidate for Kandinsky's first true abstraction is a perfectly square oil painting titled *Picture with a Circle*, now in the State Museum of Art in Tbilisi, in the Republic of Georgia. In 1935, Kandinsky mentioned this painting in a letter to a New York dealer describing the paintings he had left behind in Russia. "Among these," Kandinsky noted, "was my very first abstract picture of 1911 (this is the very first abstract picture to have been painted)." This would appear to be an unequivocal statement, but somewhat confusing the matter is the fact that Kandinsky also executed an abstract watercolor (Centre Georges Pompidou, Paris) whose date remains in dispute. The piece carries an inscription by Kandinsky, added years after the fact, that gives the date as 1910. However, it is obviously a study for an oil painting of 1913, *Composition VII* (private collection). Scholars disagree as to whether Kandinsky dated this watercolor accurately, and there seems to be no objective form of evidence that will ever fully resolve this problem.[10]

Thus, the evidence suggests that Dawson preceded Kandinsky as an abstract painter, although with less certainty than in the case of Dove. *Prognostic*, an oil painting, precedes Kandinsky's first abstraction in oil by about one year. On the other hand, if Kandinsky's first abstract watercolor was truly executed in 1910, his first venture into pure abstraction was quite close in date to that of Dawson's work. To know which was first we would have to know the time of year when Kandinsky painted the piece, but unfortunately, there is no information on this point. Probably Dawson, who produced his first abstractions early in the year, was the earlier of the two, but one can know for certain only that Dawson produced abstract oil paintings about one year earlier than Kandinsky did.

But the real dilemma, in any case, goes deeper and cannot be solved through documentary evidence. It lies in the very concept of abstraction itself, and in the impossibility of pinpointing what it actually is. In fact, the term "abstract painting" is surely a misnomer, since there is no such specific, perfect, platonic entity as an "abstract" painting—merely paintings that have been abstracted from reality to a greater or lesser degree. We can afford to wonder whether Dove's paintings are truly abstract. After all, they clearly show trees, cows, and houses. Figural references, however, also remain in Kandinsky's so-called abstractions, or even in paintings that are conventionally titled "non-objective." A painting that represents a white square on a white square, or is painted entirely blue or black, contains references to realities or entities of some sort, albeit very generalized ones. That is, we can determine that such paintings come closer to representing, or at least "connecting," to certain kinds of realities than other ones. Indeed, a purely abstract painting, if such a thing were possible, would be a painting that had no meaning, since it would connect with nothing, and thus would be without significant interest.[11] In the end, the notion of a purely "abstract" painting will always remain something fundamentally insubstantial. Consequently the search for the first abstract painting is in some sense a search for a chimera—or at least, a search for something that depends heavily on questions of definition. I would argue that Dawson was the first painter to create a language of abstract form that was expressively as rich as representations of the real world. But such an assessment, it should be made clear, depends heavily on subtle nuances in the way in which terms are defined.[12]

The fact is that all abstract paintings represent something, just as numbers represent something, although, in a fashion somewhat analogous to numbers, abstract paintings represent things in a peculiar way.[13] What is remarkable about numbers is that they are useful for describing specific things, such as a plate of apples or a gaggle of geese, but at the same time they are not specifically tied to any single set they describe. Thus, number is at once one of our most effective tools for describing reality, and for dealing with reality in a logical and pragmatic way, and at the same time it is something that stands apart from reality and exists in a separate realm. We tend to consider that people such as engineers, who work regularly with numbers, are particularly sensible and practical; at the same time we are aware that numbers do not really exist in quite the same fashion as physical objects, but have a curious "ghost existence" that is never physically tangible. It seems no accident that Dawson was mathematically gifted, and had an almost inborn sense of kinship with numbers and geometric shapes, since the idea of "abstraction" in many ways runs parallel to the notion of working with number, or with numerically generated geometric forms.

Like number, abstraction involves identifying a generalized essence that is part of what we see, but also touches on something beyond it—and so in some way expresses the essence of other things as well. Thus, abstraction, while in one sense simple—in its simplification of form—is also complex, since its meaning is not specific and limited but multivalent. Abstract paintings point to things beyond themselves, since they aim to extract some fundamental essence that lies beneath the surface of things. If they are abstract in a large enough sense, they may point to a kind of "universal force," or even "soul" that underlies everything that exists. Part of the excitement of the earliest abstract paintings, particularly the work of Kandinsky and Dawson, is that they are truly cosmic in their ambitions, and seem to explore the very essence of being itself.

The style we think of as "abstraction" was in many respects not so much a complete break with past procedures as a change in the weight of emphasis. This shift, nonetheless, results in creating something quite distinct from what existed before, both in its meaning and its impact. In viewing a nineteenth-century painting, the act of recognition comes first, and we then move on to explore a painting's formal aspects. In viewing a modern abstraction, we first take note of the patterns of color and shape, and only afterward start guessing what thing or concept the painting is meant to represent or evoke.

To a large degree, the early "abstractions" of Kandinsky and Dove seem abstract not because they do not represent something, but because the image is

FIG. 4 Wassily Kandinsky (Russian, 1866–1944), *Improvisation 21a*, 1911. Courtesy of Städtische Galerie im Lenbachhaus

cleverly distorted and camouflaged. Once things are explained to us, however, we can generally make out the nature of the image without difficulty. Many of Kandinsky's canvases, for example, as mentioned, contain riding horsemen, Saint George and the Dragon, the Last Judgment, and similar subjects, generally set in a mountainous landscape. We may not recognize these elements at first, but once they are pointed out to us they are quite evident, and if we look back to Kandinsky's work we can follow a logical process by which these elements were gradually disguised. Similarly, Dove's *The Ten Commandments*, the first group of abstract paintings that he exhibited, appeared to early viewers to be lacking in representational references, although today it is not hard to recognize houses, trees, and other elements.

Notably, however, because these images are camouflaged, they often seem more alive and interesting than more literal images, and speak to our emotions directly. By reducing the specificity of detail, these images engage our imaginations more actively.[14]

At one level, then, the excitement of an abstract painting is like that of a game of hide-and-seek. The act of visual searching encourages a process of engagement, and makes looking an active process. At its best, however, abstract painting can go further, since it can seemingly disclose an occult, mysterious, new dimension to reality, much as a mathematical formula can reveal the nature of physical forces. Kandinsky, Dove, and Dawson, at some point, all alluded to a "spiritual" dimension of their effort, and indicated that their quest was for an essence of the cosmos that was hidden

FIG. 5 Arthur Dove (American, 1880–1964), *Nature Symbolized No. 1* or *Roofs*, 1911/12. Courtesy of Fiona and Michael Scharf

beneath the skin of outward appearance. By simplifying and purifying the image, by removing the distraction of detail, these artists felt that they could move closer to this spiritual basis of reality.

Dawson's painting *Prognostic* makes further progress in this direction than the works of either Kandinsky or Dove, since the paintings of Dove and Kandinsky disguise only a single image. This leaves the viewer with the nagging suspicion that once the hidden subject has been identified, the whole meaning of the painting can be explained and its mystery deflated. One could argue, on the other hand, that Dawson's triptych is more conceptually radical, since his design suggests multiple translations into physical reality and opens up a much wider range of meanings.

We can read the meaning of *Prognostic* in several ways. The most obvious reference is to a mountain landscape, with cloud forms behind (the horizontal line near the base of the central panel seems to define a mountain lake, on whose smooth surface the mountains are reflected). Some writers have suggested that the scaffold-like shapes perhaps evoke the gridded structure of high-rise buildings. In addition, Dawson noted that the image can be interpreted in another way, as an engineer's drawing board, with parabolas and differentials laid out (the short black lines were suggested by pen, pencils, and erasers lying on the drawing board's surface).[15]

Significantly, these two meanings interconnect, since Dawson seems to suggest that nature develops from the same mathematical concepts that the engineer plots: that mountains, clouds and lakes are products of geometry and number. Rather neatly, Dawson portrays how numbers and shapes evolve from the simple to the complex. In the background we find simple shapes, such as squares and circles. Evolving from these are more complex patterns, such as parabolas and complex curves.

Prognostic might well have been titled "God's Drawing Board," since it imagines the universe from the point of view of a Creator setting out to design it. The fact that Dawson conceived his painting as a triptych is no accident (although unfortunately, the three parts of this triptych have been separated, and will only briefly be rejoined in the present exhibition). Triptychs in Western art carry a strong message, since they are almost always used for religious altarpieces, generally ones that show Christ or God the Father in the center, flanked by saints or donors. By painting a triptych, Dawson indicated that his message was essentially a spiritual or religious one, and indeed, the yellow sky in the central panel can be read as an explosion of divine energy from heaven. ("All of my paintings are spiritual," Dawson once noted petulantly in his journal, when a viewer praised his *Prayer Loft*, of 1921, [pl. 60] as particularly uplifting).

Much of the excitement we find in Dawson's painting lies in the fact that it does not portray a physical fact—we experience reality as a plan, as a diagram, as a possibility—as a prognostic of what will someday take place. Its electric quality derives not only from the remarkable "rightness" of Dawson's shapes—which indeed do seem to evoke a remarkable range of natural forms—but also from the playfulness with which they dance upon the surface. Rather than being bound to physical reality, and forced to literally transcribe it, the artist penetrates to underlying geometric principles and participates in the actual growth and vital flowering of the forms and shapes. As Dawson noted in his journal, painting thus becomes a fully creative enterprise—a way of making something that had never before existed.

Chicago and Modern Art

How was it that Dawson, who was seemingly so isolated, managed to develop, so quickly and confidently, many of the central principles of non-objective art? In some ways, this question will always be a riddle. But certainly it is relevant to note that while Dawson was indeed isolated from the centers of modern painting, in another sense he was located at the very heart of the modern revolution. To grasp this paradox it is helpful to step back and consider what we mean by the term "modern," and just where the evolution of the "modern" took place.

The term "modern" has two rather different meanings, and much confusion has been caused by failing to distinguish between them. When applied to art, it generally refers to a series of innovative movements (originally centered in France, chiefly in Paris, but eventually spreading to Munich, Moscow, and other centers) that transformed realistic representation. Loosely speaking, these movements progressed from singling out particular aspects or brief moments of reality, as in French Impressionism, to self-consciously transforming reality in a fairly arbitrary fashion, as in Analytic and Synthetic Cubism, or later, in even more "abstract" forms of modern painting. For a good part of the nineteenth and twentieth centuries, the issue of "abstraction" was central to the most exciting and inventive modern movements, although it would be risky to maintain that the progress of modern art can be reduced to some sort of lockstep march toward this goal.

When applied to life itself, however, the term "modern" possesses a somewhat different meaning, and refers to the development of new technologies, mass-production, large corporations, new forms of advertising, transport, and distribution—a new kind of mass culture. While this development also took place in Europe, it occurred most intensely and most creatively in the United States. It is striking how many of the major "modern" inventions—the telephone, the light bulb, the elevator, the refrigerated railroad car, the radio, the television set—were either conceived in the United States, or first turned into a practical product in this country. Something about the scale of the United States, its rawness and newness, and its lack of territorial borders or deeply ingrained traditions, made it particularly well-suited for ventures that required organizing material and manpower to launch a new product or to conduct production on an enormous scale. Even in cases such as the automobile, in which Europeans made many of the key theoretical breakthroughs, it was in the United States that the product was first developed for a mass market.

Viewed in broad terms, the Europeans took the lead in creating modern art, whereas Americans took the lead in shaping modern life. Indeed, to a very large degree, these two developments occurred separately. A Chicago meatpacker like Philip Armour (for whom the engineering school Dawson attended was named) would surely have been as bewildered by one of Kandinsky's abstractions as Kandinsky would have been repelled by Armour's sledgehammers and meat cleavers.

In one art form, however, Americans played a central role, namely architecture—an art that exists just at the nexus between artistic expression and the rational handling of practical affairs. Moreover, by a strange quirk, it flowered primarily in a single city—Chicago. When Mrs. O'Leary's cow kicked over a lantern, and started a fire that leveled a city of 200,000 people, it created a unique opportunity to build a modern metropolis on modern principles from the ground up. Between 1890 and 1910, Chicago architects, particularly Louis Sullivan and Frank Lloyd Wright, established the hallmarks of modern architecture: the skyscraper, the free-flowing house with an open plan, the use of new materials such as plate glass and steel structural supports, and an entirely new look that dispensed with old-fashioned ornament and was clean, sleek, and practical, like a well-designed machine. Later in the century, these ideas were perfected by a gifted group of Europeans—Walter Gropius, Mies van der Rohe, and Le Corbusier—who created the familiar "white box" look known as the International Style. But the foundations of modern architecture, and its essential principles, were first developed in the United States, and one could contend that as artistic expressions, the best work of Sullivan and Wright has never been surpassed.

Looking at things in this way allows us to understand Dawson's "isolation" from a different perspective. Though extremely distant from the major centers of modern painting, Dawson was right at the center of American architecture, and indeed, throughout most of the period of his greatest productivity, he was working as an architectural engineer. (Viewed globally, Dawson thus becomes fascinating as arguably the first figure to combine the two very different streams of modernist thinking, which finally, in the second half of the twentieth century, merged to create what we now think of as "modern life.")

While Dawson was at the center of modern architecture, he was not quite at the center of that center. Holabird and Roche, the firm for which he worked, figure briefly in most histories of the Chicago skyscraper, since these architects produced some beautiful and eminently practical steel-framed buildings. In fact, their Tacoma Building, designed in the year of Dawson's birth, is generally regarded as the first steel-framed modern skyscraper, and is usually considered the most important large Chicago building until Sullivan's Carson, Pirie, Scott and Company department store of 1903. Sadly, however, Holabird and Roche did not long maintain this high level of innovation, as much of their production was commercial hackwork of the falsest and dullest conceivable character. Dawson's first assignment for them was to trace some plates from a book of Louis XVI interiors, and scale them to fit the ballroom of a Chicago hotel. His journal is filled with grumblings about the stupidity of his drafting assignments, such as "the ridiculous Monroe building—who wants a medieval, Italian building on Michigan Ave?" It irked him that Martin Roche was primarily a salesman and "will not spend more than a few seconds either looking at designs or discussing the idea that a breakaway from the accepted conventions would be progressive." In various mutterings in his journal he outlined his own vision of what the firm should have been doing, in an expression of the concept of "form and function" that runs parallel to the thinking of Sullivan and Wright.

> Our skyscrapers are sound in interior bones and plan but our elevations are fraudulent and conceal that sound interior. The faces of our buildings are imitative in design and imitative of material and the ornamentation bears no relation to the steel and concrete behind it.

Similarly, he stated:

> It is discouraging, to me, to think of a life as an architect trying to convince the public to accept an expression of the fact that current construction is of steel column, beam, and wind bracing enclosed for fireproofing and habitation and mounted on bed-rock for security. Decoration could be unlimitedly varied, but external appearance should definitely express the structure . . .

Somewhat surprisingly, despite the seeming parallelism of their views, Dawson did not speak highly of Wright in his journals, no doubt because he knew Wright's work chiefly through that of an incompetent follower, Albert Chase Arthur. He seems to have thought somewhat more favorably of Louis Sullivan, and it is tempting to suppose that he had read Sullivan's *Kindergarten Chats*, with its mystical but compelling discussion of organic form and physical structure. Yet surely it is relevant that Dawson's work on skyscrapers occurred just when the artist was making his key breakthroughs as a painter, since his jottings show his concern for the internal essence of the building that was so often masked by a veneer of decoration. In 1909, for example, just about the time he started work on *Prognostic*, he noted that: "I am drawing up full size details of hollow tile cornice section showing the steel hooks and heavier steel connections to the roof beams, learning much about construction detail and fire-proofing ordinances. I got hold of a copy of the building code, which I have read carefully."

Many of Dawson's drafting assignments crossed the boundaries of engineering and architecture. He seems to have often worked on those parts of large buildings in which terra-cotta and decorative tile joined with structural steel and fireproofing materials. Thus, he dealt with the juncture between surface appearance, or surface ornament, and internal structure. According to customary divisions, the design of the structural steel skeleton was primarily an exercise in "engineering," that of the surface cladding one of "architecture."

Engineers, Architects, and Artists

The concepts of engineering and architecture play a fundamental role in Dawson's paintings, and, indeed, in large part explain why he developed something that moved beyond the usual conventions. Architectural drafting teaches a variety of principles for distorting the appearance of forms in order to emphasize one or another conceptual aspect. For example, isometric projection treats architectural form three-dimensionally, but without perspective diminution, in order to create a drawing that will produce precisely accurate measurements, which can be measured off by a builder on any spatial axis. Similarly, orthographic projection enables a draftsman to determine the shape of an unseen or foreshortened side of a three-dimensional object from the information provided by the sides that are visible. Essentially, the procedure is one of unfolding the three-dimensional object so that each object is laid out flat and parallel to the drawing surface

FIG. 6 *Differential Complex (Study for Prognostic)*, 1910 (pl. 17)

or picture plane—a process that has obvious parallels with European Cubism.

Engineering also taught Dawson to explore reality more deeply, to consider not only the tangible substance of a form but also its invisible properties. Engineers think of physical matter not in terms of its shape or surface but rather in terms of the internal lines of force that run through it. They use mathematical and geometric principles to chart the configuration of these forces. Dawson's most significant painting, *Prognostic* is constructed chiefly of parabolas, which play a key role in engineering calculations. The ideal shape for physical support is the parabolic arch, while the pattern of stresses assumes a shape that is its exact inverse, the catenary curve. (The Catalan architect Antoni Gaudí, who worked with parabolic arches, filled his studio with strings loaded with weights, so that he could study their catenary curves). In purely mathematical terms, the shapes of parabolas are intriguing, for while they can be calculated by mathematical means, they are not regular in the same sense as a circle or a square (fig. 6, pl. 17). The great Greek mathematician Apollonius of Alexandria studied the pattern of these shapes by imagining them as angled cross sections through regular platonic solids. Later, the French mathematician René Descartes developed trigonometry, and showed how parabolas could be generated by alge-

FIG. 7 *Wall of Arches*, 1910 (pl. 13)

braic formulas that were plotted with coordinates on a Cartesian grid. Dawson was clearly familiar with such Cartesian thinking, and indeed in *Prognostic* the parabolas are placed against a background of squares, like those of graph paper, as if they have just been plotted according to some Cartesian formula.

Certainly, *Prognostic* presents Dawson's purest rendition of the parabolic shape, but in fact, parabolas and similar complex curves are central to the artist's painting of all periods—something that distinguishes his work from that of the European Cubists. In fact, Dawson's fascination with parabolas points toward something fundamental about his kind of abstraction, which made it conceptually rather different from European Cubism, even on those rather rare occasions when the visual form is similar. Artists such as Pablo Picasso and Georges Braque thought of lines as a way of demarcating space, and of delimiting and defining spatial planes. Dawson, on the other hand, thought of lines themselves as constituting some sort of invisible force, like electricity, or gravity, or the invisible but mathematically calculable stresses that run through a bridge or building. In other words, his paintings are conceived like architecture, or like an engineer's diagrams. This also explains another peculiarity of Dawson's work, the way in which his shapes almost always build upward, like a building. Dawson's paintings on the whole tend to convey a sense of ascendency, blossoming like a plant.

Indeed, a concept that illuminates Dawson's process is one in which architecture takes on an organic life. This idea provides the basis for another of Dawson's paintings of 1910, *Wall of Arches* (fig. 7, pl. 13), which is more obvious than *Prognostic* conceptually. In this piece, the traditional Roman arches of an aqueduct or bridge become flexible and varied in configuration, as if they were made of rubber and had been deformed through some kind of seismic pressure or squeezing. This allows them to become less apparent, more chaotic, more varied in their shape—and to strike a more interesting midpoint between order and chaos.

Shortly afterward in 1910, Dawson expanded on the same general idea in *Going into Mountains* (pl. 12), which also focuses on arch-like curves, but handles them with greater freedom and representational ambiguity. Some of the curves still look like the arches of a bridge, aqueduct, or arcaded structure, but others might be grottoes, or rounded hills, or the upward-thrusting branches of a tree. Our confusion about what they represent, and whether we should read them as pushing up or pressing down, is a large part of Dawson's message—that an arch-like arrangement, albeit eccentrically deformed by other pressures, is a commonality that defines the structural configuration of a great variety of physical things. In short, Dawson's background in architecture and engineering encouraged him to think about structure in fundamental ways, and provided an avenue toward abstraction.[16] It was not the only approach, however, for Dawson's exploration of reality went even deeper than a search for underlying physical forces or structures. Dawson also was clearly intrigued by the basic principles of mathematics, a discipline that is at once "real" and "symbolic."

I have devoted my attention primarily to *Prognostic*, since it strikes me as Dawson's most complicated early painting, yet it represents only one pathway of his exploration of "abstraction." *Prognostic* represents a kind of "cosmic abstraction," tied to nature, or at least to the natural laws by which nature operates.

Dawson also made two paintings at this time, *Xdx* (pl. 18) and *Coordinate Escape* (fig. 8, pl. 19), that do not represent objects, at least not those of the natural world, and thus might be described as "non-objective," or as abstractions of an even purer type. As I have already suggested, however, any form of "abstraction" can be construed as "representation" in some sense. Indeed, in these two paintings Dawson shrewdly raises questions about the nature of representation itself.

At some intuitive level, Dawson seems to have recognized that things that are self-referential present a challenge to the usual laws of logic. *Coordinate Escape* and *Xdx* suggest a playful and curious conceit, namely that the signs and variables of an equation are themselves an expression of the equation that they symbolize. Thus, they exist in an intermediate realm, between that of things that are real and things that are simply abstract symbols—that is, between things that stand for themselves, and things that can stand for any meaning arbitrarily attached to them. Critical here is whether Dawson was creating signs or a representation of signs. In a sense he was doing both, in which case his paintings are not unlike the paintings produced in the 1950s by Jasper Johns that portray letters, numbers, targets, and the like, in which sign and symbol become subject, and serve both as themselves and as representations of themselves.

FIG. 8 *Coordinate Escape*, 1910 (pl. 19)

Parallels with Kandinsky

From what source or sources did Dawson derive his ideas? Did he come up with them independently in Chicago, or was there some way in which he knew of artistic developments in Europe? The question carries weight since its answer affects our judgment of both Dawson's credibility and his significance as an artist. If Dawson borrowed from European sources, he provided no hint of this in his journal. Presumably, Dawson built his ideas about abstract painting from some existing body of ideas. Where can that body be located? Was he influenced by European sources or American ones? A close reading of Dawson's statements illuminates these issues.

Several scholars have noted that there are parallels between Dawson's ideas and those that Kandinsky expressed in his book *On the Spiritual in Art*, first published in 1914. Indeed, some writers have even suggested that Dawson's comments on abstract art could not have been written in 1910 since they must have been based on Kandinsky's statements. In truth, however, the similarities between the writings of Kandinsky and Dawson are of a rather general nature. Their wording never matches, statement for statement. In fact, the two artists express themselves so differently that the ideas only seem similar if we present them in a paraphrase that extracts the substratum of commonality that they share. The themes they shared were rather broad. Both Dawson and Kandinsky felt that painting should not imitate the surface of reality but should explore something deeper and more fundamental, and both felt that painting had an affinity with music. They built up their arguments in a strikingly different fashion.

Kandinsky believed that the basic reality of things was spiritual. His book contains many references to Theosophy and other occult doctrines, and his main interest lay in unlocking the spiritual essence of things. In several passages he argued that music, like painting, should connect with this underlying spiritual aspect of reality, but he showed little interest in investigating the parallels between the two art forms.

Dawson began developing his ideas about painting from a different starting point. As we have seen, his training as a mathematician and engineer resulted in a deep attraction to mathematical principles of order. He recognized that music and architecture used these principles "abstractly," that is, they did not depend on a direct imitation of nature. He sought to devise a new form of painting that would do the same thing, a kind of painting that would be based not on "imitation" but on "invention." Of course, since such "invention" depended on locating the inner essentials, or "essences" of art-making, there was certainly a spiritual dimension to Dawson's enterprise. But from the passing comments Dawson made in his journal, it is clear that he was neither a regular churchgoer nor a devotee of mystical or theosophical doctrines. The spirituality of Dawson's work was simply an outgrowth of his search for fundamental principles, and it was closely associated with his love of geometry and numbers.

Dawson's American Sources

As it happens, Dawson's statements are less like Kandinsky's than like those of various American writers. We can find a remarkable parallel with Dawson's comments in a fictional conversation created by William Dean Howells for his most famous novel, *The Rise of Silas Lapham*, written in Boston in 1885, two years before Dawson was born. In the following passage, the young suitor of Lapham's daughter, Tom Corey, addresses the architect of Silas Lapham's new mansion:

> "Well," said Corey, "you architects and the musicians are the true and only artistic creators. All the rest of us, sculptors, painters, novelists, and tailors, deal with forms which we have before us; we imitate, we try to represent. But you two sorts of artists create form. If you represent you fail."[17]

While it is presented in passing, and its tenets are not pursued further, this little dialogue wonderfully suggests the line of argument that would be advanced twenty years later with the development of modern art. Howells (or his character) does not go so far as to advocate a form of non-representational visual art, but the notion is implicit in these remarks. Surely, if architecture and music become a failure when they represent things, painting could also be considered a failure when it does so. Moreover, a non-representational form of painting, one that could "create form," would in some sense be "higher" than one that merely represents.

Howells' dialogue is interesting both because of the early date at which it was written and because of the casual way it is dropped into the novel, as if the ideas presented were already familiar to his readers. Certainly, by the early years of the twentieth century, the notion of a visual harmony in painting that functioned in a way comparable to music was common currency, in large part due to the influence of the American expatriate painter James Abbott McNeill Whistler, who promoted this idea energetically in his lectures and writings as well as in his art. To emphasize this aspect of his work, he often gave his paintings musical titles, such as *Symphony* or *Nocturne*.

Whistler's musical analogies were often elaborated and developed by writers of the period. For example, the Chicago collector Arthur Jerome Eddy (who purchased one of Dawson's paintings in 1914) wrote a book on Whistler in 1903 in which he argued that an artist should compose his paintings abstractly, like a musician. According to Eddy, color should be organized into chords, and should be "arranged in harmonies to please the eye as music pleases the ear."[18] As Eddy explained:

> There is a music of color even as there is a music of sound, and there should be a delight in color composition even as there is a delight in sound composition; and this delight should be something fundamentally distinct from any interest in the subject of the composition. The subject may be a man, or a woman, or a field, or a tree, or a wave, or a cloud, or just nothing at all—mere masses or streaks of color; the perfection or imperfection of the color arrangement remains the same.[19]

Similarly, according to Eddy, line should be beautiful in a way quite separate from what it served to represent. A line could be significant and beautiful even if it were purely abstract. As Eddy argued:

> There is an art of pure line as there is an art of pure form and of pure color. It is just as possible to make a lot of meaningless lines which please the eye in their curves and endless variety as it is to please the eye with combinations of colors . . . Why should there be anything more, if to please the eye were the painter's intention?[20]

This passage could easily be construed as an argument for a wholly abstract form of painting.[21] In another passage, Eddy went so far as to propose that paintings became better when they were less tied to physical appearance: "Generally speaking, the more abstract the art the higher it is; the purer and freer it is from imitation or suggestion of natural effects, the nobler its attainment."[22]

In short, by around 1900, many writers believed that painting would become better and more "spiritual" if it could become more abstract, less bound to physical images. Just how this goal was to be achieved was not very clear, but two writers of this period made significant advances in addressing this issue. The first of these was Arthur Dow, whose book *Composition*, first published in 1893, explained how composition could be analyzed and developed in an essentially abstract manner. The second was Denman Ross. His book *A Theory of Pure Design*, though turgidly written, provided a virtual manifesto for abstract art. Interestingly, Ross' book first appeared in 1907—just around the time that Dawson began to abandon representation and move into the practice of non-objective art. Its timing suggests that it may have provided the little push that sent Dawson over the edge into pure abstraction.

Both Dow and Ross did not just present abstract theory. They also made diagrams and suggested exercises and work projects. Their books provided practical, usable manuals for young and aspiring abstract painters. As Randy Ploog proposes (see his essay in this catalogue), Dawson probably developed his principal ideas about abstract art after absorbing the theories of these two writers.

Arthur Dow's *Composition*

Until recently, histories of American modernism have given Arthur Dow less attention than he deserves. His writings influenced a whole generation of American modern painters, and fundamentally shaped the effort of artists as different as Grant Wood and Georgia O'Keeffe. The reason for this is simple. Dow's own work as a painter and printmaker, while not unpleasing in its sense of pattern, was mostly quite dull. His importance rests almost entirely on his little book titled *Composition*, which revolutionized American art education. Widely distributed and extensively used in schools, *Composition* shaped the thinking of young artists throughout the United States, and altered the course of twentieth-century art.

Born in Massachusetts, Dow encountered Post-Impressionism while studying painting in France. The single greatest influence on his work was that of Oriental art, particularly Japanese prints, which he absorbed through the teachings of the distinguished scholar and collector Ernest Fenollosa, who served as curator of Oriental art at the Museum of Fine Arts in Boston. The introduction to *Composition* boldly opens with the declaration that Leonardo da Vinci was wrong about the purpose of painting, because he had erroneously supposed that paintings should imitate or represent the natural world. According to Dow, abstract design—what he termed "composition"—as evidenced in Japanese prints, provided the underlying basis for all great art.

As a means for creating such abstract arrangements (whose harmonies he compared to the harmonies of music), Dow singled out three elements in particular:

FIG. 9 *View from Woods*, 1905 (pl. 1)

line, color, and what he called *notan* (a Japanese term for an arrangement of light and dark). This "trinity of power," he maintained, provided the tools to build all visual forms.[23] Thus, for Dow, great painting was fundamentally rooted not in imitating the natural world, but in the mastery of abstract principles. As he wrote: "Abstract design is, as it were, the primer of painting, in which principles of Composition appear in a clear and definite form. Nature will not teach composition."[24]

Dow's book was energetically promoted by its publisher, Prang, in a national publicity campaign that was aimed particularly at high school art teachers. Dow himself lectured in Chicago several times; a large group of women from Chicago attended Dow's summer school in Ipswich, Massachusetts; and the Chicago office of Prang organized a summer course for teachers based on Dow's principles. It seems very likely that Miss Dimock, the high school art teacher who provided Dawson with his only formal art instruction, introduced him to Dow's theories, which were then at the forefront of progressive art education in Chicago.

As important as the statements made by Dow were the little diagrams that illustrated his book—which schematized simple representational elements, such as trees or houses, and showed how they could create very different effects according to how they were placed on the page. Indeed, many of Dow's diagrams are purely abstract, and simply show how a rectangle can be divided up proportionally in various harmonious ways. As Randy Ploog points out, many of Dawson's early paintings—including his night sky series, his view of the log house at the farm, a scene of cattle, and his *View from Woods* (1905, fig. 9, pl. 1)—are remarkably similar to illustrations in Dow's book, and could easily have been made as applications of Dow's principles. Although Dawson seems never to have directly copied a plate from Dow, the number of similarities in his work to Dow's illustrations suggest that he was making use of Dow's text.

Denman Ross' *A Theory of Pure Design*

Whereas Dow's teachings and diagrams align closely with the earliest paintings by Dawson, the works of Denman Ross help to explain his forays into pure abstraction. Born in Cincinnati, Ross pursued his entire professional career at Harvard, where he served first as an instructor in the department of architecture, and then as a lecturer at the Fogg Art Museum. Independently wealthy, Ross collected art enthusiastically, donating fifteen hundred objects to Harvard and eleven thousand to the Museum of Fine Arts in Boston. He was also an accomplished painter, though his efforts as an artist were directed less toward the actual physical object than toward seeking to understand and elucidate the underlying principles of visual design according to scientific principles. Ross' experiments as a painter provided the raw material for his most significant writing. In the early years of this century, he produced four manuals in which he grappled with different aspects of visual order, of which the most provocative was *A Theory of Pure Design*. This book argues for the creation of a purely abstract form of art.

Ross opened by proposing that beauty derives from the mind's perception of order, and that this order provides the spiritual essence of art. Therefore, it is necessary "to study Design in the abstract, Pure Design." He wrote, "The purpose of Pure Design is to achieve Order in line and spots of paint; this with no other, no further, no higher motive; just for the satisfaction, the pleasure, the delight of it."[25] Like Dow, Ross deplored the slavish imitation of nature. Instead, he proposed that artists create "a synthetic reproduction" that would extract fundamental elements and arrange them in new combinations. "There should be no direct imitation, no copying. We must not depend so much upon the memory as upon the imagination."[26]

Ross also suggested that it might be possible to construct design from purely abstract principles without going through the extra step of referring to nature.[27] As Ross wrote:

> The application of Design in the various Arts and Crafts is well understood and appreciated. The possibility of Pure Design, pure Art, followed for the sake of Order and Beauty, with no purpose of service or of utility, is not at all understood or appreciated. I think of Pure Design as I think of Music. Music is the arrangement and composition of sounds for the sake of Order and Beauty, to give pleasure to the ear of the composer. Pure Design is the arrangement and composition of line and spots of paint for the sake of Order and Beauty, to give pleasure to the eye of the designer.[28]

Indeed, Ross became rapturous when he reflected on the possibilities of an art of this abstract sort, which would no longer relate directly to the physical world:

> The designer must be able to think in tones, measures and shapes precisely as the composer of music thinks in the sounds of voices and instruments . . . He will follow the suggestion of his imagination as it leads him into the world of tone-, measure-, and shape-ideas. This world must be as wonderful as the world of musical sounds. We know something of that in the revelations which the great composers have given us in their compositions. Of the possibilities of Pure Design, we can only guess what they may be.[29]

Recently, the scholar Marianne W. Martin has noted that "a statement such as this could almost have come a few years later from the pen of Kandinsky, save that the mystical fervor of the Russian artist is lacking."[30] One might say the same thing of Dawson's jottings in his journal, which treat the concept of a purely abstract form of art in a similar way. It is reasonable to suppose that Dawson had read Ross' book, which was available in the library of the Art Institute of Chicago. Certainly, writers such as Dow and Ross provide much closer parallels with Dawson's statements than does Kandinsky.

Ross' book also attempted to give visual form to his theories. It contains hundreds of diagrams and exercises, showing such configurations as a row of arches, a pattern of black dots and bars, or a series of amorphous dots and dashes. To be sure, none of these diagrams are visually captivating as works of art in themselves. In fact, Ross seems to have considered them chiefly as exercises. Yet what is significant here is not the artistic merit of Ross' diagrams, but rather their remarkable parallels with the work of Dawson (who had considerably greater skill than Ross in developing interesting abstract effects). Ross' diagram of arches, *Red Fort*, might have inspired Dawson's *House and Arch;* Ross' diagram 228 contains dots and bars that appear in Dawson's painting *Prognostic*. Ross' diagram of sharply cusped curves anticipates Dawson's *Discal Procession* (fig. 10, pl. 14). Finally, Ross' diagram of diagonal lines calls to mind paintings by Dawson such as *Tilt* or *Figures in Orange, Yellow and Pink*.

FIG. 10 *Discal Procession*, 1910 (pl. 14)

Dawson's artistic advances over Dow and Ross are pronounced. But his art was not produced out of thin air. Earlier American writers and artists had set down a foundation for his accomplishments. Whether or not Dawson was in contact with European modernists, American sources fit more closely with his work and thinking.

Dawson's Trip to Europe

Dawson's remarkable achievement in these early paintings of 1910 was abruptly broken off by a trip to Europe, which began in mid June. Just what Dawson saw in Europe and how it affected him has always been a problem for scholars of his work, since his style of painting shifted dramatically after his return. While in Europe, Dawson managed to see some modern and Cubist painting, albeit very briefly. Thus, after his return, he was no longer a truly isolated figure, but had been directly exposed to the virus of modern painting.

Dawson's journal indicates that he began planning this European trip soon after he started working with Holabird and Roche. He was encouraged by his fellow draftsmen, Smith and Frederick C. Lebenbaum, who "have told me I must go to Europe to get the most experience in art appreciation." Before long, Dawson was saving every penny that he could—for example, carrying a sandwich to work in his pocket, to avoid the expense of purchasing lunch He made visits to the library to read up on the places he would visit, and constructed a special traveling case to hold a small watercolor kit, as well as to carry wooden panels and materials for oil painting. (Artfully designed, the kit included a special frame at the top, to hold the panels apart while the paint was drying). A first reference to Gertrude Stein appears in Dawson's journal before he visited Europe—she was mentioned by Lebenbaum, who also provided a list of pensions where he could stay. Dawson noted in regard to Lebenbaum: "He has given me a letter to a Mrs. Stein in Paris and tells me I must visit her."

Dawson's journey lasted six months and took him through England, France, Switzerland, Italy, and Germany. The itinerary suggests that he was almost equally as interested in architecture as he was in painting, for he devoted roughly as much time to each. The tour opened in England, where he visited the cathedrals at Durham, York, Lincoln, and Peterborough. He also took walking trips through the countryside, stopped off at Oxford and Cambridge, visited museums in London, and made a trip to Stratford in homage to Shakespeare. He then crossed over to France, visiting the cathedrals at Amiens, Rouen, and Beauvais.

Continuing on to Paris, he was overwhelmed by the Louvre, which struck him as "inexhaustible." He discovered, however, that at the pension where he was staying: "Mention of pictures or artists usually hushes the conversation temporarily. The theatres and eat spots raise the most talk."

For a week or so, Paris served as a center from which Dawson made side trips to other cities in France. He then moved on to southern Germany, where he traveled down the Rhine. From Germany he went to Switzerland, and did extensive walking through the Alps. These long walks finally carried him into Italy, where he resorted to railroad travel once again, visiting most of the principal art centers, including Milan, Pisa, Siena, Rome, Naples, Florence, and Venice. He then returned to Paris by train. After a brief stay, he returned to Germany, where he visited Munich, Dresden, and Berlin and studied their collections of old masters. He finally sailed from Bremerhaven on November 19, arriving in New York about ten days later.

Early on, Dawson discovered that it was difficult to keep up a rapid pace of seeing things and still record his impressions. One English cathedral seemed to blend with another, at least in his descriptions, and within a few days of his arrival he was noting that "a diary is impossible," or observing regretfully that: "Reading the last few pages [my] comments seem trite and common place but do recall to me the circumstances of my journey." As to be expected from this extensive list of the places Dawson visited, his journal makes miscellaneous reading. It contains remarks about such diverse topics as the gutters on the channel boats that effectively flushed away the vomit of seasick passengers; the slugs he encountered littering the ground at the forest of Fontainbleau; his disappointment in Raphael's *Sistine Madonna* in Dresden, which struck him as large but not one of the artist's best; his amazement at the density of the mosquitos in Venice; or his observation, which takes on ominous overtones in retrospect, that nearly all the men in Germany seemed to have joined the army.

Comments about museums that he visited are almost equaled by notations about pretty girls who caught his eye. Indeed, one of the striking aspects of the journal is that surprisingly little of his account directly relates to paintings, and only a small fraction of that to modern art. This fact makes it unlikely that the journal was concocted to support his artistic claims.

Dawson's interest in seeing paintings seems to have grown over the course of his journey. During the first weeks of his trip, spent in England and northern France, he focused mainly on visiting cathedrals, and noted in his journal how impressed he was by the structural logic of French Gothic. But the final months of his trip, in Italy, France, and Germany, were devoted almost entirely to viewing paintings in museums. By that point, the passages about art in his journal chiefly concern painting. For example, in mid November, while in Dresden, he observed: "I am beginning to settle on favorites: Tintoretto, Rubens, Poussin, Delacroix, Turner, Constable. I think I have been most affected by Cezanne . . ."

Nearly all the paintings Dawson saw were by old masters, and he was distinctly put off by an exhibition of contemporary painting that he visited in Venice, which assembled realistic canvases in a bravura style that to Dawson's eye looked merely sloppy. Nonetheless, Dawson did record three encounters with contemporary work that profoundly affected his artistic direction: a meeting with John Singer Sargent in Siena; a visit to Gertrude Stein in Paris; and a trip to Ambroise Vollard's gallery in Paris, where he was able to see paintings by Cézanne. While one could easily paraphrase Dawson's description of these events, it is even more fascinating to absorb them through the artist's own words, with their curious mixture of perceptiveness and innocence.

John Singer Sargent

Dawson encountered John Singer Sargent at the Saccaro pension in Siena, where he arrived on September 19, 1910.[31] As he recorded, "The distinguished looking man sitting across from me at the dinner table is John S. Sargent. Sitting next to him is his sister. They are formal and very polite and seem interested in my tales of wild west Chicago." This meeting provided him with his first opportunity to observe a professional painter, and Dawson clearly looked closely, for his statement, while brief, is one of the more insightful descriptions of how Sargent executed his paintings:

> I have now been sketching in places where I run into Sargent. Without being obtrusive I've had chances to see him work. I realize how little I know about the mechanics of painting. Above all Sargent's painting looks masterfully easy. But I notice one thing. At the start of a painting he is very careful and then as it develops he lays on the paint with more freedom. When about done he looks at it with piercing eye and making a stroke *here* and another *there*, gives the whole a look of spontaneous dash. Although nine-tenth[s] of the work is very careful indeed, there is a look of bold virtuosity when the thing is done. But with all the good things he does there are occasional lapses into something very common-place.

FIG. 11 Gertrude Stein, ca. 1905. Yale Collection of American Literature, Beinecke Rare Book and Manuscript Library

He also had an opportunity to discuss the underlying principles of painting with Sargent, a matter on which it proved that they had very different ideas:

> . . . Sargent has more than once asked if he could see what I was doing. It pleased me that he should take any notice at all. Casual meetings have sometimes led to discussions. He is in favor of portrayals of sunlight. He says "like Sorolla" (who ever that is) and I try to point out the value of invention, novelty, originality, the intensive effort to compose. I suppose I am influenced by admiration of composers of music. Of the masters of painting, Sargent brings up Hals and Titian. I suggested to him: VerMeer as the most conscious as well as the most intuitive painter. I wish that in my paintings I could place everything in the right spot, and position, and attitude, and relation to every other thing in the picture.

Indeed, the contrast between their two approaches was almost humorous, although Sargent invariably was polite, listened carefully, and looked with great attention. As Dawson wrote:

> Sargent today looked long at my small wood panel. "What is it," he asked. "It is from a theme suggested by the corner of the fountain, and the jar below it, but is not an attempt to make a copy of either," I said. When I was about to take back the little panel of wood, he said "No, let me look at it." This pleased me beyond any praise I had received at any other time from anyone. He never said at any of these meetings that I was on the wrong track.

This meeting strikingly juxtaposes a major master of the nineteenth-century vision with a young disciple of the modern one. The way that Sargent and Dawson thought and looked at things was fundamentally different. As Dawson noted:

> S's piercing, slightly protruding eyes seem to see like some physics instrument, but he is blind to some of the things I see. When I pointed out a particularly determined slant in the painting at the Museum, he considered it the product of ignorance. I thought that Micharino definitely made it because the picture required it.

Gertrude Stein and Ambroise Vollard

For all their differences of opinion, Dawson clearly enjoyed his meeting with Sargent, and later recalled it affectionately as an important moment for him. But an event of more obvious relevance to Dawson's later work was his meeting in Paris with Gertrude Stein. At the time he had fallen in with an Englishman named Whitley, who knew something about modern art. As Dawson commented in his journal entry for November 2, 1910:

> An Englishman here, Whitley, is a good companion. We did the Louvre together. He is full of information on recent art trends. He speaks of "cubists" attracting attention.
>
> I do not know much about Miss Stein. Whitley has told me she is becoming known to a few as a writer having a novel style and as being a collector of many things being talked about in Paris. I shall call on her with Lebenbaum's letter for I am sure he will want to know I did so.

Shortly afterward, Dawson noted:

> I have called at Miss Stein's on Rue de Fleurus, showed my letter to the long-skirted woman who answered the bell. She spoke English like an American, didn't bother to read the letter and informed me that Miss Gertrude was busy that afternoon, but would be at home Saturday evening.

Very likely, the woman who met Dawson at the door was Alice B. Toklas. Dawson's journal continues:

> Telling Whitley about it, he suggested we call together and also suggested I take along a wood panel to show. He said Saturdays brought a mixture of nationalities to Miss Stein's, but, while there was much confusion and the light was not good, one could see an extraordinary jumble of paintings, a few of them remarkable and well worth examining.

When they arrived:

> Whitley introduced me to the hostess, a fat woman sitting in a very large chair. A brief conversation with Miss Stein let her know that I was a fellow draughtsman of Lebenbaum's, but that I was more interested in painting than architecture. I told her that I had been in Paris earlier this year and that I was glad to be here again; could not stay long because money was running out, and I was afraid of not getting home without making a desperate call to the U.S. for funds. After some time she beckoned me to her chair. With some diffidence I showed her my little painting which I had carried under my arm. Looking at it for a while steadily she passed it to a bearded Frenchman who said a few words in comment, raised his eyebrows and with just a suggestion of a bow returned it to me. Then came the surprise. "Can I have this," said Miss S. "Do you mean buy it," I asked smiling, and thinking I would gladly give it to her. "Yes," she said. "Would 200 fcs. be right." "Yes." This is the first painting I ever sold. I told her it had no title. But I had called it, to myself, "Statement." She turned to the long-skirted woman who had met me at the door and said "Wouldn't this be nice for Christmas for—. I did not know who that was.

It would be interesting to know the name of the bearded Frenchman, who was clearly a favorite of Miss Stein (Matisse, for example, wore a beard during this period). As with other passages in the journal, part of the fascination of the account is the curious blend of naiveté with astute observation. From our present perspective, for example, it seems downright irreverent to describe Gertrude Stein as "a fat woman sitting in a very large chair" (fig. 11). But Dawson was only twenty-two, and simply jotting down reminders of his general impressions.

From the standpoint of his art visually, what Dawson did a few days later was probably even more significant. Whitley took him to a dealer—obviously Ambroise Vollard—who showed him a group of paintings by Cézanne. As Dawson recorded:

> The following Monday, due to my interest in the Cezannes at Miss Stein's, Whitley took me to a dealer on Rue Laffitte to see some of Cezanne's paintings. Whitley was a walker so we walked to

the shop which had nothing about it that seemed to advertise its purpose. The window was empty. The dealer was polite, but as the conversation was in French, I got very little of it. The few paintings he showed impressed me extremely. I wanted to see more, but he was very slow [to] bring each out. Finally he told Whitley of a coming appointment so we left, myself thrilling as we went. My mind has been full of the few things I saw. One painting I cannot forget, a late one and apparently unfinished. The arbitrary black lines, the tying of knots, the emphasis these made in showing where the parts were important to the composition, and the great variety of altered forms were very instructive to an understanding of inventive pictures, and gave me a big lift in support of what I was trying to do in my own work. One thing I noticed was the invariable success of Cezanne's color.

Arthur Davies and Albert Pinkham Ryder

Arriving in New York on his return, Dawson also took time to make an important contact. As he wrote on roughly November 31:

> Next day: Looked up Arthur Davies, the Kellogg's friend. He gave me some time in his studio, said he had seen my little sketch for the larger "Germinal," and really gave a good look at my little wood panels and the snap shots of "Flowering Twilight." He was complimentary—wanted to know if a move to New York were possible. His own work is dreamlike and very original. After an hour (how I wish I had a studio like his) we visited Albert Ryder—a very exhilerating time there. He is a great artist. I felt extremely elated when he looked lengthily at my paintings and photos.

They also visited the studios of other artists, whose work displayed "clever craftsmanship." Dawson noted that "one discussion was about the 'wild men' of Paris. I may have seen something of those mentioned, without having thought of them as wild."[32]

But it seems to have been the visit with Ryder that left the strongest impact. As Dawson noted later:

> I can't get over thinking of Ryder. He is a great inventor of shapes, haunting impressions of those inner feelings which he has and which I can feel with him. He seems, however, close to his end, doing little except repainting, touching, and burnishing. His studio was a picture of awful disorder.

Dawson's "'Museum' Paintings"

After the dramatic breakthroughs that Dawson achieved in his first abstract paintings, it is difficult, but unfair, not to see his later career as something of an anticlimax. Hilton Kramer has perceptively noted the irony in the fact that Dawson came back from the European centers of modern art in many respects a less radical figure than he was before he left Chicago.[33] After he returned to the United States in early December 1910, Dawson did not go back to the pure abstraction he had been exploring earlier, but began making figure paintings in a style that scholars have generally described as Cubist. A major theme of these works is an effort to reinterpret the old masters. Yet one could argue that the best of these paintings, while not as important as *Prognostic*, are "better" as paintings—more fascinating as visual puzzles, more artfully contrived, more rewarding to intensive visual study. It took Dawson several years, however, to become fully confident in his new approach to art, which reached a peak of accomplishment around 1913.

In his later years, Dawson was somewhat apologetic about this return to the figure, and blamed it partly on his meeting in New York with Arthur Davies. In October of 1967, for example, in a statement for an exhibition at the Schoelkopf Gallery, Dawson said of these figural abstractions: "These I might not have done if Arthur Davies had not urged me and encouraged me in that direction." Indeed, Dawson says the same thing in his journal of the time, although more cryptically. Next to his first discussion of this series, on December 15, 1910, he commented that "Meeting Davies was a great stimulant."

The motives for this shift ran deeper, however, and Dawson's journal contains a number of hints about his reasons.[34] On December 15, 1910, Dawson noted, "I am sketching for projects, thinking much about Rubens and Tintoretto, and the Cezannes in Paris. And Ryder's paintings haunt me." A few weeks later, on January 2, 1911, he wrote, "Sketches are developing plans for 'museum' paintings. These rely somewhat on those last themes that came from so much looking at paintings in the galleries, and on conversations about new trends."

Quite a number of thoughts are compressed in these brief entries. The phrase "'museum' paintings" is particularly suggestive, and seems to carry more than one level of meaning. Before going to Europe, Dawson had seen only one museum, the Art Institute of Chicago, whose collections were considerably less impressive in 1910 than they are today. Clearly, Dawson's visit to Europe had inspired him, like Cézanne, with the wish to make paintings "like those found in the museums." In addition, Dawson's paintings were "'museum' paintings" in another sense—that is, they were largely based on old master compositions. Art historian Mary Mathews Gedo calculates that three-quarters of the paintings that Dawson produced in 1911 and about half of those produced in 1912 derive directly from old masters.[35] By 1913, this was considerably less true—although as Dawson's paintings grew more abstract, his sources often grew more difficult to recognize. Paintings such as *Passed Correlations* (1913, fig. 15, pl. 43), for example, are surely based on old master sources, although the specific paintings Dawson was looking at have not yet been established.

FIG. 12 *Portrait*, 1910 (pl. 21)

Dawson's "Cubism"

Dawson's painting between 1910 and 1913 has usually been referred to as Cubist, and in a very loose sense this is correct, but Dawson's "cubism" took a form that was rather different from what was happening in France. Scholars have made much of Dawson's alleged dependence on Picasso, but in fact, Dawson's journal makes it clear that his only opportunity to view Picasso's work came when he visited Gertrude Stein for a single evening. This would have given him a chance to see that Cubism existed, but scarcely time to grasp its visual language properly. Indeed, at this point, Stein's collection was still largely dominated by pre-Cubist works, such as the famous portrait that Picasso made of Stein in 1905. Dawson's cubism is only loosely related to Picasso's work or what was happening in France, and was largely an independent invention of his own—resulting from what anthropologists describe as "stimulus diffusion."[36]

This becomes apparent when we ask ourselves a simple question: was Dawson's cubism of the Analytic or Synthetic type? At the time that Dawson visited Gertrude Stein, Picasso's *Demoiselles d'Avignon* was only two years old, Analytic Cubism was still new, and Synthetic Cubism had not yet been invented. But Dawson's cubism does not closely resemble Analytic Cubism, with its dense networks of vertical and horizontal lines and its constant allusion to transparent volumes and shifting planes. Even in its subject matter it is different, since nearly all of Dawson's "cubist" paintings present figure compositions, rather than the still-life arrangements favored by Picasso and Braque, or half-length portraits of single figures (fig. 12, pl. 21). In fact, Dawson's approach is closer to Synthetic Cubism, in its frequent use of flat patterning. But it is not quite the same as Synthetic Cubism either, since Dawson's shapes do not have distinct boundaries, in contrast to the Synthetic Cubist paintings of Picasso and Braque (which began with actual cut-out shapes and almost always can be translated back into paper cutouts even when the shapes are created with paint rather than with collage).

Also unlike a Synthetic Cubist, Dawson does not work with shape and color alone, but makes extensive use of superimposed black lines.These suggest directional movement and sometimes appear to indicate edges, but they never follow the complete outline of the form, tending, rather, to break off ambiguously. To a large degree, in fact, Dawson's outlines seem to be derived not so much from Picasso or French painting as from his use of parabolas and other curves in his earlier painting *Prognostic*. As in *Prognostic*, Dawson's lines in his work from this period are not simply edges but express some inner essence, or flow of forces, that gives spiritual or mathematical meaning to the object. The disjunction between color and line in Dawson's cubism seems to relate to his experience as an architectural draftsman, with lines placed as if Dawson had laid a sheet of tracing paper over the image and deftly summarized the most vital features of the form.[37]

As early as 1967, Karl Nickel, the curator at the Ringling Museum of Art who mounted the first exhibition of Dawson's work in recent times, offered a still-cogent assessment of how Dawson's artistic language stood apart from European Cubism.

> These pictures may be described as "Cubist," in a sense, though the resemblance to properly Cubist pictures seems superficial . . . Dawson does not follow the Cubists, but runs parallel, beginning from Cézanne as they do. His paintings must be seen as an independent American approach to the problems of pictorial construction announced in late Impressionism.[38]

The first paintings that Dawson made after returning from Europe look particularly different from the European examples. They are less like Picasso's Cubism than like the expressively deformed early figure paintings of Willem de Kooning and Arshile Gorky. Essentially, Dawson was accentuating and embellishing the linear surface of a traditional realist work, slightly dissociating the line from the form and creating a visual tension between line and plane. These lines undulate strongly, and in general, the forms Dawson created are not so much cube-like as flame-like. Abraham Davidson has observed that the rhythms of these paintings flicker and swim "as though a movie projector were suddenly jammed and the boundaries of the figures repeated in multiple overlaps."[39]

One of Dawson's most successful early paintings in this style is *Lucrece* (1911, fig. 13), which as Mary Gedo has noted, is based on a painting by Peter Paul Rubens, *The Capture of Samson*.[40] Dawson, however, focused simply on the female nude, removing the other figures, and retitled the piece to suggest that the woman rather than the man is the victim. Here the flame-like character of the forms ties in with the meaning of the painting, which is basically erotic. (The flames grow hottest in color and most intense in the most erotic portions, reaching a peak of intensity around the subject's thighs.) A portion of the painting that clearly gave Dawson trouble was the placement of the arms of the figure, for which he could find no single satisfactory position. In the end, he decided to show it in more than one position, which created a sense of blurred motion.[41] Both the flame-like forms Dawson favored, and this interest in capturing the effect of motion, call to mind Italian Futurism more than they do Parisian Cubism. Futurism, however, was generally not well known in the United States, so if some Futurist influence reached Dawson in Chicago, it was probably through an intermediate source.

Dawson's first paintings in this mode seem to have been tentative affairs, in which realist outlines are only slightly distorted. Even with *Lucrece* one feels that Dawson was still struggling for a satisfactory system for breaking up shapes. By the time he produced *Madonna* (pl. 22), however, which is also dated 1911, Dawson had begun fragmenting the internal shapes of his compositions in a startling and fascinating manner. Unfortunately, his working drawings have been lost, but it is likely that he worked from tracings, like an architect, and that like an architect or engineer, he was interested in creating room-like shapes and also in finding the bearing lines of the compositional structure. Dawson employed an interesting technique in these works, one not found in European Cubism—the use of white outlines as well as dark ones. Probably, this device was inspired by architectural blueprints, which contain white lines against a dark background.

Viewed as pure abstractions, these paintings are generally quite pleasing, but to follow Dawson's thinking it is often helpful to juxtapose them with their sources. *Madonna*, which uses Leonardo da Vinci's *Virgin of the Rocks* as a springboard, is a case in point. To a large degree, Dawson was interested in using this source to create a purely arbitrary pattern of shapes, a kind of jigsaw puzzle arrangement that disguises and camouflages the underlying form rather than revealing it. Through a pattern of block-like shapes, for example, he makes the proper left hand "float" in front of the body, so that its attachment to the arm or body is no longer clear. In certain places, however, Dawson was interested in revealing the understructure of the form more emphatically than was done in the original painting. In particular, he created cutouts in the center that allow us to see through the figure's clothing and in essence "undress" her.

By 1913, Dawson no longer needed a model and was generating equally interesting patterns of form from his own imagination. As Dawson later noted, "Before the end of 1912, I was moving toward non-objective themes and their elaboration and, in that winter, was painting that way." The best example of this abstract direction is the painting *Wharf under Mountain*, of 1913 (pl. 34), which appeared later that year in the Armory Show, and must have been completed before the exhibition reached Chicago. The title was given to the painting by Walter Pach, who thought the work resembled a schooner at a wharf, with a mountain behind it. While Dawson accepted the titled, he confessed, "That I did not see in it," and in a letter of the 1960s, written when he sold the work to Ralph Norton, he made it clear that he conceived the painting as a pure abstraction.

In just one instance before the Armory Show, it seems likely that Dawson used a modernist picture as a source. Several scholars have suggested that his *Woman in Brown* (1912) is a reworking of Picasso's *Portrait of Gertrude Stein* (1906, The Metropolitan Museum of Art), which he had seen two years earlier in Paris.[42] The parallels between the two works are unmistakable, though Dawson also made a number of significant changes in his portrait—rotating the head, manipulating edges, and reversing elements in several places, as if turning over a sheet of tracing paper. It is not clear how Dawson was able to reproduce the composition of this painting so accurately, short of having a photographically perfect visual memory. Possibly he had made a sketch when he visited Gertrude Stein, but he may have found a reproduction of some kind.[43] In any case, Dawson's "cubist" language is very different from that of Picasso, a fact that slightly deflates the notion that Dawson was powerfully influenced by Picasso's work. It is has more resemblance to the Constructivism of Naum Gabo and Anton Pevsner, though this parallel is one of similar thinking rather than influence. Since Constructivism was invented in Russia, Dawson could hardly have known of its development, particularly since the movement began a year later than this picture was made, in 1913.

FIG. 13 *Lucrece*, 1911. Oil on canvas. Museum purchase, Collection of The John and Mable Ringling Museum of Art, the State Art Museum of Florida

The Armory Show, 1913

In the period from 1908 to 1913, the principal venue for seeing modern art in the United States was Alfred Steiglitz's gallery in New York, located in the attic of an old brownstone at 291 Fifth Avenue. There, Stieglitz held exhibitions of drawings by Rodin (January 1908) and Matisse (May 1908 and again in February 1910), Cézanne's watercolors (March 1911), watercolors and drawings by Picasso (March 1911), and sculpture and drawings by Matisse (March 1912). Stieglitz also showed the work of forward-looking American artists, including John Marin, Max Weber, Arthur Dove, and Georgia O'Keeffe. For those who did not live in New York, it was diffiult to learn of these activities. Occasionally some of the works Stieglitz exhibited were also reproduced in his magazine *Camera Work*, accompanied by innovative writing by figures such as Gertrude Stein. However, this magazine also was by no means

FIG. 14 Pablo Picasso (Spanish, 1881–1973) *Woman with a Mustard Jar*, 1910. Haags Gemeentemuseum, Netherlands. Photo courtesy of the Bridgeman Art Library

easy to obtain, and reached only a small circle. It remains unclear whether Dawson was aware of Stieglitz's ventures during this time, particularly since Stieglitz is never mentioned in his journal.

Only seldom did adventurous art reach Chicago. In fact, the only occasion when it did was in March 1912, when the W. Scott Thurber Galleries mounted Stieglitz's exhibition of the work of Arthur Dove, including his first group of exhibited abstractions, *The Ten Commandments*. This attracted a good deal of attention in the Chicago press, although again, Dawson never mentioned the event in his journal. Thurber's death shortly afterward, in September 1913, brought a close to the activities of the only gallery in Chicago that had seriously promoted modern art.[44]

Consequently, as far as is known, the first time Dawson saw modern art was in 1913, when an enormous "International Exhibition of Modern Art" was brought to the Art Institute of Chicago. Referred to as the Armory Show because it opened at the Sixty-ninth Regiment Armory in New York, the exhibition had originally been intended to showcase avant-garde American art, for example, thework of the painters of the Ashcan school. In the end, however, the American offerings were overshadowed by the radical experiments of European painters, particularly the Cubists, and received almost no critical attention. When the exhibition opened it was widely ridiculed in the press, but it also created a media sensation, and thousands of visitors flocked in to see the strange new horrors.

Before the Armory Show, modern art was known to only a small circle of Americans. Afterward, it was the subject of discussion almost everywhere. Before the Armory Show, the social realism of the Ashcan school seemed boldly radical. Afterward, it seemed timid and slightly old hat. The most controversial works in the exhibition were the Cubist paintings— particularly Marcel Duchamp's *Nude Descending a Staircase* (1912, Philadelphia Museum of Art), which was singled out by the press and the public as an emblem of the absurdity and strangeness of the new art. For Dawson, the Armory Show marked a turning point, since it provided his first opportunity to see Cubism and other forms of the new art on a wide scale and with sufficient time to actually scrutinize and study the work.[45]

While nominally organized by a committee, the exhibition was selected principally by two or three people, the most significant of whom was the artist Arthur B. Davies, whom Dawson had met briefly in New York. On December 16, 1912, Dawson noted in his journal that Davies had invited him to send some paintings to the Armory Show, and that "Bennet" (whoever Bennet may have been) had sent him a newspaper clipping announcing the enterprise. But Dawson's best paintings were stored at "The Humps," and were not easy to get to, and others that he liked were still unfinished. Moreover, even if he went to the expense of collecting and shipping the paintings, he doubted that they would be accepted, given the competition from other well-known American and European painters. On January 26, 1913, Dawson wrote the following, which suggests the character of his work at this point:

> Nothing on hand that I can send. Two pictures I like, both very "abstract" (that is a word I hear more and more now adays) I hope to finish soon. A dozen others are almost ready. These are themes and elaborations making shapes that seem to give out those peculiar feelings: what are they—awe, mystery, reverie (I can't find the words). Whatever they are, these feelings are produced entirely by the shapes and colors that are not those of any visible or external objects.

Dawson's reaction to the clipping sent by "Bennet" is also worth noting, since it indicates that at this stage his knowledge of European developments was very vague, a fact underscored by the works themselves. As Dawson stated:

> The paper mentions several names unknown to me, mostly French. I recall talk at Miss Stein's. The name Matisse sounds familiar and I think that Picasso was in the talk, too. With all the great quantity the promoters would not particularly want me from way out here in Chicago.

Nonetheless, Dawson clearly looked forward to the exhibition with excitement. On March 16, he noted that it would open in another week, and on March 25, the day after the exhibition opened, he described his enthusiasm for the new work:

> (March 25): The Armory Show opened yesterday at the Art Inst. Today I have had a good look. I stayed long and looked and looked. It was with great difficulty that on coming out I could convince myself that I hadn't been thru a dream.
>
> (March 27): The Chicago newspapers are putting out the strangest headings and the silliest comments. The articles in the newspapers sound far more crazy than are the pictures which they are shouting about. "Crazy-quilt," "Lumber factory," "Nasty," "Lude," "Indecent" are the common descriptions. Such terrible misunderstanding when, to me, there isn't an insincere work shown and almost everyone is fitting it into the stream of progression that in art has never stopped, nor broken away at anytime to discard the qualities that make fine art.
>
> These are without question the most exciting days of my life. The works of Matisse and Kandinsky are extremely important in breaking open the avenues of freedom of expression. I am feeling elated. I had thought of myself as an anomaly and had to defend myself, many times, as not crazy; and here now at the Art Institute many artists are presented showing these very inventive departures from the academies.

He also commented, "I look back to my discussion with Sargent and wish he could see this exhibition. Maybe he would see what I meant."

Dawson's attentive study of the paintings soon brought him into contact with another one of the organizers of the exhibition, Walter Pach. He wrote on March 25:

> The man with the moustache and tremulous hands who seemed in constant attendance saw me as the most lingering of spectators. Engaging me in conversation I found him most interesting and informative. His name is Walter Pach. I asked him about prices and was amazed to find how low prices are, except of course the Cezannes and the paintings of one or two others now dead. He says he is a close friend of Arthur Davies and on hearing my name said that Davies had told him to be sure to look me up.

Pach came to the family home a few days later. As Dawson described:

> Walter Pach called on us yesterday evening. He said he was tired and hadn't expected the visit to be anything but tiresome, but that Davies insisted that a major project in Chicago was to see what Dawson was doing. Pach was, he said, amazed. The fireplace board in the living room caught his eye. When I brought out "Germinal" and "Flowering Twilight" he seemed fascinated. He said he was not a "complimenteur," but the compliments he gave the things I showed him gave me great pleasure. I brought out the one I had just varnished. This should have gone to the Armory in N.Y. It wasn't titled. He gave it "Wharf under Mountain." *That* I had not seen in it."

On April 4, 1913, Dawson recorded,"Walter has taken the "Wharf under Mountain" with him and said that when no one was looking he would have the men hang it." And shortly afterward, under the same date, he continued:

> Walter said he had no trouble getting the painting hung, but if any of the staff should notice it, it might have to come down. He said that so far none of the boss men had come anywhere near the show. I bought every newspaper everyday and searched thoroughly for any mention of the added item. I could find none."[46]

Added at the last minute, Dawson's painting did not appear in the catalogue of the Armory Show, and it was apparently not mentioned in any of the reviews of the exhibition.[47]

Besides having the chance to display his own work—this was the first time Dawson had actually had one of his paintings in a public exhibition—Dawson was able to purchase a painting by Marcel Duchamp from the Armory Show. In his book *Queer Thing, Painting*, published in 1938, Walter Pach noted that he was startled by Dawson's naiveté in regard to the pricing of the works, and that he seemed to have no knowledge whatsoever of their respective values. The first painting he asked about, a landscape by Cézanne, was the most expensive canvas in the exhibition, priced at $50,000, whereas the next was a figure piece by Marcel Duchamp that cost only $160. Initially, Dawson had hoped to purchase Picasso's *Woman with a Mustard Jar* (1910, fig. 14, now in the collection of the Gemeentemuseum, the Hague), which was priced at $324, but his savings amounted to only $220 and his father was unwilling to lend him the difference. Consequently, he purchased a figure painting by Duchamp, *Nu (esquisse)* of 1911, now generally titled *Sad Young Man on a Train*, for $162, as well as a smaller painting, *Return from the Chase* (1911), by Amadéo de Souza Cardoso, whose price is not recorded, but which must have cost only a few dollars.[48]

Dawson's Work of 1913

The year 1913 was the most prolific year of Dawson's career—no doubt in part because of the adrenaline put into his system after viewing the Armory Show, and perhaps also because, for the better part of the year, he was unable to land a steady job and had a large amount of time in which to make paintings. The work of this time is also consistently high in quality. But assessing Dawson's stylistic development and sorting out the crosscurrents of influence during this year presents a particularly daunting challenge, since some of the artist's paintings of 1913 were produced before the Armory Show, and others after. A few of those made after the exhibition show the influence of what Dawson had learned there. For example, Dawson noted that his three *Hercules* paintings were influenced by Marcel Duchamp—and one might add that they are also highly reminiscent of Picasso's *Woman with a Mustard Jar*. Finally, Dawson was able to look closely at European modern art, and his own work quickly reflected this influence.[49]

What complicates the problem, however, is that even after the Armory Show, Dawson often seems to have continued with his own internal development, and gleaned only a general kind of emotional boost from his new art historical knowledge. A case in point is the remarkable painting titled *Passed Correlations* (fig. 15, pl. 43). Dawson put this at the very end of his list of paintings for 1913, which would suggest that it was his last work of the year. But it is hard to imagine a painting that is further from any European prototype than this canvas. Instead, it is one of the most remarkable examples of Dawson's architectural "Puzzle Pictures," in which he transforms an old master source into a "room plan" of perplexing shapes. (A device he used, perhaps derived from architectural room plans, consists of pivoting the outline off the form on which it rests, similar to the way in which an architect indicates a door.)

Over the course of his career, Dawson developed various quasi-Cubist languages, but certain qualities remain constant. In all his paintings, line is strongly asserted and, in general, Dawson made lines that detach themselves at least slightly from the forms they represent, so that they do not simply delineate edges but take on an independent expressive character. As suggested earlier, this handling of line seems to relate to Dawson's work as an architect and engineer. His lines are like those an engineer calculates when figuring the internal forces that run through a block of steel or stone, and like an engineer, he often treats them as if they were traced overlays that float above the surface of the picture. Indeed, Dawson often uses shapes that resemble the "force line" of an engineer, although in his work the lines usually do not press downward, but push up, in a kind of ecstatic gesture. Dawson is also drawn to bud and cusp-like curves that blossom upward like a flower. Unlike the Analytic Cubists, who preferred straight lines that they employed to articulate interleaved planes, Dawson likes lines that wiggle and bend in space. Thus, the line itself, rather than the space it defined, is his focus of interest. Even when he does use straight lines, as he did in *Passed Correlations*, he emphasizes the point at which the lines join, and the resulting angle.[50]

In his use of color, Dawson tends to work logically, establishing a central color "chord" and applying it throughout the picture. Many of these chords consist of hues that are fairly close to one another, such as pink, brown, and tan—one of his favorite harmonies. In other cases, however, he uses bolder juxtapositions, which come close to opposing hues on the color wheel, such as the contrast of red and green. Dawson's colors never span the entire spectrum, but encompass a more limited and controllable set of variables (although occasionally

FIG. 15 *Passed Correlations*, 1913 (pl. 43)

he breaks away from the central color chord for a moment, to add extra energy to the effect). Whatever the degree of contrast, distinctions of hue and of color temperature are employed to create a sense of space that is complexly layered, like different levels of a sculptural relief. Each color serves a highly specific demarcating function, the way colors on a map work.

Dawson's triptych, *Prognostic*, introduced one of the artist's most effective devices in handling form, which crops up repeatedly throughout his career—the concept of the "ghost form," in which the central block of the form is less solid than its outline, like a ghost whose edge can be discerned but whose center is transparent. Like so many of Dawson's devices, this one seems to have its conceptual root in his work as an engineer, for to an engineer the form itself is often less significant than the energy or force—whether the force that runs through it is electricity, physical stress, or gravity. To most of us this seems like an inversion of reality, but to Dawson this way of thinking seems to have come naturally.

Thus, for Dawson, lines and edges are more real than the form itself. ("I have the strong feeling, on looking at the masters," Dawson noted, "that the most recognizable communication is in the lines.") Where Dawson varied frequently throughout his career was in his use of shading. Some of his most significant paintings, such as *Passed Correlations*, employ completely flat, map-like shapes. In other cases, he used tonal gradation to create complicated spatial nuances—in some instances, to create a kind of secondary picture-puzzle that lies underneath the one formed by the outlines. Because of these differences, his paintings often look very dissimilar to one another. But what unites them, and what separates Dawson's work from European Cubism, is his handling of edges. For Dawson, it is the edge that activates the form. In this respect, his work differed greatly from the Analytic Cubism of Picasso, for whom line itself was not primary (which is why he made all his lines straight) but served instead as an indicator of underlying relationships, volumes, and planes. Picasso's Analytic Cubist paintings have an elaborately mottled surface—every brushstroke stood for a decision about modulating space—whereas in Dawson's work the surfaces are often rather flatly painted and it is the wiggly, restless contour that enlivens the design.

Dawson's paintings from 1911 to 1913 show a progressive increase in skill and subtlety in handling these internal areas. At first, he seemed trapped within his boundaries of line, like a child filling in the outlined areas of "paint by number." As his work developed, however, he found that he could create interesting effects by highlighting or shading one or another side of these outlines, or again, by running a color underneath the outline. He often used both these devices in one picture to create a feeling of transparent planes in intricate overlays. Dawson's paintings of 1912 suggest that he went quite far toward developing these devices on his own, but certainly his use of them becomes dramatically more effective and complex after he attended the Armory Show and was able to study the work of Picasso and other Cubists.

Disillusionment with Architecture

Dawson left Holabird and Roche while the Armory Show was running. It is not clear whether he resigned or was fired. During the next few years he worked for a variety of architectural and design firms, but these jobs paid poorly and none of them lasted very long. In each instance, he felt frustrated by the shoddy quality of the work.

In April 1913, Dawson took a job with a furniture company called W. K. Cowan, under an architect named Arney. He soon found that the company cut corners to save expenses. Trouble in complying with building codes, and evidently, low profits, caused the firm to discontinue its architectural remodeling division at the end of May, leaving Dawson out of a job.

Around May 25, 1913, he met a young architect, Albert Chase McArthur, a disciple of Frank Lloyd Wright, who was just starting up his own firm. Very quickly, Dawson discovered that McArthur "knows practically nothing about construction or specifications," and that his designs were third-rate. As Dawson observed: "It is distressing to work with McArthur—his designs have no merit whatever and I have to draw up details of construction of houses that I wish would never get built." Around July 5, Dawson resigned his position, agreeing to forfeit his pay for the month of work he had put in.

At the end of July, he took a job with the Nachtegal Manufacturing Company in Grand Rapids, Michigan, as head of the building department. His first project was to remodel a bank in Logansport, Indiana. He developed a plan that combined plate glass and structural steel, but when his insistence that the cracked wall of the bank was structurally unsound, and needed additional steel support, led to disagreements over cost, Dawson resigned the position after only one week of work.

After that, he did some drafting work for a friend named Smith, whom he had met while working with Holabird and Roche. He found the experience "a dull rut," however, and resigned sometime in March or April 1914.

Judging from the comments in his journal, it seems a shame that Dawson was not able to develop his architectural talents. He clearly combined a remarkable grasp of structural necessities with interesting ideas about design and decoration. But Dawson always confessed that he was a poor salesman, and his string of dismal experiences made him feel that painting would be a better outlet for his talents. As he wrote in his journal, "The artist painter has an advantage in that he can conceive, start in and complete a design without having a client already backing the production. The architect can make all the designs he chooses but is foiled in completing his work by lack of a client." This rapid rotation of jobs was obviously frustrating for Dawson, and disillusioned him with architecture, though it did leave him long periods of time during which he was free to paint.

To emulate Carrie Nation and swing a hatchet on everything in sight is the first impulse that seizes one on his first inspection of the cubist exhibition.

—Anonymous art critic,
Milwaukee Free Press, April 1914

Exhibitions and Sales of 1914

While Dawson is not listed in the catalogue for the Armory Show, the following year he showed in several exhibitions that are better documented. In December 1913, he received a surprise letter from Walter Pach stating that he and Arthur Davies were organizing an exhibition at the Montross Gallery in New York of the most modern recent American art. ("He thinks Stella and I are the most abstract," Dawson noted.) The final exhibition, *The Fourteen*, included work by Davies, William Glackens, Kunk McRae, George F. Of, Pach, Maurice Prendergast, Morton Schamberg, Charles Sheeler, Joseph Stella, Henry

Fitch Taylor, Allen Tucker, and Howard Coluzzi, as well as Dawson's painting *Wharf under Mountain*.

His single most important showing occurred at the Milwaukee Art Society, through his friendship with Dudley Crafts Watson, a high school classmate of his brother Mitchell. Watson is first mentioned in Dawson's journal in December 1913, at which time Dawson noted that his friend had just accepted the directorship of the Milwaukee Art Society and that "this may be a chance for some showing of my work." About a year later this hope was realized, when Watson invited Dawson to send some work for an exhibition he was organizing called *Paintings and Sculptures in "The Modern Spirit."* The exhibition was a curious hodgepodge, featuring the work of several European moderns (but not Picasso) alongside Chicagoans such as Dawson. But it did include several of Dawson's most striking paintings, among them *Germinal*, *Figures in Action* (1912), and his early triptych, *Prognostic*. (It also had several works by the Post-Impressionist landscape painter Jerome Blum, who became acquainted with Dawson around this time.)

Watson clearly set out to create a slightly scandalous sensation, modeled on the Armory Show, and due to is lively promotion, the exhibition attracted a good deal of attention in the press, though much of it was mocking or inaccurate. The *Milwaukee Sentinel* carried a headline stating, "Latest Art Show Staggers Natives," while the *Milwaukee Free Press* blared, with telegraphically fractured grammar, "Cubist Art on Exhibition, Gallery Visitors Giggle, Wild Canvases Fascinating." The most interpretive reaction came from the *Milwaukee Journal*, which paraded the headline, "Big Cubist Art Exhibit Looks Like Grandmother's Crazy-patch Quilt Gone Wrong." The first sentence of the attached article declared, "To emulate Carrie Nation and swing a hatchet on everything in sight is the first impulse that seizes one on his first inspection of the cubist exhibition."

For the first time in his life, Dawson's work was singled out for special notice, and he even was described as one of the best-known modern painters (in fact, at this stage virtually no one had heard of his work). This attention seems to have beeen paid, in large part, because someone—apparently Luci Blum, Jerome Blum's wife—had told a reporter that Dawson's canvas *Prognostic* was a portrait of Dudley Watson. As a result, the *Milwaukee Free Press* carried a photograph of the piece that took up two columns and soberly cited Luci Blum's statement: "It is an unmistakable portrait of Mr. Watson. It suggests admirably his versatility, his energy, his quick grasp of subjects and ceaseless activity. The heavy cubes and cones near the center indicate the substrata of strength and stability in his character." "They are having great fun with it," Dawson noted in his journal, and for his part, Dudley Watson seems to have felt pleased that he had awakened the art lovers of the community out of what he described as "their dormant state."[51]

While none of the reviews showed any insight into Dawson's intentions, the clippings have value as one of the chief independent records of what Dawson had produced at this stage—and as evidence that *Prognostic* must have been executed at a reasonably early date. The one standoff created by the exhibition was caused not by the radical style of Dawson's work but by the fact that one of his early paintings represented Adam and Eve, and the exhibition committee felt that this display of nudity should be removed lest it corrupt the morals of small children. Watson came to Dawson's defense, but for a moment things were tense, and Dawson and Blum threatened to remove all their pictures. Finally, the committee relented, after observing a group of schoolchildren trooping past the work in question, without bothering to turn their heads.

In this same period, Dawson made the only two known sales of his work, other than his first sale to Gertrude Stein. The first of these was to Arthur Jerome Eddy, the author of a book on Whistler, as noted earlier, as well as of an even more daring account of modern art, *Cubists and Post Impressionism* (1916). Eddy owned an enormous collection of modernist canvases, including at least twenty-five paintings by Kandinsky. Despite his enthusiasm and support for modern art, however, few painters seem to have liked Eddy very much, apparently because of his strange personal deportment and the way in which he haggled over prices. Dawson's journal entry of May 25, 1914, describing his visit, is curiously unenthusiastic:

> Have been to Eddy's and have seen his big collection of paintings which he has hung in nearly every room in the house. It is somewhat indiscriminate . . . Cezanne is strangely missing and Picasso is represented only by a small, early, pointillist picture of an old Spanish woman. What a fine collection he could have with his money. One would think he would have

FIG. 16 *Brown Equation*, 1919 (pl. 58)

something of Cezanne, or Van Gogh, or De Gas, or Gaugin. There is a little feeling as you look at the paintings with Eddy, of the possibility of the collection being to him a practical joke.[52]

At Eddy's request, Dawson left two paintings with the collector, to consider for purchase. But by the time he finally sent his payment, some five months later, Dawson had shifted his energy from painting to agriculture, and used the money to buy a team of horses for his farm. Sadly, both paintings are now lost. One of them, titled *Rotor* (1913), seems to have been unusually interesting. A twenty-four inch pentagon, it was perhaps the earliest shaped canvas by an American artist, preceding Frank Stella's shaped canvases by nearly fifty years.[53]

Dawson also sold two additional paintings that year. In February 1914, he sold one of his "brown abstractions"of the previous year to Dudley Grant, an impecunious friend of his brother Mitchell, who paid him a mere five dollars—not quite enough to cover the cost of canvas, stretchers, and paint.

In addition, he sold a painting from 1908, *Flowering Twilight*, to a gentleman named E. F. Bennet, who seems to have seen the work in New York when it was shown in the exhibition *The Fourteen* at the Montross Gallery. (This was evidently the same Bennet who earlier had sent him a clipping announcing that the Armory Show would be coming to Chicago.)

During this period, Dawson also hoped to create a mural for the Ludington State Bank, located not far from his farm, but in July 1914, W. G. Wing, the president of the bank, wrote to say that the project would be delayed until funds for it were available. Soon afterward, Dawson became involved in establishing his fruit farm, and in the end the mural was never executed.

The Fruit Farm

Around this time, a shift major shift occurred in Dawson's life: he married and moved to the family property in Michigan, transforming adjacent land into a fruit farm. By May 1914, Dawson had given up all hope of making a living in architecture, and was beginning to dream of a country existence. He noted that he had loaded the library table with books on country life, from Thoreau's *Walden* to publications on farm management. His fate was sealed not many weeks afterward, when he attended an ice-cream social at the local schoolhouse and sat two desks away from a farm girl named Lily Boucher, just seventeen years old, who struck him as "the prettiest girl in the room." He arranged a date for the next Sunday afternoon, and confided to his journal: "I am in love with Lily Boucher. This is the first time I have thought seriously of married life. May be she is too young and, too, how can I support two or even one."

The romance flowered. In October 1914, Dawson purchased fifty acres from a farmer who had land just to the south and in the spring of 1915 he began planting it with hundreds of cherry and other fruit trees. On July 29, he married Lily Boucher, and on the first of December he noted that she had become pregnant. On July 11, 1916, his son Gerard was born, followed by two daughters, Hope (born December 1, 1917) and Carolyn (born January 31, 1921). Dawson's journal from this point on mainly concerns farmwork: purchasing land, trees, livestock, a Ford automobile, a new mower, a drill, and a harvester; hiring extra help; planting, pruning, and tending his fruit trees; and spraying and picking the fruit. Financially, the first few years were very difficult. The First World War increased the demand for farm crops, however, and by 1936, Dawson had paid off all his debts and was beginning to reap a clear profit.

Occasionally there are references to paintings or sculpture, such as his canvas *Loft* (1920) or *Prayer Loft*, which he considered one of his best works. But the entries become spaced farther and farther apart. In July 1939, after a gap of seventeen years, he noted that he had discovered the journal lying in a stack of wood and cardboard sketches and that "very little painting or carving was done for more than a dozen years." In an earlier entry, written on January 3, 1921, he commented with some regret on his decision to become a farmer and his abandonment of painting.

> It's a big laugh how I ever got onto a farm. The thought was developing over a good many months and was clinched after I met Lili. Here was a farm girl and here was a prospective farmer. This much is certain; farm life has its pleasures, but they are not the intense pleasure that art can bring. As to work, the two don't mix.

By this time the art world had completely forgotten Dawson, and even some of his old friends had ceased to think seriously about his paintings. One of his last entries mentions receiving a copy of Walter Pach's book *Queer Thing, Painting,* which described meeting Dawson at the Armory Show, and wrote sympathetically of his enthusiasm for what was shown there, but completely passed over his own work as a painter. There is an unmistakable sense of hurt in the last line of Dawson's entry: "How could Walter change his mind about my work and ignore me as a painter, make me only a 'young architect?'"

The Late Work

Around 1914, Dawson's work changed in character. The sort of intricate, subtle compositions he had produced in 1913 suddenly disappear to make way for paintings that are generally considerably simpler, with less elaborate shapes. In fact, many of these paintings even revert to a much earlier look, similar to the still-life paintings Dawson made in 1906, when he was just becoming fascinated by art. In addition, his artistic development ceases to form a clear trajectory at this point, but becomes episodic and increasingly uneven, with longer spaces between major pictures. The reason for this shift is not difficult to guess. Dawson was now hard at work trying to start up his fruit farm in Michigan, and he no longer had much time for painting. Some writers have suggested that Dawson's talent vanished at this point, and that his later work is of no interest, but this judgment is questionable. Some of the

FIG. 17 *Three Trees at Culvert,* 1914 (pl. 49)

later paintings are wonderfully original and inventive, though less complex than the work he produced at his peak. *Letters and Numbers,* of 1914 (a kind of punning poem in paint, pl. 44), *Brown Equation,* of 1918 (at once a still-life and a mathematical formula; fig. 16, pl. 58), and *Deep Sea Flowers,* of 1922 (a weird, underworld vision of fantastic, glowing shapes; pl. 62), are all remarkable conceptions. Indeed, in some cases the simplicity of these works becomes an advantage, as in *Three Trees at Culvert* (1914, fig. 17, pl. 49), whose marvelous bareness gives a startling tension to the spatial ambiguities and to the relationship between the vertical trees and the horizon. Mary Gedo has suggested that this last piece was based on a painting by Picasso, but it is unclear how Dawson could possibly have known the Picasso work in question, and it seems equally likely that he was going back to ideas he had explored in his 1908 work *The Dreamer* and revising them in light of his more recent discoveries.

Several writers have made biting comments about Dawson's retreat from art into farming, viewing it as evidence of a failure of nerve, and as proof of something weak and unsure about his character. Dawson himself later had some misgivings about his decision, but by any ordinary standard he was exceptionally successful in his later years. He had an enduring marriage, successfully raised three children, and became extremely prosperous. Even though farming was never a particularly lucrative profession, Dawson became a millionaire—at a time when a million dollars was still a large amount of money. In this period, Dawson pursued hobbies that interested him, such as botany and astronomy, and made improvements to the property around his house, for example, planting gardens (including one with flowers that bloomed at night) and constructing a small golf course. Moreover, Dawson did not cease to be an artist. He produced remarkable artistic work up to the end of his career, though not at the same pace as before.

Dawson's Sculpture

Dawson started to focus on sculpture as his career as a painter was winding down, and he was devoting much of his energy to starting up his fruit farm. The first journal entry to discuss sculpture at length is one from September 25, 1913, although he clearly made sculpture earlier, since this entry mentions some previous projects. While brief, Dawson's notation describes at least four different sculpture projects in wood and stone. There was a block of cast cement that the artist planned to carve into a freestanding piece; another flat slab of cement that he was carving into two dancing figures; a warped piece of pine that he intended to paint and carve; and the stump of an old plum tree that he had saved and planned to chop and saw into unusual shapes. Perhaps what is most striking is the variety of projects he describes. He was mixing techniques, including carving, casting, and painting; he was using a variety of materials, including cement and wood; and he was moving back and forth between "carved paintings," reliefs, and freestanding sculptures. From this time on, sculpture received an increasing amount of Dawson's attention, and in some years he produced more sculpture than painting.

Dawson turned to sculpture for various reasons. The most important seems to have been his discovery that while a piece of sculpture took longer to produce than a painting, it was easier to work on it intermittently, with constant interruptions. Unlike brushes, chisels do not need to be cleaned, so it was easy to pick up or break off work at a moment's notice. Moreover, the physical challenges of making a piece helped refocus his attention on an interrupted project.

An additional factor was one that Dawson himself never stated directly, but that must come to the mind of anyone who reads the last section of his journal. Both in practical and spiritual ways, making sculpture was very similar to the process of pruning trees. Dawson was unusually skillful at tree-pruning, which requires a quick, intuitive grasp of a number of complex and simultaneously operating variables—issues of weight, balance, and support; assessments of the healthiness of each branch; and finally, judgments about the overall shape of a tree, in the round, much like a freestanding sculpture that reaches upward toward the sunlight. With sculpture he applied very similar principles in the realm of pure imagination.

Unfortunately, Dawson's sculpture is largely ignored in critical writing about his work. Most of the sculpture is late, and thus it belongs to the period when Dawson's artistic creativity was supposedly on the wane. Most of it was executed during the period when he had ceased to keep up his journal, or made entries only very infrequently. Thus, we have few verbal clues about what he was attempting, and must rely almost entirely on the visual evidence. Following these purely visual clues is difficult at this stage, since Dawson's artistic projects were often disrupted by his work on the farm, and this gives an episodic quality to his artistic progress. Finally, since Dawson's sculptural conceptions were difficult to fabricate, there are frequently long lapses between when he first conceived an idea and when he executed it. For example, Dawson made a number of paintings between 1916 and 1918 that feature sculptural concepts, but he does not seem to have actually constructed some of these pieces until the late 1950s and early 1960s, when he produced some of his most ambitious freestanding pieces, such as *Morning Figure* (1959, pl. 72) or *Dark Word* (1961, fig. 18, pl. 73).

Dawson anticipated the future of sculpture perhaps more clearly than any American artist of his generation. Conceptually, his work provides a fascinating link between early modernist sculptors such as Henry Moore or Jacques Lipchitz, and those of the Abstract Expressionist generation, such as David Smith. In broad terms, Dawson's sculpture was innovative in three respects. First, he moved away from traditional materials toward combinations of media that are often highly original. Second, he moved away from representation toward the invention of pure forms. Third, he moved away from an emphasis on sculptural mass toward a form of drawing in space.

Technical inventiveness was essential for Dawson, since he had no access to a foundry, could not afford expensive materials, and had no tools other than those he used for farmwork. Thus, from the start, he employed a great variety of technical processes. He carved concrete, which he had mixed to be unusually soft, by adding a large amount of sand; he laminated pieces of wood; he carved shapes from wood and then used these carvings to make molds, and to cast the forms in concrete. Dawson was surely one of the earliest artists to make abstract sculptural reliefs out of sawed plywood; and he also made mixed-media constructions, for example, by combining metal rods with wooden connections to form constellation-like creations. While Dawson did not undertake welding, his use of rods and slender stems of wood often resulted in effects that were visually similar to that medium. Thus, he is an interesting transitional figure between sculptors such as Lipchitz and Moore, who were modelers and carvers, and those of the 1950s and 1960s, such as Mark di Suvero or John Chamberlain, who began to freely assemble disparate materials.

Dawson also stretched the limits of representation. As Randy Ploog has noted in his essay for this catalogue, Dawson's paintings of 1916–18 present concepts in sculpture that strikingly resemble Picasso's surrealist paintings of about 1930 (which also portray imaginary sculptures). Similarly, in his sculptural reliefs of the 1930s, Dawson took suggestions from the human figure to create ambiguous, biomorphic forms, like those found in the work of Jean Arp. Most sculptors of Dawson's generation, such as Lipchitz or Moore, did not stray far from recognizable human figures. Dawson's play of line, however, tends to take on a life of its own, so that often his figures dissolve into biomorphic shapes, like those that fascinated the

FIG. 18 *Dark Word,* 1961 (pl. 73)

Surrealists or the early Abstract Expressionists, such as Arshile Gorky.

Finally, from a formal standpoint, Dawson was unusually early in his emphasis on free-floating line, with the result that his sculpture often ceases to function as a mass and becomes a means of drawing with lines in space. The majority of sculptors who were his contemporaries (Lipchitz or Moore) produced works that focused on a single mass, although this mass is often penetrated with holes. In fact, Dawson himself seems to have started at this point, as is evident from one of his earliest sculptures, a figure from 1916. Perhaps inspired by his pregnant wife (he learned she was pregnant on December 1, 1915), *Figure* (pl. 53) consists of a human body whose center is hollowed to reveal another smaller figure inside. More often, however, Dawson's sculptures are essentially linear and considerably more open in their form. While most of these pieces are relatively late, a few surviving early examples demonstrate that this was his approach

FIG. 19 *658*, 1917 (pl. 54)

almost from the beginning. In 1917, he produced a remarkable piece titled *658* (fig. 19, pl. 54), which synthesizes the numbers from 0 to 9 into a single linear swirl. Similarly, *Three Dancing Figures*, of 1946, reduces three figures to a series of swirling arabesques. One of Dawson's most effective expressions of this style, however, was made later, around 1959, and is made up of a dancing or leaping figure, precariously balanced on one leg, composed from a single undulating line. Although, as mentioned, Dawson did not work in welded steel in the manner of Picasso or David Smith, he produced amazingly similar effects of line with other materials.

By the 1940s, Dawson had become relatively prosperous, and in 1949 he began spending the winter months in Saint Petersburg, Florida. At this time, his productivity as a sculptor increased markedly. Looking at this work presents a historical problem exactly opposite of that posed by Dawson's early paintings. If the early work is perplexing because it seems too early, his later work is bewildering because it takes little note of contemporary work, and to a large degree simply picks up where Dawson had left off decades earlier. In fact, some of the pieces of the 1960s are essentially realizations of concepts that he had expressed in painted form some forty years earlier. Given their early conception but late execution, it is hard to know where to place them in relation to the work of Dawson's contemporaries; but considered in juxtaposition with other sculpture produced in the 1960s, Dawson's work from this time can be compared favorably to that of artists such as Reuben Nakian, Theodore Roszak, Seymour Lipton, and Herbert Ferber.

Issues of Sincerity and Authenticity

At this stage we are finally ready to consider the credibility of the story of Dawson's career. Both the dating of Dawson's work, and the veracity of his journal, have caused scholars anxiety for some time. Having surveyed Dawson's life and art, it is now worth examining whether we are dealing with truth or with a remarkable fiction. Of necessity, such examination involves repeating some of what already has been presented, but from a slightly different perspective.

A first step toward confronting the issue of dating is to consider the painting by Dawson whose date is most important, the triptych *Prognostic*—since this single painting is quite sufficient by itself to establish Dawson's place as a major figure in art history. Dawson stated that he painted *Prognostic* sometime in the first five months of 1910, before he left for Europe. All existing information seems to strongly support this early date. It is true that *Prognostic* and the group of paintings associated with it are not mentioned by title in Dawson's intermittent journal. But the journal does have early statements indicating Dawson's interest in a purely abstract form of painting, and several forms of evidence substantiate an early date for his triptych.

First, all three panels of the triptych are dated 1910 on the front—and are dated in a fashion that, according to museum conservators, looks like part of the original paint surface. (Technical examination reveals no evidence that the signatures are "floated.") Second, the painting was reproduced and discussed in a Milwaukee newspaper as early as April 19, 1914. It seems farfetched to suppose that Dawson was changing the dates of his work as early as 1914, or that at such an early date he was also concocting a journal to support these deceitful practices. In 1914, no one in Milwaukee, and few people anywhere, would have seen a difference of date between 1914 and 1910 as in any way significant. Moreover, none of the press reports about the painting took note of its early date or commented on its art historical significance.[54]

As has been touched on earlier, the main reason for questioning such an early date is the belief that *Prognostic* is so strikingly similar to Kandinsky's work (or to that of some other European artist) that Dawson could not have produced his painting without knowledge of these European experiments. But, as has been discussed, the most convincing prototypes for Dawson's painting are sources that were quite readily available to him in Chicago. While there are parallels between the work of Dawson and Kandinsky, they seem to derive from ideas widely circulated in the late nineteenth century, and are not so close as to suggest that one artist borrowed from the other. The more we study *Prognostic*, the more it becomes clear that it speaks with an American accent.

With *Prognostic* behind us, we can move on to the remainder of Dawson's work, and to the general plausibility of the statements that Dawson made about it. This issue is more amorphous than the dating of a single painting, since it asks us to assess the myriad relationships between some 250 works of art and hundreds of pages of documentary evidence. Two general questions need to be considered. First, are the documents Dawson produced believable and internally consistent? Second, can we establish the truth of his statements from independent sources, at least in key instances? Dawson's credibility holds up on both counts, as becomes apparent when we review each of the major sources of our knowledge about his work.

As has been mentioned, Dawson arranged for nearly all his paintings to be kept together in a group after his death, and he compiled an inventory of them, spanning the years 1904 to 1963. This list groups the paintings by year. Dawson's statement at the beginning of the inventory, that the paintings are "not always in order within the years," suggests that most of them are indeed listed in their rough chronological sequence. Consequently, the list is helpful, though not infallible, in establishing the stylistic progression of Dawson's work. The fact that Dawson dated most of his paintings, and sometimes wrote titles on the back, makes it fairly easy in most instances to match the pieces with the titles on his list. But Dawson was clearly still sorting out his work and compiling the inventory when he died, so the correspondence between the list and the paintings is not quite perfect.

Dawson's children and grandchildren remember him as a careful, meticulous man—an assessment that fits well with his training as an engineer. To them the notion that he would have altered or confused his dating seems preposterous. In general, Dawson seems to have taken care to clarify anything that might throw a skeptical scholar offtrack. For example, he carefully noted when any of his wooden reliefs were repaired or remounted at a later date.[55]

Despite intimations that Dawson could possibly have altered some of his dates, no one has ever produced solid evidence that he did so.[56] In most cases, Dawson seems to have dated his paintings at the time he finished them, using the same pigments that he had employed to produce the image.

The supposition that Dawson changed dates has been based on the assumption that his work was directly inspired by the sight of some European masterwork, particularly works by Picasso. In the majority of instances, these alleged parallels simply are not visually convincing. Those parallels that do seem quite plausible—such as the notion that *Woman in Brown* might have been influenced by Picasso's portrait of Gertrude Stein, or that the *Hercules* paintings were influenced by Marcel Duchamp—are invariably also supported by statements made by Dawson himself in his journal.

The most persuasive reason for believing that Dawson's list must be accurate lies in the paintings he made, which in themselves contain a great deal of evidence. These works do not seem to directly imitate the work of other artists, but reveal an original stylistic approach that is distinctly their own. In addition, if we follow Dawson's dating, they seem to develop from year to year in a convincing manner, which seems to tie in with what we know of Dawson's life.

The written sources also appear believable. The central document of Dawson's development is the intermittent journal that he kept, which continues regularly (though with breaks) from December 26, 1908, to December 25, 1922, and contains a few pages of additional entries that take the story to December 15, 1940.[57] Both Mary Gedo and Randy Ploog have stated of Dawson's journal that "the entire document was recopied by the artist from his original notebooks," and Gedo has gone on to claim that the whole document was "consciously pruned and shaped." Even a cursory reading of the text, however, suggests that neither of these statements is true. Without exception, even in cases in which they are slightly self-conscious in tone, the entries feel like a first draft that was not carefully revised or edited. The text is filled with awkward locutions, odd punctuation, and occasional misspellings. Indeed, the only parts that seem to have been recopied were a few passages that Dawson reproduced from his pocket travel notebook. Dawson himself indicated which passages these are, and specified those sections to which he made slight additions and those that he recopied verbatim.[58] A comparison of the journal with Dawson's more formal artistic statements reveals notable differences of tone. The journal entries are relaxed, more colloquial in language, and more specific in content. In other words, neither the tone nor the content of the journal suggests that it was highly calculated, or that its chief purpose was to buttress Dawson's artistic claims.

As it happens, the journal does not mention many of Dawson's key paintings, such as *Prognostic*, and in fact only about a quarter of the writing is devoted to discussing art. The remainder is taken up by discussion of daily doings, architectural practice, travels in Europe, and so forth. The level of minute detail in the text, such as train schedules or descriptions of fellow travelers and hotels, would be difficult to assemble unless it were written down at the time of events, and it seems most unlikely that it was contrived later. In addition, Dawson's statements often reveal an innocence or naiveté that would be hard to fabricate. He describes Gertrude Stein, for example (as noted earlier), as "a fat woman sitting in a very large chair," hardly the sort of reverent phrase we would expect in a major document of modern art. Often, Dawson's lack of awareness of major figures is surprising, as in his rather dismissive comments on Frank Lloyd Wright, whom he seems to have distrusted because he knew Wright's work through an incompetent disciple, Albert Chase McArthur. Passages of startling perception on Dawson's part are often counterbalanced by instances of naiveté or misjudgment.

Finally, there are the supporting documents. Dawson noted that an important box of documents, including letters from Arthur Davies and Maurice Prendergast, was lost when his father's house was sold. But he did manage to preserve letters from Walter Pach, Dudley Watson, W. L. Wing, and other figures, dating from the period of the Armory Show and afterward, and these consistently support the statements he made in his journal. The way these letters mesh with his statements, both on larger questions and on seemingly trivial matters of detail, lends credence to Dawson's veracity as a witness.

At some level, I like the idea that Dawson might have faked the whole thing—if only because the task of faking would have been even more remarkable than his artistic achievements. To challenge the authenticity of something is not altogether bad, since it keeps our senses alert, and encourages us to think about things with special intensity. When we are wondering about Dawson's veracity, reading the most mundane entries in his journal becomes an exciting undertaking—and our senses become even more electrically energized when we look at his artistic output. For in the end, the most significant test of the truth of Dawson's statements is the degree of "truth" to be found in his art. Here we enter even more difficult terrain, since testing artistic truth involves a kind of "logic" even more elaborate than that needed for documentary evidence—one that is so complex that it is easier simply to say that our judgments are "intuitive."

One painting, *Passed Correlations*, strikes me in some odd way as remarkable—in Dawson's words, as mysteriously *right*—although I cannot not quite figure out what it portrays. Painted in pink, beige, and tan,

trate mainly on their work, and because their language of abstract form seems particularly rich. Their work is the touchstone against which all abstract painting of the period has been measured. But in fact there are quite a number of claimants to an early role in abstract art. Frantisek Kupka and Francis Picabia may have made abstract paintings around 1911; Robert Delaunay painted his non-objective *Color Disks* in 1912. The self-taught Lithuanian artist M. K. Ciulionis may have painted non-objective pictures between 1905 and 1910. What complicates the matter is that "abstract painting" in the modern sense implies not simply "abstract form," but a particular kind of content. Thus, "decorative art" is viewed as different from "abstract art," because it is simply decorative and has no meaning. Similarly, works such as *Color Disks* come close to being "diagrams" rather than artistic statements. In short, what is most striking about the work of Dove and Kandinsky (and also about the work of Dawson) is not simply that they made "abstract" paintings, but that they demonstrated that this kind of painting could be wonderfully varied and fertile, in both visual and emotional terms.

Recent scholarship has greatly expanded our knowledge of early ventures into abstract art by numerous figures (for example, see Tuchman et. al., *The Spiritual in Art: Abstract Painting, 1890–1985).* But there has been no systematic synthesis of this material nor any serious attempt to develop categories to distinguish the various languages of abstract painting. It is notable that the most ambitious recent survey of abstraction, Mark Rosenthal's *Abstraction in the Twentieth Century*, neither provides a clear definition of abstraction nor deals seriously with the issue of who made the first abstract painting.

Writers have generally tried to confront this issue in formal terms, but in fact, it would make sense to consider it in light of "information theory," since the essential issue is to what degree an image provides information that connects it, whether through representation or some other visual link, with material objects, moods, or spiritual states. Most writers have tacitly assumed that this feat can only be achieved through "representation," but in fact, an image can "connect" with reality in several ways: it can be a diagram (a simplified representation designed to dramatize a particular idea), a representation (an image that closely conforms to visual appearance), a symbol (a visual form to which meanings are arbitrarily attached), a trace (something that provides evidence of the activity by which it was made, such as an expressive brushstroke), or a stimulant (such as a sound or color that evoke a particular reaction or mood). Most visual images communicate in more than one of these ways. The meaning of the term "abstract painting" differs slightly, depending on which of these techniques is utilized to achieve a connection with things that lie "beyond" or "outside" the specific image. The notion that visual communication might be connected with information and "language" has been explored by Natasha Stahler in her provocative essay, "Babel: Hermetic Languages, Universal Languages and Anti-Languages in Fin de Siècle Parisian Culture," *Art Bulletin* 86, no. 2 (June 1994): 331–354.

13. Some writers employ the term "non-figurative painting" (literally "painting without figures") instead of abstraction, to suggest a painting that has no illusionistic reference but is constructed of geometric shapes. This seems to me, however, a slightly artificial distinction, since some geometric paintings, for example, the early works of Piet Mondrian, are rather literally representational (although they do not usually represent human figures) and by the same token, figurative paintings may be remarkably abstract.

14. The same process can be observed in regard to the toys of children, since children often will prefer a simple wooden or Raggedy Ann doll to a perfect plastic simulacrum of the human figure. It is generally the more "abstract" dolls that are hugged and loved and "turned into something" by the child. This issue is discussed with great sensitivity by E. H. Gombrich in his essay "Meditations on a Hobby Horse or the Roots of Artistic Form," included in his book *Meditations on a Hobby Horse* (London: Phaidon Press, 1963), 1–11.

15. Dawson noted in a letter to the director of the Milwaukee Art Center in 1969: "'Prognostic' is one of seven paintings (the others smaller) painted shortly after I graduated from college where I had so many engineering and mathematics courses that the influence of this shows in the background of coordinates and the super-position of differentials. The black lines and circles thrown over these are subconsciously possibly suggested by pencils, pens, and erasers generally strewn over a student's drawing board."

16. In his essay for this catalogue, Randy Ploog has noted that the arch shapes that Dawson explored are similar to those featured in S. Edward Warren's book *Stereotomy: Problems in Stone Cutting* (New York: John Wiley and Son, 1884). Dawson spent a semester at the Armour Institute of Technology in Chicago using this book to study the arch and its variations.

17. William Dean Howells, *The Rise of Silas Lapham* [1885] (New York: MacMillan Publishing, Inc., 1962), 173.

18. Arthur Jerome Eddy, *Recollections and Impressions of James A. McNeill Whistler* (Philadelphia and London: J. B. Lipincott Company, 1903), 176.

19. Ibid., 179.

20. Ibid., 177–80.

21. Whistler's painting *The Falling Rocket* (1875, Detroit Institute of Arts), however, pushes the boundaries of representation to the point at which the subject is not evident to most viewers unless its title is given. It was this painting that inspired John Ruskin's derogatory statements about Whistler's work, which in turn incited Whistler's libel suit against the critic.

22. Eddy, *Recollections and Impressions of James A. McNeill Whistler*, 205.

23. Dow noted that Fenollosa recognized "music to be, in a sense, the key to the other fine arts, since its essence is pure beauty."

24. Arthur Wesley Dow, *Composition: A Series of Excercises Selected from a New System of Art Education* (Boston: J. M. Bowles, 1899), 24. Continuing this line of thought, Dow stated that the artist "must learn the secret as Giotto and Francesca, and Kanawoka and Turner learned it,

by the study of art itself in the work of the masters and by continual creative effort."

25. Denman Waldo Ross, *A Theory of Pure Design: Harmony, Balance, and Rhythm* (Boston and New York: Houghton, Mifflin and Company, 1907), 5.

26. Ibid., 190.

27. One of the admirers of Ross' writing was the influential English critic, Roger Fry, who noted that with Ross' help he was able to "dispense once and for all with the idea of likeness to Nature." Denys Sutton, ed, *The Letters of Roger Fry*, vol. 1 (London: Chatto and Windus, 1972), 235. Also see Roger Fry, *Vision and Design* (New York: Brentano's, 1921), 21.

28. Ross, *A Theory of Pure Design*, 6.

29. Denman Ross, "Design as a Science," *Proceedings of the American Academy of Arts and Sciences* 36 (March 1901), 374, cited in Martin, "Some American Contributions to Early Twentieth-century Abstraction," 162.

30. Martin, "Some American Contributions to Early Twentieth-century Abstraction," 162.

31. As Randy Ploog notes in his essay for this catalogue, Sargent's presence in Siena at this precise time is confirmed by other sources. For example, William Blake Richmond, a British artist living in Florence, recorded in his diary on September 11, 1910, that Sargent had visited him before leaving for Siena. See Simon Reynolds, *William Blake Richmond: An Artist's Life, 1842–1941* (London: Michael Russell, 1995), 306–307.

32. The phrase "wild men" has a specific reference, for in May 1910 the American humorist Gelett Burgess had published an article titled "The Wild Men of Paris" in *Architectural Record*. The conversation Dawson mentions was clearly a response to this piece.

33. Hilton Kramer, "Art: Manierre Dawson, a Kandinsky," *New York Times*, April 10, 1981, 19.

34. On January 2, 1911, Dawson wrote in his journal, "Davies would be pleased to think that I haven't forgotten his advice to do figure painting. But I haven't been thinking of that advice. The urge had causes before that."

35. See Mary Mathews Gedo, "Modernizing the Masters: Manierre Dawson's Cubist Trasliterations," *Arts Magazine* 55, no. 8 (April 1981): 143.

36. A good example of stimulus diffusion is the Cherokee alphabet. Chief Sequoyah, who devised it, did not know how to read, but he knew that the Europeans had an alphabet. After thinking about the matter carefully, he invented a Cherokee alphabet of his own, in some ways superior to the European one. Rather than having twenty-six letters, it had eighty-six, the result being that each letter truly stood for a single sound, and was not ambiguous, in contrast to the European model. Sequoyah's alphabet was not a true "copy" or "replica" of the European one, which he himself did not know how to read, but a separate invention, inspired by the fact that he knew that alphabets existed even though he was not exactly sure how they worked. Dawson's cubism was produced in a similar fashion—it was a kind of "Cherokee cubism."

37. Signs played an important role in the early Cubism of Picasso and Braque, beginning around 1911, when words such as "BAR," the names of drinks in cafés, or the names of composers in pictures containing musical instruments, add an associative meaning to the painting. Later on, in their collage, these artists often used a portion of an object, such as the fragment of a newspaper title, to signify the whole. Dawson also was fascinated by signs, beginning as early as 1910 when he painted *Xdx*, in which various symbols exist both as abstract shapes and as allusions to an algebraic equation. In *Letters and Numbers*, of 1914, he explored the interplay between the meaning of letters and numbers and their existence as abstract shapes. Nonetheless, what is striking is that, while at times their philosophical concerns were similar, Dawson's handling of this material is very different from that of the French Cubists. Whereas Picasso and Braque draw mainly from newspaper headlines and advertisements, Dawson drew chiefly from the formulas of engineers. In addition, Picasso and Braque interwove these signs with the other elements of the paintings, unlike Dawson, who preferred to give them an autonomous life of their own.

38. Karl Nickel, "Introduction," in *Manierre Dawson: Paintings 1909–1913*, (Sarasota, Fla.: John and Mable Ringling Museum of Art, 1967), 6.

39. Abraham A. Davidson, *Early American Modernist Painting, 1910–1935* (New York: Harper and Row, 1981), 264.

40. Gedo, "Modernizing the Masters," 142.

41. On January 2, 1911, Dawson stated in his journal, apparently in reference to this painting: "At a loss to choose the proper angle for the arm at the left of the picture, I am getting the idea of presenting two or three positions and leaving these all in the picture. This does not look unreasonable and I think adds motion, though I usually think of motion, in a static picture, as belonging to that produced by directional relations of lines."

42. The chief discussion of the parallel between the two works is found in Earl A. Powell, III, "Manierre Dawson's 'Woman in Brown'," *Arts Magazine* 51, no. 1 (September 1976): 76–77.

43. The painting itself is not dated, but *Woman in Brown* figures on Dawson's list as a work of 1912 and it appears to be mentioned in Dawson's journal in an entry of January 1, 1912. Mary Gedo has noted that Alfred Stieglitz reproduced Picasso's *Portrait of Gertrude Stein* in *Camera Work* in June 1913, and has proposed that Dawson used this as his source. See Mary Mathews Gedo, "The Secret Idol: Manierre Dawson and Pablo Picasso," *Arts Magazine* 56, no. 4 (December 1981): 119. This would suggest that Dawson lied about the date of his canvas. But Dawson had actually seen this painting a few years before, and could have sketched it at that time. In addition, he may have gotten an image of the piece from some other source. During this period, for example, Dawson corresponded with Arthur Davies, who was organizing the Armory Show (unfortunately, Davies' letters to Dawson have been lost).

44. Shortly after the Armory Show, in July and August 1915, the Art Institute of Chicago held an exhibition of twenty-five paintings by Albert Bloch, all borrowed from the collection of Arthur Jerome Eddy. Bloch had shown his work in both Blue Rider exhibitions and had been closely associ-

ated with Franz Marc and Wassily Kandinsky. His Expressionist paintings might well not have appealed to Dawson. This exhibition also does not figure in Dawson's journal.

45. For an account of the Armory Show, see Milton W. Brown, *The Story of the Armory Show* (New York: The Joseph Hirshhorn Foundation, 1963; distributed by New York Graphic Society). Dawson is mentioned on pages 182 and 293.

46. In the 1960s, Dawson, who at that time was spending winters in Sarasota, Florida, drove to West Palm Beach in his station wagon and sold this painting to the Chicago steel magnate Ralph Norton, for his museum.

47. On January 30, 1969, Dawson described this same incident in a letter to the director of the Norton Museum of Art in West Palm Beach, Florida, which had just acquired the painting in question. At that time he stated:

> The "Wharf" was one of a series of blue pictures painted in Dec 1912–Jan'13 along with the brown ones at the same time. Davies had invited me to show this painting in the "Armory," but no frame or box was ready and I had my days filled with my architectural designing and drafting and I didn't realize at that time how important it would have been to get forward. When the show came to the Chicago Art Inst. in Feb, Walter Pach who was in charge for the "Association" found, after a few days, that he was the sole gallery boss, so suggested that I let him take it and get it hung in the American Room. He did that. It had been untitled. He called it "Wharf under Mountain" altho for me it had no reference to a wharf. This was the only non-objective abstraction in the American Room.

48. For nine years the Duchamp hung over the mantelpiece in Dawson's father's home in Chicago, but in March 1922, when Dawson badly needed money for his farm, he sold it back to Walter Pach. It eventually made its way to the Peggy Guggenheim Collection in Venice. The year before his death, Dawson donated the Souza Cardoso to the Hackley Art Museum in Muskegon, Michigan, the museum that was closest to his fruit farm. On October 2, 1968, Dawson wrote a letter donating the painting, which also described how he purchased it from the Armory Show. See Shirley Reiff Howarth, *European Painting: Muskegon Museum of Art* (Muskegon, Mich.: Dana Printing Company, 1981), 76 and 82.

49. Around the time of the Armory Show, Dawson also seems to have had greater access to reproductions of European modernist works, no doubt because modern art had become a widespread topic of discussion. Thus, for example, Mary Gedo has proposed—I think correctly—that Dawson's *White Tower*, of 1913, was based on Picasso's *The Reservoir, Horta de Ebro*, of 1909. See Gedo, "The Secret Idol," 120. Picasso's painting was reproduced in *Camera Work* in August 1912, and it seems likely that Dawson learned of the painting from this source.

50. Some of Dawson's later sculptures specifically address this issue. They are made with an armature of metal rods connected by wooden dots. This creates web-like patterns in which the inner substance of form disappears and the linear edge becomes the form.

51. In 1923, after Dawson had shifted most of his energy to fruit farming, Watson held a second showing of Dawson's paintings—this time a one-man show of twenty-seven paintings, the first solo show of Dawson's career. This second showing of his work, however, failed to stir up the excitement generated by the first, and Dawson does not seem to have been very interested in the response. Most of the paintings were small because of the difficulty of shipping them to Milwaukee from the farm.

52. Evidently, Dawson was a quick study, for just a few months before he had been unfamiliar with the work of Picasso or almost any other modern painter. After studying the Armory Show, however, he had clear ideas about how to properly present the history of modern art.

53. The shape of the painting is known from a sketch that Dawson made in his inventory notebook. Its significance was first recorded by Mary Gedo, in "Manierre Dawson: The Prophet in His Own Country," *American Art Review* 4, no. 3 (December 1977): 124, as well as in her article "Modernizing the Masters," 145, note 24.

54. In addition, the letter Dawson wrote about the painting being sold to the Milwaukee Art Center, although it was penned years after the fact, describes the painting in a way that sounds convincing, both biographically and psychologically. Dawson's assertion that the painting was largely inspired by his training as an engineer seems to fit very well with the forms that appear on the canvas.

55. As Dawson noted in his inventory, he remounted several of his early reliefs on Novoply, a product first released in 1951 that he began using a year later.

56. The only misdated paintings are a few small early works, which remained in the family, separate from the rest of Dawson's estate. On these, Dawson's widow seems to have inscribed dates after her husband's death. Since these additions were made with a ballpoint pen and are often obviously inaccurate, they are not difficult to discern.

57. In many instances, Dawson would add to one of these entries a day or two after the date of the original heading, as is apparent from the phrasing of the text.

58. The book itself bears an imprint and date that seem to place it in Chicago at just about the time that Dawson penned his first entry, on December 26, 1908. The volume is imprinted with the name of the Boler-Vawler Company, located in the Chicago Tribune Building, and it also has several patent dates, starting with April 11, 1899, and ending with May 15, 1906.

OVERLEAF Manierre Dawson in his studio with the center panel of *Prognostic* (1910, pl. 16) in background (1966). Courtesy of the Peter Lockwood Collection, Arlington, Texas.

THE FIRST AMERICAN ABSTRACTIONIST

Manierre Dawson and His Sources

RANDY J. PLOOG

Manierre Dawson defies many of the conventional canons concerning the development and dissemination of modernism in the early twentieth century. With no formal art training except for a high school art class, and working without access to an avant-garde artistic community, this civil engineer from Chicago was one of the most progressive and innovative artists in the United States throughout his career. By 1909, the same year Max Weber became the first American to embrace European Cubism, Dawson had developed his own geometric style. In the spring of 1910, he completed a group of seven non-representational paintings that pre-date Arthur Dove's first abstractions by at least a few months, making them the earliest known abstract paintings produced by an American artist. In 1913, he constructed and painted wooden reliefs that were unlike anything that could be found in American art at the time, three years before Hans Arp produced his painted constructions. Beginning in 1913 and continuing through 1918, Dawson experimented with cast-concrete sculptures and shaped canvases, and incorporated letters of the alphabet and numerical characters as compositional elements. By the end of the decade, he was painting a series of daring, stark, linear compositions. Finally, in the 1950s and early 1960s, he worked with new composite wood products, which he laminated together into a thick medium from which to fabricate abstract sculptures.

According to the traditional history of modernism, Dawson could not have achieved many of these early accomplishments without prior knowledge of contemporary (or in some cases, later) events in Europe. Yet he did achieve these accomplishments in Chicago and in Michigan, without relying on relevant European developments. Through a careful examination of his work, his writings, and his life, many of Dawson's sources can be identified and his evolution as an artist can be understood. The purpose of this essay is to explain Dawson's creative development by tracing his accomplishments to their sources within the context of his biography.

All extant material pertaining to Dawson's career is mutually supportive. The majority of Dawson's paintings bear the date on the front of the work. With very few exceptions, these dates are confirmed in the artist's inventory of paintings and sculptures. Distinct aspects of his life, his training in civil engineering, his career as an architectural draftsman, and his move to Michigan are all reflected in his art. In addition, Dawson kept a personal journal in which many specific events described between 1908 and 1922, the most crucial period of his career, are verified by independent documentation, such as correspondence from friends, newspaper accounts, and exhibition records. Most important, however, the thoughts and ideas recorded in his journal precisely parallel his evolution as an artist as revealed through the development of his oeuvre.

The aesthetic philosophies that Dawson cultivated in his youth laid the foundation for the rest of his career. As he wrote in 1911:

> In trying to answer the questions that are repeatedly thrown at me, "What does it mean?" "What does it represent?" I have to start with a statement that sometimes helps. "Art is a human invention. In nature there was no art except that all creations of the almighty are part of that almighty. "Art" as a word for us to use describes the invention of that part of creation that is man. All nature is bearing down on us day after day. We cannot avoid it. Every form that we could use is there. But away from nature and in the seclusion of the mind we can invent arrangements to be found no where else. One answer to the question, "What is it," is to point to the picture and say, "It is *that*." "It exists nowhere else."[1]

Dawson described his creative process as the pursuit of "the phantoms of imagination."[2] His primary objective was to make his pictures "look right." Armed with such an attitude and with practically no academic fine-art training to overcome, he was free to experiment and invent with few restrictions.

FIG. 1 The Dawson Family. Front row (left to right): George, Sr., Lovell, Grandmother Dawson, and Eva. Back row (left to right): Aunt Kate Manierre, George, Jr., Manierre, and Mitchell. Mitchell Dawson Collection. Courtesy of the Newberry Library, Chicago, Illinois

Early Life

Manierre Dawson was born the second son of George E. Dawson and Eva (Manierre) Dawson. He was given his mother's maiden name, apparently in honor of his maternal grandfather, who was then seventy-five years of age. Edward Manierre had been a successful merchant who served as alderman of Chicago's First Ward before being elected City Treasurer for three consecutive terms in the 1850s.[3]

George E. Dawson was the descendent of farmers and blacksmiths in rural central Illinois. From these humble origins he rose to become a well-educated, widely traveled, and cultured gentleman who spoke and read six languages. Largely self-taught, he was a teacher of the classics and a high school principal before traveling in Europe and becoming an attorney in Chicago.[4] In addition to languages, literature, and the law, one of his favorite pastimes was music. Through his participation in a mixed chorus he met Eva Manierre, a pianist who had studied for two years in Vienna. George and Eva were engaged in the summer of 1885 and were married the following September. The two settled in one of Chicago's most prosperous neighborhoods. George, Jr. was born in December 1886, and Manierre followed a year later. The household quickly grew to include the elder George's mother, Eva's sister Kate, and two more sons; Mitchell was born in 1890 and Lovell in 1897 (fig. 1).[5]

FIG. 2 Manierre Dawson, *Night Sky with Moored Sailboats*, c. 1904. Oil on wood. Private Collection

FIG. 3 James Abbott McNeill Whistler (American, 1834–1903), *Nocturne: Blue and Gold—Southampton Water*, 1872. Oil on canvas. The Stickney Fund, 1900.52. Photo courtesy of The Art Institute of Chicago

As their older sons reached adolescence, George and Eva sought to offer them recreation and a change of environment by taking them on vacations in the country. This practice led to the purchase of a small fruit farm near Ludington, Michigan, which would be used by the family as a permanent summer retreat. Not only was the farm an escape from the city, but it kept the two older sons busy repairing the buildings, caring for the peach orchard, and selling the harvests. The hilly farm, which they nicknamed "The Humps," quickly came to be associated with the Dawsons' most pleasant family memories, except for one tragic event in 1904 when Manierre's brother George, Jr. drowned in a nearby lake.[6]

After the loss of the Dawsons' eldest son, parental aspirations were focused on Manierre. With a year of high school remaining at the time of his brother's death, Manierre was already devoting considerable time and effort to painting, an interest he had demonstrated from a very early age.

Early Paintings: 1904–05

Dawson's earliest surviving oil paintings are a series of small wooden panels depicting night-sky effects, such as *Night Sky with Moored Sailboats* from 1904 (fig. 2). Each of these moonlit scenes conveys a somber mood, no doubt reflecting the grief the artist experienced as a result of his brother's recent death. As a group, these paintings represent a concerted study of a single subject, evidence of a remarkable seriousness of purpose for a young artist. Moonlit landscapes were popular subjects during the last decades of the nineteenth century, the most notable examples being the nocturnal scenes of James Abbott McNeill Whistler. Following his death in 1903, Whistler was the subject of many tributes and exhibitions. In fact, Whistler's *Nocturne: Blue and Gold* (fig. 3), which was acquired by the Art Institute of Chicago in 1900, has a strong resonance in Dawson's *Night Sky with Moored Sailboats*.

Dawson received his only formal art instruction in a high school art class during his senior year at Chicago's South Division (Wendell Philips) High School.[7] It was through this course that he was introduced to the formalist aesthetics of Arthur W. Dow, which shaped Dawson's approach to art for much of the rest of his career. Dow was a painter turned art educator, whose most influential publication, *Composition*, first published in 1899, was an instructional manual for art teachers. In it, Dow encouraged the expression of beauty over representation, rejecting the prevailing method of teaching art through "nature-copying," with its courses in cast-drawing, perspective, and anatomy that suppressed self-expression. Through such training, Dow believed, "The picture painter is led to think of likeness to nature as the most desirable quality for his work," consequently judging his art by "a standard of Realism, rather than of Beauty." As an alternative, he proposed that every work of art be "regarded as primarily an arrangement, with Beauty as its raison d'etre." According to Dow,

> Abstract design is, as it were, the primer of painting, in which principles of Composition appear in a clear and definite form. Nature will not teach [the artist] composition. He must learn the secret as Giotto and Francesca, and Kanawoka and Turner learned it, by the study of art itself in the works of the masters and by continual creative effort.[8]

Immediately after its publication, *Composition* began to be promoted through a nationwide advertising campaign led by the Prang Educational Company. Dow's "new system of art education," as the book was subtitled, was especially popular in Chicago. His theories were the subject of exhibitions, workshops, and magazine and newspaper articles, and in March and December 1900, Dow gave lectures in the city on his ideas.[9] Beginning in 1904 and continuing through the summer of 1905 (a period that corresponds to Manierre's senior year in high school), Dawson's paintings find thematic and compositional parallels in the illustrations in Dow's book. A clear example of this is *Night Sky with Moored Sailboats*, which is similar to of one of Dow's illustrations (fig. 4).

While his earliest paintings draw directly from such illustrations in *Composition*, Dawson's works from 1905 reflect a more profound comprehension of Dow's theories. *View from Woods* (pl. 1), which was probably painted at The Humps in the summer of 1905, for example, combines the accentuated verticality of Dow's illustrations of trees (fig. 5) with his close-up views of flowers (fig. 6). Rather than reveal any direct borrowing, however, this painting demonstrates a thorough assimilation of Dow's design principles. In *View from Woods*, the subject is compressed into the extreme foreground so that it extends off the picture plane, essentially resulting in a two-dimensional pattern, just as in Dow's illustrations. With dark leaves against a bright sunlit background, *View from Woods* exemplifies the design tenet that Dow described with the Japanese term *notan*. Pertaining to the arrangement of light and dark, *notan*, along with line and color, belonged to Dow's trinity of power—the three most important elements of design as derived primarily from Japanese *ukiyo-e* prints. Under the influence of Dow's *Composition*, Dawson's early work quickly progressed from the romantic imitation of natural effects to an emphasis on two-dimensional design.

Ash Heap (pl. 2), also ascribed to 1905, was probably painted in the fall of that year, after Dawson's return to Chicago from the Michigan farm. Consisting of a pile of ashes, a discarded can, a pair of suspenders, and four lemons against a stockade fence, the subject is one that typically would have been seen in the alley behind Dawson's Chicago home. This gritty scene is the type of subject that earned a group of contemporary, though somewhat older, East Coast artists the title of the Ashcan school. These realist artists, including

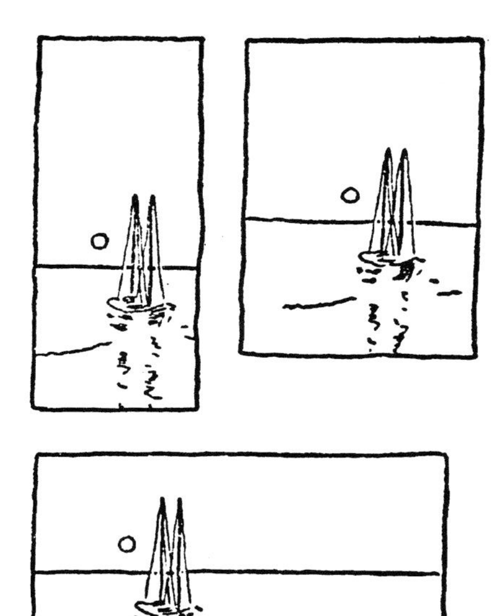

FIGS. 4, 5, 6
Arthur W. Dow.
Illustrations from
Composition, 1899,
p. 35, 26, 48

FIG. 7 Everett Shinn (American, 1876–1953), *The Rag Picker*, 1909. Pastel on paper. Private Collection

Robert Henri, John Sloan, Everett Shinn, and George Luks, depicted dirty city streets and alleys as they saw them—a revolutionary concept for American art at the time—and frequently participated in the annual juried exhibitions organized by the Art Institute of Chicago.[10] Shinn, who executed several scenes of vagabonds rummaging through waste heaps, such as his pastel drawing entitled *The Rag Picker* (fig. 7), also exhibited a watercolor of the same title in the Art Institute's Annual Exhibition of Watercolors by American Artists in 1905, the same year Dawson painted *Ash Heap*. Thus participation by the New York realists in the Chicago exhibitions could very likely have provided a source of Dawson's acquaintance with their work before he painted *Ash Heap*.

Architectural Training: 1905–09

In the spring of 1905, weighing his father's wishes for him to pursue a professional career against his own creative desires, Dawson enrolled at Chicago's Armour Institute of Technology. He advanced through the four-year program and received a bachelor of science degree in civil engineering, but he was never truly committed to his studies. Six months before his graduation, he started to keep a personal journal. His first entry begins, "All these days of hard study at Armour Tech, where I am taking a course in civil engineering, are brightened by continuing the making of pictures on weekends, in the past especially a delight during summer vacations." Later in the same entry he added, "Engineering has some fascinations, but if I could choose a life work it would be the painting of pictures."[11]

Through 1906, 1907, and part of 1908, while he was enrolled at Armour Tech, Dawson produced a group of paintings of invented scenes—perhaps containing autobiographical allusions—that included *Children and Ghosts* (1907, pl. 5) and *The Dreamer* (1908, pl. 7). Unlike anything he had done before, these fantastic landscapes represent Dawson's first attempts at painting from his imagination. He described these works as "somewhat cartoon-like, multi-figure, primitive arrangements which often amused the viewer, yet were painted in all seriousness."[12] In their visionary subject matter, they recall the work of Arthur B. Davies, although Dawson's paintings are generally flatter and less illusionistic than Davies' art from that time. As Dawson noted in his journal, he knew of Davies' work through Kate Kellogg, a friend of his mother who had shown him "some small dream-like sketches" that Davies had left with the Kellogg family.[13]

In *Children and Ghosts*, the adults observe the children from a distance, the title of the painting reinforcing the suggestion of separate realms for children and adults. Although the presence of the three adults suggests a triangular relationship, a household of three young adults, two women and one man, was the norm for Dawson. The reference to ghosts in the title indicates some contemplation of death, and perhaps thoughts of his deceased brother. In *The Dreamer*, a likely metaphor for the artist sits alone observing a couple under a tree while a group dances in the distance.

Many aspects of these fantasy landscapes and of the still-lifes painted during the same period, were derived from Japanese *ukiyo-e* prints. The steeply vertical mountains in *Children and Ghosts*, the silhouetted dancers in *Steps* (1907, pl. 6) and *The Dreamer*, and the almost leafless tree in *The Dreamer* all have precedents in Japanese prints. Likewise, Dawson's still-life from 1906 entitled *Aspidistra* (pl. 3) has many qualities in common with Utagawa Hiroshige's *The Cape of the Moon (Tsuki no Misaki)*, from his series *One Hundred Views of Edo* (fig. 8). The exaggerated perspective, the unmodulated colors, and the simple patterns contribute to the flattened effect in both compositions.

This emphasis on two-dimensional design was precisely the quality of Japanese prints that Dow had espoused in *Composition*. In addition, Dawson was also able to view Japanese art, especially *ukiyo-e* prints, firsthand in Chicago. The city had a devoted nucleus of Japanese print collectors, including Frank Lloyd Wright. In 1905, Wright traveled to Japan expressly to acquire prints, returning with several hundred Hiroshige woodcuts. The following year, his acquisitions were exhibited at the Art Institute.[14] The

FIG. 8 Utagawa Hiroshige, (Japanese, 1797–1858), *The Cape of the Moon (Tsuki no Misaki)*, from the series *One Hundred Views of Edo (Meisho Edo Hyakkei)*, 1857. Woodblock print. Clarence Buckingham Collection, 1939.1485. Photo courtesy of The Art Institute of Chicago

exhibition of Wright's Hiroshige prints in 1906, which included *The Cape of the Moon*, coincided with the year in which Japanese influence became most apparent in Dawson's paintings.

As Dawson began his senior year at Armour Tech, a dramatic change in his approach to painting occurred that established the direction his work would take for years to come. After making contemplative landscapes such as *The Dreamer* during the first half of 1908, he began painting reductive geometric compositions before the end of the year. A notable aspect of this change was his increased emphasis on formal considerations, an interest that led directly to his first abstract paintings in 1910. In December 1908, he declared in his journal, "This winter I am very hard at work Saturdays and Sundays on several arbitrarily constructed paintings of arranged figures, blocking things out without rhyme or reason other than to make the picture look *right*."[15]

FIG. 9 Richard W. Bock, *Head of Thor* (Model for the J. Fletcher Skinner residence fountain, Oak Park, Illinois), c. 1909–10. Cast concrete with inlaid mosaic, 15 inches. Photo courtesy of The Richard W. Bock Sculpture Collection, Greenville College, Greenville, Illinois

One of the "arbitrarily constructed paintings of arranged figures" to which Dawson referred is *Germinal* (1909, pl. 9). The work was given its title—an obvious reference to Emil Zola's novel of the same name—by Manierre's brother Mitchell.[16] The painting's apparent depiction of a subterranean world whose inhabitants reach for the surface makes his choice understandable. Zola's novel, which tells the story of French coal miners striking for better working conditions, is rich with symbolism of the birth of the labor movement sprouting from the earth. However, this was probably not Manierre's intent when he painted the picture. Tombstones in the extreme upper left-hand corner of the painting indicate that Dawson's intended setting was a cemetery, and the figures might be interpreted as the deceased—souls reaching for the heavens.

Dawson's geometric treatment of the figures in *Germinal* has been compared to the Cubism of Pablo Picasso and Georges Braque, but its real origins were in Chicago architecture. Geometricized organic forms were a common characteristic of architectural ornament in Chicago and other American cities during the first decade of the century. Frank Lloyd Wright, in particular, geometrically abstracted botanical forms in his ornamental designs, especially in his leaded glass windows.[17] While Wright derived his designs from plants, Richard W. Bock, a sculptor who worked with Wright on many projects, geometricized the human form. In fact, Bock conceived his angular figure of Thor (fig. 9) as a fountain for the J. Fletcher Skinner residence in the Chicago suburb of Oak Park, in 1909, the same year Dawson painted *Germinal* and *Scarp* (pl. 8).[18] As a resident of Chicago and as a student at Armour Tech, Dawson had ample opportunity to see examples of the geometric style derived from organic forms utilized by both Wright and Bock.

Architectural Motifs and American Influences: 1909–10

In May 1909, Dawson graduated from the Armour Institute of Technology and within one month was employed as a draftsman by the Chicago architectural firm of Holabird and Roche. At the same time, utilizing a geometric style similar to that of *Germinal* and *Scarp*, he produced a series of paintings that took architectural motifs, particularly arches, as their primary theme. Using the arch as a point of departure, the paintings in this series became progressively abstract during the first half of 1910.

Dawson's fascination with the arch and its evolution to the arc form in his paintings grew out of his training in civil engineering. The masonry arch was a basic structural device employed by civil engineers at that time. The civil engineer was expected to be able to determine the exact shape of each side of each stone within a structure. The most complex aspect of this process was defining the curved surface of a stone. An entire semester-long course in stereotomy, the study of descriptive geometry as applied to stone-cutting, was required by the Armour Tech civil engineering program.[19] The textbook for that course, S. Edward Warren's *Stereotomy: Problems in Stone Cutting*, exclusively addressed the arch and its variations.[20] Through this specialized application of descriptive geometry, solutions are determined mechanically in drawings. Dawson's paintings of floating and fragmented arches, such as *Wall of Arches* (1910, pl. 13) and *Going into Mountains* (1910, pl. 12), could have been inspired by

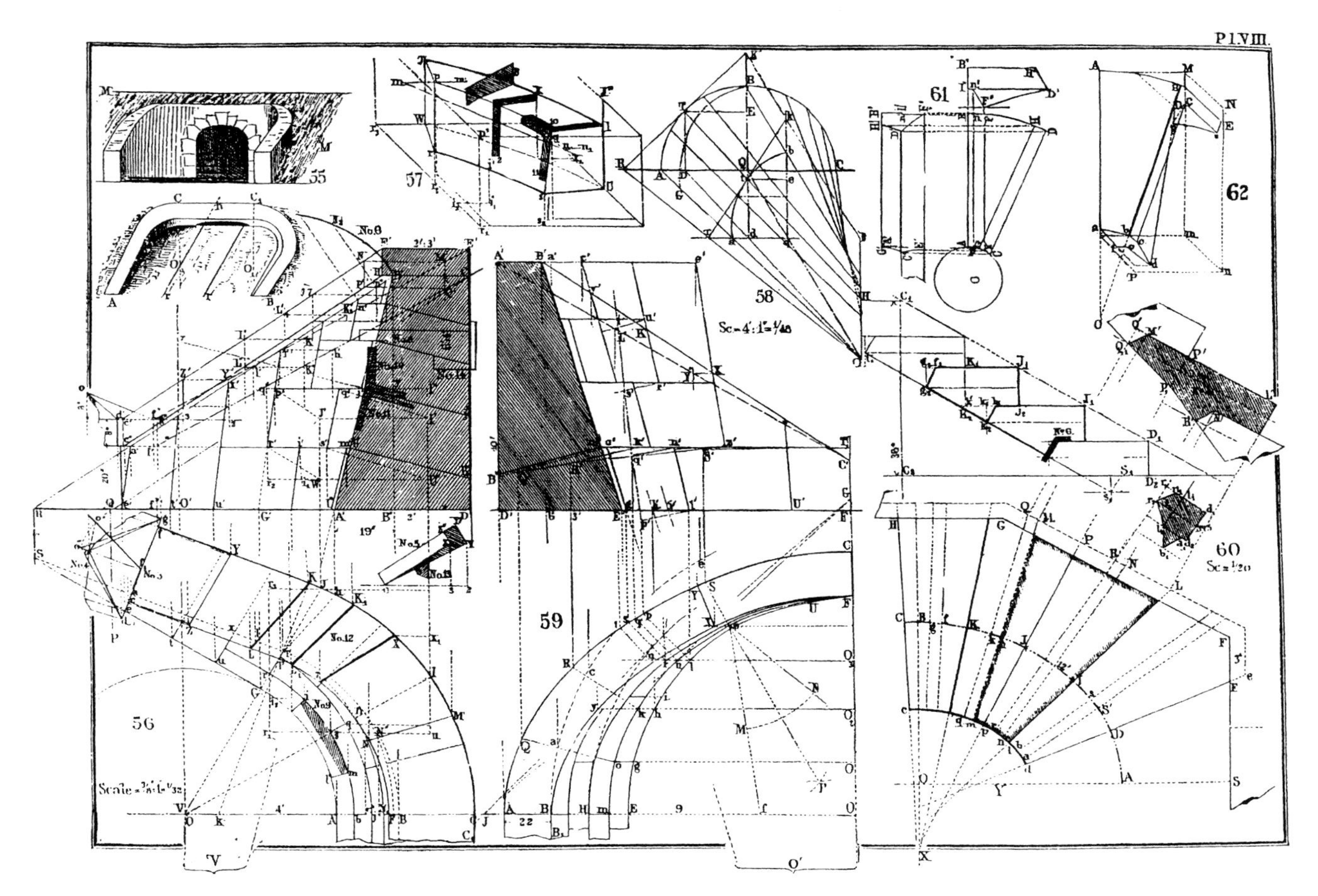

FIG. 10 S. Edward Warren, Plate VIII from *Stereotomy: Problems in Stone Cutting*, 1885

his stereotomy exercises. In fact, both of these paintings resemble plates in Warren's textbook (fig. 10).

Dawson's development that began with his representation of the arch in *Wall of Arches* and *Going into Mountains* culminated in a triptych titled *Prognostic* (1910, pl. 16). The abstract arc forms in *Prognostic* reflect Dawson's preoccupation with the mathematical calculations required for the arch, which he had to study in his civil engineering courses. In addition to mechanically defining curved surfaces through descriptive geometry, Dawson also had to express the same curved surfaces as equations through analytic geometry. Analytic geometry involves algebraic equations whose solutions are parabolic or hyperbolic arcs according to coordinates plotted (or superimposed) on a grid defined by *x-y* axes. Most of Dawson's non-representational paintings of 1910 contain curvilinear forms juxtaposed with some portion of a grid. In *Differentials* (pl. 15), *Differential Complex* (pl. 17), and *Prognostic*, the most prominent curved forms are roughly parabolic arcs. In *Xdx* (pl. 18) and *Coordinate Escape* (pl. 19), also painted by the spring of 1910, the grid is present only as vertical and horizontal axes. In addition, Dawson's titles for most of his abstractions include mathematical terms, such as "differential" and "coordinate"; and "Xdx" is an algebraic expression in itself. In a letter to the director of the Milwaukee Art Center after the museum bought the central panel of his triptych in 1969, Dawson wrote, "Prognostic is one of seven paintings painted shortly after I graduated from college where I had so many engineering and mathematics courses that the influence of this shows in the background of coordinates and super-position of differentials."[21] In the same letter he added, "The black line and circles thrown over (Prognostic) are subconsciously possibly suggested by pencils, pens and erasers generally strewn over a student's drawing board."[22]

During roughly the same period, from late 1908 to mid 1910, Dawson gradually formulated a personal rationale for non-representational art that had origins that went beyond his training in engineering. In December 1908, while he was still a student at Armour Tech, Dawson reflected in his journal:

The boys in the civil engineering department were asking me "What do you say art is?" I could say that it is an attempt to fix forms by painting or sculpture that have given me an emotion, hoping to find some who reacted as I did to these shapes and colors presented on canvas or in some plastic material. Music is an art which to many is easier to appreciate with some emotion. It has many means—comparative pitch, time, combinations and sequence. It can produce in most people some feeling that could be called an appreciation of art.[23]

A year later, in January 1910, when he was employed by Holabird and Roche and just as he was beginning his non-representational experiments, Dawson observed:

Many times in the D-room [drafting room] we discuss what is good or bad in architecture. Sometimes I have mentioned my paintings and what I am trying to do. All the boys agree that architecture is a human invention and is artificial. They can all understand how inventive music is. But when I say that great art in painting does not represent or copy nature, some say that the closer to nature the greater the art. That is not my understanding. We are influenced by nature because we are born into it, but great art must come from within oneself and is thus from nature only in that one is part of nature.[24]

Engineering provided him with many of the motifs he used during this period, and Dow's theories furnished a foundation for his aesthetic thought, but Dawson could not have reached his most progressive ideas or arrived at non-representational painting from these sources alone. Another publication that must be considered a source of many of Dawson's ideas is Arthur Jerome Eddy's book, *Recollections and Impressions of James A. McNeill Whistler*. Eddy, a Chicago attorney and art collector, was so impressed by Whistler's paintings at the World Columbian Exposition in 1893 that he sought out the artist to commission a portrait. His book, published upon Whistler's death in 1903, attempted to explain the artist's life and his aesthetic theories. Dawson's statements parallel Eddy's explanation of Whistler in two important aspects: they both relate painting to music and they are very similar in their views on the relationship between art and nature.

The analogy between painting and music has a long history and was widely discussed and accepted by 1908 when Dawson began recording his thoughts in his journal. However, Eddy was original in his use of the music analogy as a justification for non-representational painting. He wrote:

. . . there is a music of color even as there is a music of sound, and there should be a delight in color composition even as there is a delight in sound composition; and this delight should be something fundamentally distinct from any interest in the subject of the composition. The subject may be a man, or a woman, or a field, or a tree, or a wave, or a cloud, or just nothing at all—mere masses and streaks of color; the perfection or imperfection of the color arrangement remains the same.[25]

Concerning art and nature, Eddy proposed that "One should never confound art with nature; they are antithetical terms. There is not art in nature; there should be no nature in art."[26] However, he also conceded that "Nature is never left entirely behind, and some arts are more dependent upon her than others; but, generally speaking, the more abstract the art the higher it is; the purer and freer it is from imitation or suggestion of natural effects, the nobler its attainment."[27] Like Eddy, Dawson considered nature an undesirable, yet unavoidable, influence on artists.

Although in his book Eddy provided the basis for Dawson's rationale for non-representational painting and contributed to many of the most forward-looking statements recorded in the artist's personal journal, he never proposed putting this theory into practice; he presented the concept of abstract art only as a theory in defense of Whistler. Another book published a few years later, however, did advocate the practice of purely formal art and very likely was the impetus for Dawson's decision to paint abstractly.

As a student in civil engineering and, after June 1909, as an employee in an architectural firm, Dawson was likely to have been introduced to Denman Waldo Ross' *A Theory of Pure Design*, an instructional manual published in 1907.[28] The body of the book consisted of hundreds of diagrammed exercises that methodically demonstrated the formal elements and how to use them to achieve desired effects. Ross, an instructor of design theory at Harvard University, was a friend of Dow and his book was loosely modeled after Dow's *Composition*. Unlike *Composition*, however, which reproduced representational works of art, Ross' illustrations were exclusively non-representational diagrams. While the concept of "pure design" was a topic of much discussion in architectural education early in the century, Ross was the first to present a thorough treatise on its practical application. In his book he stated, "The purpose of Pure Design is to achieve Order in line and spots of paint; this with no other, no further, no higher motive; just of the satisfaction, the pleasure, the delight of it."[29] Believing that in actual application, the elements of design were often obscured by representation, he advised, "It is worth while, therefore, for those who wish to bring Design into their work, whatever that is, to study Design in the abstract, Pure Design, so that they may know, before they undertake to use it, what Design is."[30] Essentially a summary of the direction Dawson's work was beginning to take in 1908, Ross' statement was probably the immediate inspiration for Dawson's non-representational experiments of 1910.

In his conclusion, Ross recommended that the student of pure design study order as "revealed in nature and achieved in Works of Art" through "analysis and synthetic reproduction." The analysis should consist of the visual isolation and definition of each of the formal elements that contribute to the sense of order. By "synthetic reproduction," Ross meant:

> . . . a reproduction of the effect or design, whatever it is, following the images which we have in mind as the result of our analysis. The reproduction should be made without reference to the effect or design which has been analyzed. There should be no direct imitation, no copying.[31]

This statement, too, precisely encapsulates what Dawson did over an extended period. In 1910, Dawson described one of his paintings as being "from a theme suggested by the corner of the fountain, and the jar below it, but is not an attempt to make a copy of either,"[32] which almost paraphrases Ross' book. From 1911 to 1913, Dawson produced a number of paintings based on compositions of old master works, not by copying them but by translating them into his own semi-abstract style. Following Ross' instructions, he analyzed examples of design in nature and in works of art and reproduced the "effect" of those designs in his own paintings, but never directly imitated or copied his sources. In addition, some elements in Dawson's abstractions of 1910 appear to have been inspired by Ross' diagrams. For example, the distinctive dots and bars in *Prognostic*, and its amorphous abstraction, have precedents in figure 228 of Ross' book (fig. 11).

Fig. 228

FIG. 11 Denman W. Ross, Figure 228 from *A Theory of Pure Design*, 1907

FIG. 12 Manierre Dawson, *European Landscape*, 1910. Watercolor on paper. Private Collection

As Dawson was formulating his rationale for non-representational painting in Chicago, Wassily Kandinsky was doing the same in Munich. Dawson's *Prognostic*, of 1910, has been repeatedly compared to Kandinky's first abstractions of a few years later. However, an even more compelling comparison can be made between the ideas of these two artists. Kandinsky's notations on abstraction were published as *Über das Geistige in der Kunst* in early 1912, and translated into English as *Concerning the Spiritual in Art* two years later.[33] Although the nature and extent of the similarities between their ideas are complex, the affinities can be summarized as three basic precepts: that art appreciation can function on a level other than the conscious intellect; that painting need not represent or copy nature but should come from within; and that music is an appropriate analogy for painting. How these two artists on opposite sides of the Atlantic simultaneously arrived at similar constructs of non-representational art may not be entirely coincidental. The sources of Dawson and Kandinsky's ideas may have had common origins. The American proponents of formalist aesthetics—Whistler, Dow, Eddy, and Ross—all had exposure to Europe and, in some cases, mingled with the European theorists Charles Blanc, Maurice Denis, Adolf Hölzel, and Wilhelm Worringer, who provided a conceptual foundation for Kandinsky.

Dawson's European Voyage: 1910

On Dawson's first day of employment at Holabird and Roche, the young engineer was mistakenly assigned a table in the design department of the firm. Many of his colleagues there had studied at the Ecole des Beaux-Arts in Paris and they quickly convinced him of the value of a European tour. Dawson began saving money and looked forward to the following June when, having completed one year with the firm, he would be eligible for a leave of absence. His departure for Europe on June 17, 1910, interrupted work on his first series of non-representational paintings.[34]

As far as his employers and his father were concerned, this six-month tour of Europe was for the purpose of studying architecture, but Dawson had planned his itinerary around the major art collections and hoped for opportunities to paint.[35] He sought out the important architectural monuments, but for most of his trip paintings and painting were his highest priorities.[36]

Dawson left Chicago by train bound for Montreal, where he boarded the *S.S. Canada* for Liverpool.[37] He meandered through England to London, and then crossed to France, visiting the Amiens cathedral on his way to Paris. After two weeks in Paris, much of which was spent in the Louvre, he traveled by train to Cologne and afterward went by boat down the Rhine to Mainz. He continued to follow the river south to Basel, and then headed east to Zurich. From there he set out on foot southward across Switzerland. Stopping only to sketch in watercolor (fig. 12) and to have his shoes repaired, he reached the Italian border two weeks later. After visiting Milan, he spent the night in Pisa on his way to Siena.[38]

On his arrival in Siena on September 19, Dawson found he was the only American in his pension. Two days later, however, he learned that the distinguished-looking man sitting across the dinner table was the expatriate American painter John Singer Sargent, who was accompanied by his sister.[39] The Sargents, according to Dawson, were formal, polite, and appeared interested in his tales of "wild west Chicago." After meeting over dinner, Dawson experienced many chance encounters with Sargent in the streets and museums of Siena during the following week. On one occasion, Dawson was able to observe Sargent at work. On another, Sargent asked to see Dawson's latest effort. Dawson was flattered by Sargent's interest in his work but his record of their discussions highlight the differences in their opinions.

After eleven days in the city, Dawson had to force himself to leave Siena to resume his tour. Following two weeks in Rome, Dawson accelerated the pace of his travels, visiting Naples, Pompeii, Viterbo, Orvieto, and Perugia within a week. He spent a few days each in Florence and Venice before making a second visit to Paris.[40]

Returning to Paris, Dawson took advantage of a letter of introduction to Gertrude Stein provided to him by one of his colleagues at Holabird and Roche. Informed by the woman who answered the door that Miss Stein would be home that Saturday evening, Dawson returned on that date with one of his recently painted panels under his arm. He introduced himself to his hostess and, with some hesitation, showed her the work. To his surprise, Stein offered to buy it for 200 francs—Dawson's first sale of a painting.[41]

At Stein's apartment, Dawson admired the Cézanne paintings in her collection, and the next Monday sought out a gallery on Rue Laffitte, probably Ambroise Vollard's, where he saw more works by the French artist.[42] Of the Cézanne paintings he saw in the gallery, Dawson wrote, "the great variety of altered forms were very instructive to an understanding of inventive pictures, and gave me a big lift in support of what I was trying to do in my own work."[43] Undoubtedly, Dawson considered the Cézannes, especially the late works, as validation of his own geometric reductive style in *Germinal* and *Wall of Arches*. He made no mention of any other modern masters while in Europe, although he certainly could have also seen paintings by Picasso and Braque at Stein's or Vollard's. In fact, the mask-like face in *Portrait* (1910, pl. 21) may have been inspired by Picasso's portrait of Gertrude Stein that hung in Stein's apartment.

The modest windfall from Stein's purchase of his painting allowed Dawson to extend his stay in Europe for three more weeks. From Paris he visited Munich, Dresden, and Berlin before boarding the *S.S. Friedrich der Grosse* in Bremerhaven on November 19 for the journey home.[44]

Return to the United States: 1910–12

Ten days later, Dawson arrived in Hoboken, New Jersey, and made his way to Manhattan. The next morning, with an address provided by Mary Kellogg and examples of his European paintings and photographs of his earlier works in hand, he called on Arthur Davies. Davies gave Dawson's pictures "a good look" and advised him to paint the human figure. After visiting for an hour, Davies took his guest to call on Albert Pinkham Ryder and introduced him to other friends. Ryder's health had begun to decline, but Dawson was exhilarated by just meeting the aged master. He later wrote in his journal, "I can't get over thinking of Ryder. He is a great inventor of shapes, haunting impressions of those inner feelings which he has, and which I can feel with him."[45] Dawson was humbled by the "clever craftsmanship" demonstrated by some of Davies' other artist friends, but conceptually he was more progressive than his New York hosts.

FIG.13 Leonardo da Vinci (Italian, 1452–1519). *The Virgin of the Rocks*, c. 1508. National Gallery, London, England

According to Dawson, Courbet and Ingres were the artists most frequently mentioned during their discussions. One conversation focused on the "wild men" of Paris, a reference to the Fauves and Cubists. Dawson observed that he "may have seen something of those mentioned, without having thought of them as wild."[46] From New York, Dawson traveled to Chicago by train. By mid December he had returned to his position at Holabird and Roche and was back to painting in the small spare room in his parents' home. Before the end of the month, he produced a painting on a wooden panel designed to cover the opening of an unused fireplace. The non-representational work, titled *Discal Procession* (1910, pl. 14), is stylistically akin to the angular depictions of buildings and streets Dawson executed on his European tour.

With free time during the holidays, Dawson attempted to synthesize some of the images he had seen in his travels. He noted in his journal,

> Meeting Davies was a great stimulant. I am sketching for projects, thinking much about Rubens and Tintoretto, and the Cezannes in Paris. And Ryder's paintings haunt me. . . . Sketches are developing plans for "museum" paintings. These rely somewhat on those last themes that came from so much looking at paintings in the galleries, and on conversations about new trends.[47]

This fusion of the best of what he had seen in Europe, the old as well as the new, is reflected in Dawson's subsequent paintings. Beginning in January 1911, through 1912 and part of 1913, many of his works employ motifs and sometimes complete compositions borrowed from the old masters but depicted in his own geometric style. The sources of a number of his paintings have been identified: for example, *Cumaea*, painted in 1911 (pl. 24), has its origins in Jan Vermeer's *The Geographer*; *Birth of Venus*, of 1912 (pl. 30), is excerpted from Peter Paul Rubens' *The Feast of Venus*; and *Meeting (The Three Graces)*, of 1912 (pl. 28), is Dawson's interpretation of the Pompeiian wall painting of the same title. Some of his sources were paintings that he probably saw during his travels, but others would have been known to him only through reproductions. The accuracy with which he rendered certain aspects of his sources indicates that he probably relied on reproductions for all of his borrowings, even in the case of those paintings he had seen firsthand.[48]

Dawson's selection of the old masters he paraphrased was based on composition, without regard to style, subject matter, nationality, or historic period. Through his study of their works he gained "insight into the artistry of invented shapes and composition."[49] In the spring of 1911, while working on his old master-inspired compositions, he wrote, "Time and again I have had the thought that all artists in all times past and present are trying to do the same thing, to make a picture and make it right."[50]

This fascination with composition is also evident in Dawson's treatment of his sources. He did not copy the originals precisely; he did not attempt to imitate their styles, nor did he duplicate their subjects in their entirety. On the contrary, he frequently borrowed only select figures from his sources, imposing his own semi-abstract style on the composition, which rendered it almost unrecognizable. In general, the process was one of simplification; the elimination of extraneous details and the reduction of the original composition to its most essential components. For example, in *Madonna* (1911, pl. 22), which is derived from Leonardo da Vinci's *Virgin of the Rocks* (fig. 13), Dawson flattened and geometricized forms but maintained the general compositional arrangement of the original. What at first glance appear to be random shapes actually relate to folds of drapery, landscape formations, and anatomical features. Concentrating on the dominant figure, Dawson maintained the slope of the Virgin's shoulders, the tilt of her head, and the position of her hands. The line of her chin, the area of shadow below it, the part in her hair, the curve of her eyelashes, and even the arc of her halo are all faithfully preserved. Through the process of simplification the secondary figures are eliminated, but the line of the elongated cross held by the infant Saint John remains, continuing the line of the Virgin's thumb, as it does in the original.

A similar treatment of Sir Thomas Gainsborough's portrait of Jonathan Buttall, better known as *The Blue Boy* (fig. 14), is found in Dawson's 1912 painting of the same name (pl. 33). Despite the many liberties taken, the dominant compositional elements and enough details are retained so as to make Dawson's source unmistakable. For instance, Dawson repeats the positions of the arms and the hand holding the hat. The soft curve of the plume in the Gainsborough becomes a hard right angle in the 1912 painting, but its basic form is retained.

Many other paintings from 1911 and 1912 include figurative compositions that might have been based on other, as yet unidentified, historic sources. For example, judging from its limited palette, *Cavalier* (1911, pl. 25) might derive from a portrait by Titian or one by Rembrandt. *Venus and Adonis* (1912, pl. 31) could have its origins in the work of Veronese, who painted a number of variations of that subject.

Dawson's practice of appropriating motifs from the old masters is evident from his paintings and confirmed in his journal. Less obvious is whether his treatment of these compositions owes a debt to the Analytic Cubism of Picasso and Braque, or was a continuation of his geometric style begun with *Germinal* and reinforced by his viewing of Cézanne's paintings in Paris. Dawson made no mention of Picasso or Braque in his journal entries from his time in Europe, but he certainly had opportunities to see examples of their work. Mary Mathews Gedo has argued that Picasso was a major influence on Dawson after his trip abroad,[51] but, as discussed, Dawson's process had more to do

FIG. 14 Thomas Gainsborough (British, 1727–88), *Portrait of Jonathan Buttall (The Blue Boy)*, c. 1770. Oil on canvas. Photo courtesy of the H. E. Huntington Library, Art Collections, and Botanical Gardens, San Marino, California

with the analysis and simplification of composition than with the multiple views characteristic of Analytic Cubism. The study of composition in other works of art was advocated by both Arthur Dow and Denman Ross. As he was painting his first "museum" pictures, Dawson noted in his journal, "Davies would be pleased to think that I haven't forgotten his advice to do figure painting. But I haven't been thinking of that advice. The urge had causes before that."[52] This prior urge might have been his intention to follow Dow and Ross' recommendation to study works of art, which Dawson equated with returning to the figure.

The Armory Show and After: 1913–14

When nearly two years had passed without hearing from Davies, Dawson speculated in October 1912 that his new friend had forgotten him. Less than two months later, however, he received a letter from New York that included an invitation to participate in what would prove to be arguably the most important

FIG. 15 Marcel Duchamp (French, 1887–1968) *Nude (Study), Sad Young Man on a Train (Nu [esquisse], Jeune homme triste dans un train)*, 1911–12. Oil on cardboard, mounted on masonite. Photo courtesy of the Solomon R. Guggenheim Foundation, New York, Peggy Guggenheim Collection, Venice, 1976

exhibition in the history of American art, the International Exhibition of Modern Art, known as the Armory Show. As president of the organizing body, the Association of American Painters and Sculptors (AAPS), Davies asked Dawson to send some of his "most novel" paintings.[53]

The invitation presented Dawson with a dilemma. That summer, at his father's insistence, he had taken advantage of his first vacation since his European tour to move finished paintings from his parents' house to the Michigan farm for storage. Receiving Davies' letter in December, Dawson had no opportunity to cross Lake Michigan to retrieve his works from where they were stored and as winter grew near, the uninhabited summer retreat became even more inaccessible.

Dawson, apparently recognizing the magnitude and significance of Davies' project, found most of the finished works that he had on hand unsuitable for the exhibition in one way or another. Feeling that many of these works were too small to be noticed in a large installation, he considered his one available large painting, *Meeting (The Three Graces)*, with its ancient Roman origins, too derivative for this exhibition. Recalling Davies' advice to return to the figure, Dawson judged his most recent works as too abstract for the New Yorker's taste. He frantically tried to prepare something for submission, but as the February opening of the exhibition approached, he conceded that he had nothing to send. As Dawson's first opportunity to exhibit outside his family's home, Davies' "great show" was evidently too intimidating for the young painter. After seeing newspaper announcements listing the exhibition's many European participants, he lamented, "With all that great quantity the promoters would not particularly want me from way out here in Chicago."[54]

When the exhibition came to the Art Institute, Dawson visited it repeatedly. He wrote with enthusiasm in his journal,

> These are without question the most exciting days of my life . . . I am feeling elated. I had thought of myself as an anomaly and had to defend myself, many times, as not crazy; and here now at the Art Institute many artists are presented showing these very inventive departures from the academies . . . I have learned more from this exhibition than at any previous view of old masters who had already taught me a great deal.[55]

During his visit to the exhibition on opening day, Dawson met Walter Pach, a representative of AAPS. Davies had recommended that Pach see Dawson's recent work so Dawson invited Pach to his parents' home for dinner. Pach was very complimentary of the few early paintings he saw there, but he was most impressed by an abstraction that had yet to dry. Dubbing the still untitled painting *Wharf under Mountain* (1913, pl. 34), Pach took it with him and clandestinely hung it in one of the American galleries of the exhibition, where, although undocumented, it became the only painting by a Chicago artist to be included in the Armory Show and the only abstraction among the American entries.

Dawson found the European paintings in the exhibition "entrancing." He wanted to buy Picasso's *Woman with a Mustard Jar* (1910), which had received considerable notoriety in the Chicago newspapers, but the price was beyond his means. He begged his father to lend him the money, but the elder Dawson was "disgusted by the idea of taking such a thing home."[56] Lowering his sights, he was able to acquire Amadéo de Souza Cardoso's *Return from the Chase* and Marcel Duchamp's *Nude (Study), Sad Young Man on a Train (Nu [esquisse] Jeune homme triste dans un train)* (fig. 15) without his father's assistance.[57]

In early April, while the Armory Show still hung in the Art Institute galleries, Dawson's employment with Holabird and Roche was terminated. The circumstances of his dismissal are not known, but a likely reason was his preoccupation with the exhibition and his own paintings. For the next year he moved from one unrewarding design-related job to another.

His renewed enthusiasm resulting from the Armory Show, combined with frequent periods of unemployment that provided him with time to paint, made 1913 and 1914 his most productive and innovative years for art. During this two-year period he produced more than eighty wildly diverse paintings and sculptures. An example of the direct influence of the Armory Show is his series of three paintings titled *Hercules* (1913, pl. 38), which in their figurative-abstraction and limited brown palette resemble the Duchamp that hung over the mantel in the family library.[58] The near monochrome palette of this series stands in sharp contrast to the bright and varied colors of *Figure Party-color* (1913, pl. 42); *Passed Correlations* (1913, pl. 43), with its numerous geometric facets, is dramatically different from the minimal simplicity of *Three Trees at Culvert*

FIG. 16 Manierre Dawson, *Athene*, 1913. Painted wood relief. Private Collection

(1914, pl. 49); and the lyrical line and the sensuous color of *Afternoon I* (1913, pl. 39) is a fundamental opposite of the intellectual exercise *Letters and Numbers* (1914, pl. 44), in which Dawson's engineering background reappears in the form of actual letters of the alphabet and numerical characters. Also in 1913, Dawson constructed a pentagonal canvas (the location is now unknown), which he sold to Arthur Jerome Eddy a year later.

In September of 1913, Dawson went back to the family farm in Michigan; he was unemployed and low on funds, but brimming with creative energy. When he had exhausted his supply of canvas, he painted on cardboard. When his tubes of paint grew empty, he thinned the pigment with turpentine to increase its coverage. When the paint was gone, he became even more inventive. From a partial bag of Portland cement he poured two blocks of "artificial stone," which he then carved. After a month of scavenging for materials and experimenting with sculpture, he returned to Chicago. There, Dawson envisioned cutting and assembling boards into low relief panels that could then be painted, and he wrote in his journal, "Thinking of it, it could be gruesomely elegant with the cutout boards fastened to a back with color applied to emphasize the shapes to make the thing stand stark but rough."[59] He produced two such painted reliefs before the end of the year, one of which he titled *Athene* (fig. 16).

With his confidence bolstered by the Armory Show and Pach's letters of encouragement, Dawson began for the first time to pursue outlets for exhibiting and selling his paintings. He approached dealers and made his only submission to the Art Institute's annual juried exhibition for Chicago artists, but because of the negative press that the avant-garde works had received during the Armory Show, the dealers and jurors were, in Dawson's words, "dead set against anything resembling cubism."[60] His only opportunities to exhibit came from outside Chicago.

In December 1913, a second invitation to exhibit in New York came from Davies, this time in a letter from Pach. Following the success of the Armory Show, Davies proposed an exhibition of paintings and sculptures by the fourteen American artists he considered the most important. Dawson was invited to send three pieces; Davies requested *Steps*, and Pach suggested *Wharf under Mountain*. Again, most of Dawson's paintings, including *Wharf under Mountain*, were in storage in Michigan. Unlike a year earlier, however, Dawson made a Herculean effort to retrieve the desired painting. Since the ferry across the lake had ceased operations for the winter, he took the train around Lake Michigan to Pentwater, Michigan. From there he walked nine miles in a foot of snow, located the painting, and retraced his path back to the station just in time to catch the last train of the day to Chicago. Clearly, he was no longer intimidated by the prospect of exhibiting in New York. Along with *Wharf under Mountain* and *Steps*, Dawson sent a charcoal drawing. In February of 1914, the exhibition opened at the Montross Gallery in New York before traveling to Detroit, Cincinnati, and Baltimore.[61]

While his paintings hung in the Montross Gallery, Dawson was preparing for another exhibition. A high school friend, Dudley Crafts Watson, had just been named the first professional director of the Milwaukee Art Society and wanted to bring some of the excitement of the Armory Show to his institution. Watson's exhibition, held in April 1914 and titled *Paintings and Sculptures in "The Modern Spirit,"* was an unbalanced assembly of what was available. Nine contemporary Europeans were represented by one painting each borrowed from local collections, while several East Coast artists sent three or four pieces each. But the exhibition was dominated by Dawson and fellow Chicagoan Jerome Blum, who exhibited at least forty works each. The inclusion of Duchamp was the subject of headlines announcing "Explosion of Shingles Is Coming to Our Town," a reference to the artist's *Nude Descending a Staircase* (1912), which had been described as resembling "an explosion in a shingle factory" when it was exhibited in New York a year earlier.[62] Dawson's own work did not go unnoticed. The caption for an illustration of *Prognostic* in the *Milwaukee Free Press* lampooned both the artist and the new museum director by identifying the painting as "Manierre Dawson's Cubist Portrait of Director Dudley Crafts Watson" (fig. 17).[63]

MILWAUKEE FREE PRE

Cubist Art on Exhibition

Gallery Visitors Giggle

Wild Canvases Fascinating

MANIERRE DAWSON'S Cubist Portrait of Director Dudley Crafts Watson.

Interpreter and Guide Are Needed if Visitor Would Know What He Sees.

AT THE PLAYHOUSES

Three more performances will close the engagement at the Davidson of the San Carlo Grand opera company. "Lucia"

FIG. 17 "Manierre Dawson's Cubist Portrait of Director Dudley Crafts Watson," *Milwaukee Free Press*, April 19, 1914

Encouraged by having paintings in two exhibitions simultaneously and frustrated with his latest employer, Dawson quit his job to devote more time to his art. Once his paintings were returned from Milwaukee later in the spring, he headed to Michigan for a "long, long stay" at The Humps. He quickly planted the family vegetable garden and tended to the fruit trees so that he could have some time free for painting.[64]

Life on the Farm: 1914–21

In the summer of 1914, the twenty-six-year-old Dawson attended nearby Fourth of July festivities where he met Lilian Boucher, the seventeen-year-old daughter of a local farmer, and fell in love. For the first time, serious thoughts of marriage crossed his mind but Lili's youth and his financial instability were obstacles. He wrestled with the uncertainty of his art in his journal: "I am convinced that there is something great urging

FIG. 18 Manierre Dawson, *Dark Word*, 1918. Oil on board. Private Collection

the necessity of producing paintings. So I keep on doing. Satisfaction of accomplishment can be—but no money. What to do?"[65] He had given up all hope of a career in architecture, and viewed returning to engineering as "going backwards." He considered teaching art but conceded that he did not possess the necessary craftsmanship.[66] Dawson's visits to The Humps had always been his most pleasant and most artistically productive times, so despite the hard work that would be required, he decided to try farming as a profession. That fall he purchased a fifty-acre farm bordering The Humps to the south, which he named "Southedge," and proceeded to plant fruit trees on it. In July 1915, he married Lili, and a year later a son, Gerard, was born. The following year brought a daughter, Hope, and a second daughter, Carolyn, was born three years after that.

The themes of Dawson's work during this period seem to alternate between his earlier career and his new life as a farmer and father. In 1915, only one year after his last design-related employment, his architectural interests are still evident, especially in *Profiles* (pl. 51). Underscoring the title, the shapes in the composition mainly resemble cross sections of objects, most of which appear to be architectural elements, such as wooden moldings and a newel post. Located at the lower right is what appears to be a mechanical drawing of a female torso in profile, perhaps a reference to Dawson's new bride. Seen above is a potted plant on a mantel, depicted in crisp outline and in perfect profile. The severe treatment of the leaves and the profile view of the pot is repeated in *Pot and Green Leaves* (pl. 50), of the same year.

Figure (1916, pl. 53) is intentionally ambiguous in form, but its theme is unmistakably fertility (Lili was pregnant during this first year on the fruit farm). As the title suggests, the outer shell of this carved concrete sculpture resembles a standing human figure. The exposed internal organs, however, look like a seed taking root and sending a shoot upward. In this interpretation, the head of the figure becomes an emerging sprout about to unfurl its leaves.

Dawson returned to mathematics for the subject of his relief *658* in 1917 (pl. 54). In addition to forming the title, the numerals six, five, and eight make up the largest part of the sculptural configuration. The artist mentioned this piece in his journal, but he assigned no significance to the numbers, which were apparently chosen purely for their abstract formal qualities.[67]

With the demands of the farm and his growing family, Dawson's creative pursuits were restricted by time and the financial limitations of a new business. When paint and canvas were beyond his means, sculpture became an affordable alternative since carving could be done on materials found around the farm. But carving was a time-consuming process and Dawson soon realized that the three-dimensional compositions he envisioned could be more quickly recorded in paintings than as sculptures. Once finances were stable, he began making paintings of imaginary abstract sculptures. Consisting of intertwining masses and open voids, these compositions were probably inspired by the limbs of the fruit trees that consumed much of his attention. In his later years, with more time on his hands, Dawson executed a number of painted compositions as sculptures, for example, *Dark Word* of 1918 (fig. 18), which was sculpted in 1961 (pl. 73).

Between 1918 and 1923, Dawson produced paintings that, in his words, "reduce design to the bones of the theme and its related surroundings."[68] *Brown Equation* (1919, pl. 58) and *Equation* (1923, pl. 63) exemplify his work during this period. In their austere simplicity and juxtaposition of circles and arcs with perpendicular lines, these paintings are reminiscent of *Xdx* and *Coordinate Escape* of 1910. Like the earlier abstractions, these works also have a mathematical "equation" in their titles.

Dawson reestablished contact with Walter Pach and Dudley Watson in 1921, after a lapse in correspondence of a few years. Through Pach's encouragement, Dawson participated in the annual exhibition of the Society of Independent Artists in 1922 and 1923, entering two paintings each year. Their friendship ended in 1939 when Dawson resented Pach's description of him as a "young architect" and ignored him as a painter in his published memoirs.[69] Dawson's renewed association with Watson in January 1921 resulted in a second exhibition at the Milwaukee Art Society two years later. Unlike the first exhibition, this was a solo show, the first in Dawson's career and his last until 1966. The exhibition was limited to twenty-seven small and medium-sized paintings because he could not afford to crate and ship his larger and, in his opinion, better works. Consequently, he was apprehensive about the success of the show and did not even attempt to see his first solo exhibition.[70]

In January 1921, with a third child on the way and finding time to paint a constant problem, Dawson expressed some regret about his career decisions, writing in his journal:

> It's a big laugh how I ever got onto a farm. The thought was developing over a good many months and was clinched after I met Lili. Here was a farm girl and here was a prospective farmer. This much is certain; farm life has its pleasures, but they are not the intense pleasure that art can bring. As to work, the two don't mix.[71]

Once he committed himself to his family and farm, visits to Chicago were rare. During the summer, his orchards demanded his attention and various members of his family were nearby at The Humps. During the winter, travel across or around Lake Michigan was arduous, especially with young children.

One of the rare visits to Chicago occurred in January of 1922. Dawson's parents had sold their house, which was then immediately demolished. At his first opportunity to talk to his father, Dawson inquired about a carton that he had stored in the attic of the old house. His heart sank when he learned that the carton, which contained sketches, small paintings, and letters from Davies, Pach, and Maurice Prendergast, had been entirely overlooked and presumably destroyed when the house was vacated and subsequently razed.[72]

While he was in the city, Dawson visited commercial galleries with paintings under his arms, but met with indifference. Before returning to his parents' home, he visited his brother's law office, where he happened to encounter Carl Sandburg, a client and friend of Mitchell. On seeing a painting that Dawson had named *Loft*, Sandburg suggested that the title be expanded to *Prayer Loft* (1921, pl. 60), a suggestion the artist followed.[73] A month later, Sandburg wrote to Mitchell, "Those pictures chased business out of my head. Tell your reckless brother."[74]

The Later Years: 1922–69

In 1922, Dawson stopped writing in his journal except for a few brief notations in 1939 and 1940. As a result, the details of his life and thought from this point on become more sketchy. Contrary to a widely held notion, however, he did not stop painting. In fact, Dawson produced more than ninety works, nearly a third of his total production, after 1920.

From the late 1920s through the 1940s, abstracted landscapes predominate in Dawson's paintings, with the seed or sprout form as a recurring motif. In *Two*

Arms (1926, pl. 64), a pair of limbs emerges from the soil, terminating in curled, sprout-like ovoids rather than the recognizable hands one would expect from the title. Similar swirling forms appear in the painted relief *Mex Theme* (pl. 65), from 1933, and the wall sculpture *Argument* (pl. 66), from 1946.

In January of 1948, Dawson returned to New York for the first time since 1910. The purpose of the trip is not known, but surviving relatives believe that he hoped to generate interest in his paintings by introducing himself to dealers. Perhaps the sixty-year-old artist had read about the resurgence of abstraction with the New York school and thought that he, with his long career as an abstractionist, would be favorably received. If that was indeed his intent, the trip was apparently unsuccessful. While in the city, however, he probably saw recent work by the New York Abstract Expressionists, including that of Pollock, whose latest paintings were on view at the Betty Parsons Gallery. The paintings Dawson executed after his return to Michigan, such as *Abstraction* (ca. 1950, pl. 67), resemble the biomorphic forms of Jackson Pollock and other contemporary New York artists.

In 1941, Dawson and his brother each inherited a substantial sum of money from an aunt. Dawson invested his share in the stock market and, within a few years, was able to contemplate retirement. In the early 1950s, Dawson and his wife began wintering at various locations in Florida, eventually establishing a permanent winter residence in Sarasota. Throughout the rest of his career, Dawson was primarily occupied with sculpture. In his retirement, he had the luxury of time to develop and execute the three-dimensional compositions that had haunted him during the period spanning the years 1916–18. Beginning in 1952, he experimented with a composite wood product called "Novoply."[75] Novoply offered many advantages over more traditional materials such as solid wood and marble. It was versatile and could be easily worked. Manufactured in three-quarter-inch-thick sheets, it could be cut into shapes with a saw. The pieces could then be laminated together for depth, further shaped by chisel or by grinding, and sanded to the desired finish. Left rough and painted tan, as in Dawson's *Morning Figure* (1959, pl. 72), Novoply resembles limestone. Polished smooth and painted brown, as in the sculpture *Dark Word*, it might almost be mistaken for cast bronze. But its most remarkable quality is its lightweight strength. The thin supporting limb in *Dayd* (1958, pl. 71) would have been nearly impossible to achieve in stone or even solid wood, which would likely crack along its grain.

The last entry in Dawson's inventory, a painting titled *Vision* (pl. 75), is dated 1963. As of that date, forty years had passed since Dawson's last exhibition and he had sold only five paintings during his entire career. The fact that he continued to produce even though his art had never brought him recognition or financial reward is a testament to his passion for creating. For Dawson the making of art was a righteous act. In 1910, he had recorded in his journal:

> One dictum of Christ's "Blessed are the pure in heart for they shall see God," is very appropriate for the artist. The purity can mean keeping clear of copying, clear of following fad or custom. And by all means keep out sobbing sentimentality. The artist *is* trying to see God. He is trying to make things *right*.[76]

Exhibitions at the Grand Rapids Art Museum in 1966, and at the Ringling Museum of Art in Sarasota the following year, paved the way for Dawson's rediscovery. Through the efforts of Karl Nickel, assistant curator at the Ringling at that time, Dawson was brought to the attention of New York Art dealer Robert Schoelkopf. In April 1969, Schoelkopf gave Dawson's paintings the first of many exhibitions in his gallery. Later that summer, Nickel was asked by the Smithsonian Institution to record an interview with Dawson for its Archives of American Art.[77] Unfortunately, before a meeting could be arranged, Dawson was hospitalized with an illness from which he never recovered. He died on August 15, 1969. During the last year of his life and since his death, many major museums have acquired his paintings and sculptures. In 1976, the Museum of Contemporary Art in Chicago mounted a retrospective exhibition of his work, and in 1988 the Whitney Museum of American Art presented Dawson's early abstractions.

The perception of Dawson is that he was enlightened yet innocent regarding contemporary avant-garde trends, which is borne out by Pach's description of his friend in *Queer Thing, Painting*. Dawson appreciated works by Picasso and Duchamp enough to want to own them but, according to Pach, knew nothing about the reputations of the artists. Surviving relatives describe

Dawson as a renaissance man, equally at ease discussing the plants at his feet or the constellations over his head. His titles, which held little significance for the artist, actually reveal much about the diversity of his interests and depth of his knowledge.

Although he worked in near total obscurity for more than a half-century, Dawson produced some of the most innovative works of art of his time. The circumstances of his career, his lack of formal artistic training, and his isolation from other avant-garde artists, only serve to enhance his accomplishments. Yet, it is precisely because of these circumstances that his achievements have not received the attention they deserve. Dawson was never deterred by his lack of recognition, but he did crave acceptance. As he wrote presciently in his journal:

> It would be good to be able to tell here as a matter of record, just why these certain shapes and forms and relations mean something so significant of the emotions of surprise, elation, joy, or what not, that registered at the time of conception. Only the pictures can tell. It is my intention when doing these arrangements to make a *fix* of what was seen to produce the aesthetic feeling. Later there is always some hope that others will see that I have done something *right!*[78]

Notes

The author wishes to acknowledge the generous assistance of George Mauner, Craig Zabel, Mary Mathews Gedo, Dr. Lewis Obi, Tim Foley, Dr. David Dean Brockman, Carolyn Dawson, Peter Lockwood, Hilary Dawson Schlessiger, Gregory Dawson, Kristi Wormhoudt, Carolyn Smith, Richard Ormond, David Schmidt, Emily Grosholz, and Tom Boothby.

1. Manierre Dawson, journal, April 2, 1911, copy in Archives of American Art, Smithsonian Institution, Washington, D.C. Dawson's original journal is owned by the artist's grandson, Peter Lockwood, Arlington, Tex.

2. Dawson, journal, December 24, 1917.

3. See Edward Manierre, "Old Days in Chicago: Stories from Edward Manierre" (typescript, Chicago Historical Society Collection, n.d.).

4. Much of George Dawson's training and education was independent. He boasted of teaching himself Latin and Greek languages and literature, which enabled him to pass the Unversity of Michigan entrance exam. During two years in Europe, he exchanged instruction in English for lessons in German and French. While a high school principal in Chicago, he read the law in his spare time and was admitted to the Illinois bar in June 1881, a few days before his thirty-fifth birthday. See George E. Dawson, *Autobiography of George E. Dawson* (privately printed, Peter Lockwood Collection, Arlington, Tex., n.d.), 2–105.

5. Ibid., 126, 161–162.

6. During the summer of 1904, the two eldest sons, joined by a high school friend, planned to camp for a few nights. Manierre and the friend set out across country on foot, loaded with tents and supplies, for a predetermined campsite on the remote side of Bass Lake, five miles from the farm. George, Jr., who had just graduated from high school, was eager to test a canoe he had built in the basement of the Dawsons' Chicago home. Accompanied by Mitchell, George transported his canoe by horse-drawn cart to a point on the lake accessible by road. George rigged a sail to his canoe and set out across the lake to meet Manierre and his friend while Mitchell returned the team of horses to the farm. The next morning a local farmer found George's body floating in the lake. Eva and Kate were collected by a neighbor and taken to the lake to identify the youth. An anxious but successful search was made for Manierre and his friend. A telegram was sent to George, Sr., who crossed Lake Michigan to spend the night with his family and accompany them on their ferry ride back to Chicago the next morning. Most of the family returned to the farm a week after the funeral for quiet recuperation. A family trip to the Louisiana Purchase Exposition in St. Louis planned for later that summer was canceled. See George Dawson, *Autobiography*, 180–182, 202–215. Manierre's sorrow over the loss of his brother was compounded by guilt over his inaction. Although he probably could not have changed the outcome of events, when George Jr. did not join him as expected, Manierre never voiced concern for his brother's safety.

7. While Dawson was in high school, a new building to house South Division was under construction. The students and teachers of South Division moved into the new building, which was named for Wendell Philips in August 1904, just before Dawson's senior year. Little is known about Dawson's art teacher, Miss Dimock, except what he wrote about her in his journal; he admitted to having had a crush on her even though she was twice his age, and that she frequently summered in London or Paris (see Dawson, journal, May 1, 1910). He referred to her only as Miss Dimock; however, his mother identified her as Katherine G. Dimock in a letter to Mitchell Dawson, June 15, 1928 (Mitchell Dawson Papers, Newberry Library, Chicago). From entries in the *Lakeside Directory*, Katherine G. Dimock apparently began teaching in Chicago in 1904 and continued through the 1920s.

8. Arthur Wesley Dow, *Composition: A Series of Exercises Selected from a New System of Art Education* (Boston: J. M. Bowles, 1899), 24.

9. Frederick C. Moffatt, *Arthur Wesley Dow (1857–1922)* (Washington, D.C.: Smithsonian Institution Press, 1977), 145. Also in 1900, the School of the Art Institute added to its summer schedule a course based on Dow's principles specifically for secondary school teachers. See *Chicago Evening Post*, April 21, 1900. Dawson's art teacher certainly had sufficient opportunity to be trained in Dow's theories and she undoubtedly conveyed them to her students.

10. Peter Hastings Falk and Andrea Ansell Bien, *The Annual Exhibition Record of the Art Institute of Chicago, 1888–1950* (Madison, Conn.: Sound View Press, 1990) s.v. "Henri, Robert"; Sloan, John"; "Shinn, Everett"; and "Luks, George."

11. Dawson, journal, December 26, 1908. Dawson began keeping a personal journal in December 1908 and continued to record entries in it until December 25, 1922, with a few additional comments added in 1939 and 1940.

12. Dawson, journal, December 26, 1908.

13. Dawson, journal, May 1, 1910. Kate Kellogg's older sister Alice and Davies had been very close friends as classmates at the School of the Art Institute. Alice Kellogg's relationship with Davies was apparently a serious one. Her letters from Europe to Kate in 1887 and 1888 repeatedly reveal her thoughts of "marrying Arthur." Alice Kellogg to Kate Kellogg, Archives of American Art, Smithsonian Institution, Washington, D.C.

14. Julia Meech and Gabriel P. Weisberg, *Japonisme Comes to America: The Impact on the Graphic Arts, 1876–1925* (New York: Harry N. Abrams, Inc., 1990), 190–191. The Art Institute's exhibition of Hiroshige prints from Wright's collection was accompanied by a small catalogue authored by Wright. See Frank Lloyd Wright, *Hiroshige: An Exhibition of Colour Prints from the Collection of Frank Lloyd Wright* (Chicago: Art Institute of Chicago, March 1906).

15. Dawson, journal, December 26, 1908.

16. Dawson noted in his journal that his brother Mitchell named *Germinal* upon its completion in February 1909. (Dawson, journal, February 7, 1909). Mitchell was an attorney and joined his father's firm, but he also emulated his father's love of literature, becoming a published author of poetry and children's stories.

17 . Wright wrote that his window designs were "deduced from some plant form that has appealed to me." Frank Lloyd Wright, "In the Cause of Architecture," *Architectural Record* 23 (March 1908): 161. James M. Dennis and Lu B. Wenneker have described the method used by Wright as "an 'analytic' process of starting with actual plant forms and abstracting them into geometric components." James M. Dennis and Lu B. Wenneker, "Ornamentation and the Organic Architecture of Frank Lloyd Wright," *Art Journal* 25 (fall 1965): 6.

18. Bock's fountain is dated circa 1909–10 in Brian A. Spencer, ed., *The Prairie School Tradition* (Milwaukee: Milwaukee Art Center, 1979), 167.

19. Armour Institute of Technology, *14th Annual Yearbook, 1906-07* (Chicago: Armour Institute of Technology Press, 1906), 23.

20. S. Edward Warren, *Stereotomy: Problems in Stone Cutting* (New York: John Wiley and Son, 1884).

21. Dawson to Tracy Atkinson (director, Milwaukee Art Center), letter, April 6, 1969, Milwaukee Art Museum Collection.

22. Ibid.

23. Dawson, journal, December 26, 1908.

24. Dawson, journal, January 2, 1910.

25. Arthur Jerome Eddy, *Recollections and Impressions of James A. McNeill Whistler* (Philadelphia and London: J. B. Lipincott Company, 1903), 183–184.

26. Ibid., 215.

27. Ibid., 205.

28. According to accession records, the library of the Art Institute of Chicago received its first copy of *A Theory of Pure Design* in April 1907, the same month it was published. Dawson frequented this library during his lunch breaks while employed at Holabird and Roche. Though no records survive to confirm the fact, the Armour Institute of Technology probably received a copy of the book around the time of its publication as well, and Dawson, as a student there, could have easily encountered it.

29. Denman Waldo Ross, *A Theory of Pure Design: Harmony, Balance and Rhythm* (Boston and New York: Houghton, Mifflin and Company, 1907), 5.

30. Ibid., 7.

31. Ibid., 190.

32. Dawson, journal, September 21, 1910.

33. Excerpts from Kandinsky's *Über das Geistege in der Kunst* appeared in English in "Extracts from 'The Spiritual in Art,'" *Camera Work* no. 39 (July 1912): 34.

34. Dawson, journal, September 5, 1909–June 17, 1910.

35. For oil paintings he had secretly prepared wooden panels to fit precisely into the lid of his suitcase, along with a frame to hold them while they dried. For watercolors he took a small box of colors and pads of paper that fit into his coat pocket.

36. Dawson, journal, September 26, 1909.

37. Dawson described leaving Chicago by train on June 17, 1910, boarding the *S.S. Canada* that evening, and the ship embarking sometime during the night. On June 26, 1910, he recorded "First day in England" (Dawson, journal, June 17, 1910, and June 26, 1910). The New York Maritime Register confirms the departure of the *Canada* from Montreal on June 18, 1910, and its arrival in Liverpool on June 26, 1910 (New York Maritime Register, June 29, 1910).

38. Dawson, journal, June 26, 1910–September 19, 1910.

39. Dawson, journal, September 19–30, 1910. Sargent's presence in Siena that September is documented by a British artist living in Florence, William Blake Richmond, who wrote in his diary on September 11, 1910, that Sargent had visited him before leaving for Siena. See Simon Reynolds, *William Blake Richmond: An Artist's Life, 1842–1921* (London: Michael Russell, 1995), 306-307.

40. Dawson, journal, October 1–November 2, 1910.

41. Dawson, journal, between November 2 and November 14, 1910. Dawson identified the colleague who provided him with the letter of introduction to Gertrude Stein as Lebenbaum. (He noted that Lebenbaum's parents were well-to-do and had given him a few years in Paris [Dawson, journal, September 17, 1909]). Frederick C. Lebenbaum was Dawson's colleague; he was trained at M.I.T. and at the École des Beaux-Arts in Paris. See *Biographical Dictionary of American Architects (Deceased)*, Henry F. and Elsie Rathburn Withey, eds. (Los Angeles: New Age Publishing Co., 1956), s.v. "Lebenbaum, Frederick." Dawson later wrote that the letter addressed to Stein was actually written by

Lebenbaum's mother (Manierre Dawson to Milton W. Brown, letter, undated, ca. 1964).

42. Ambroise Vollard's gallery was at 6 Rue Laffitte. The paintings Dawson saw probably remained in Vollard's storeroom after the Cézanne exhibition that the dealer hosted that summer. *Figures de Cézanne* was scheduled to be on view in Vollard's gallery from June 27 to July 23, 1910, but Guillaume Apollinaire, writing in *L'Intransigeant* on September 27, stated that the paintings could still be seen at that time. See *Apollinaire on Art: Essays and Reviews, 1902–1918*, ed. LeRoy C. Breunig, trans. Susan Suleiman (New York: Viking Press, 1972), 104–105.

43. Dawson, journal, November 2, 1910.

44. The departure of the *S.S. Friedrich der Grosse* on November 19 and its arrival in Hoboken, New Jersey, on November 29, recorded by Dawson, is confirmed by the New York Maritime Register of November 30, 1910.

45. Dawson, journal, between November 30 and December 5, 1910.

46. Dawson, journal, between November 30 and December 5, 1910. Dawson's use of the phrase "wild men" might be an indication that he or his New York hosts had seen the article by Gelett Burgess, "The Wild Men of Paris," *Architectural Record* 27 (May 1910): 400–414.

47. Dawson, journal, December 15, 1910 and January 2, 1911.

48. Dawson's practice of borrowing compositions was first noted by Earl A. Powell III in his article "Manierre Dawson's 'Woman in Brown,'" *Arts Magazine* 51, no. 1 (September 1976): 76–77, but was examined in more detail by Mary Mathews Gedo, "Modernizing the Masters: Manierre Dawson's Cubist Transliterations," *Arts Magazine* 55 , no. 8 (April 1981): 135–145.

49. Dawson, journal, July 23, 1910.

50. Dawson, journal, April 2, 1911.

51. Mary Mathews Gedo, "The Secret Idol: Manierre Dawson and Pablo Picasso," *Arts Magazine* 56, no. 4 (December 1981): 116–124.

52. Dawson, journal, January 2, 1911.

53. Dawson, journal, October 25 and December 16, 1912.

54. Dawson, journal, between December 16, 1912 and January 26, 1913.

55. Dawson, journal, March 27, 1913 and April 4, 1913.

56. Dawson, journal, April 4, 1913.

57. Milton W. Brown, *The Story of the Armory Show* (New York: Abbeville Press, 1988) 264, 318. In 1921, Dawson sold the Duchamp to Pach, who sold it to Peggy Guggenheim in 1942. It now hangs in the Peggy Guggenheim Collection, Venice. Dawson still owned the Souza Cardoso in 1968, but its current location is not known. See Manierre Dawson to Robert Schoelkopf, letter, July 18, 1968.

58. Dawson, journal, April 4, 1913.

59. Dawson, journal, October 5, 1913.

60. Dawson, journal, October 5, 1913.

61. The core of this exhibition was drawn from a show organized by Davies for the Art Society of Pittsburgh. The exhibition traveled under different titles from the Montross Gallery in New York, to the Detroit Museum of Art, the Cincinnati Museum, and the Peabody Institute of Johns Hopkins University in Baltimore. In addition to the work of Davies, Pach, and Dawson, the exhibition included examples by Joseph Stella, Charles Sheeler, Morton Schamberg, William Glackens, Maurice Pendergast, Walt Kuhn, E. L. McRae, George F. Of, Henry Fitch Taylor, Allen Tucker, and Howard Coluzzi. For a thorough study of this exhibition, see Laurette E. McCarthy, "The Modernists on Tour: A New Look at a Historic Show," *Archives of American Art Journal* 37, nos. 3 and 4 (1997), 2-26.

62. "Explosion of Shingles Is Coming to Our Town," *The Wisconsin*, April 9, 1914.

63. "Manierre Dawson's Cubist Portrait of Director Dudley Crafts Watson," *Milwaukee Free Press*, April 19, 1914.

64. Dawson, journal, May 31, 1914.

65. Dawson, journal, July 4, 1914.

66. Dawson, journal, July 4, 1914.

67. Dawson, journal, January 6, 1917.

68. Dawson, journal, January 3, 1921.

69. Pach did not admire Dawson's later work and their friendship began to deteriorate in the early 1920s. When Pach's memoirs were pubished in 1939, Dawson was offended by his friend's reference to him as a "young architect." See Walter Pach, *Queer Thing, Painting* (New York and London: Harper and Brothers Publishers, 1938), 157. Overlooking Pach's glowing compliment concerning his high regard for Duchamp's work in 1913, Dawson wrote, "How could Walter change his mind about my work and ignore me as a painter, [and] make me only a 'young architect?'" Dawson, journal, December 26, 1939.

70. Dawson, journal, December 25, 1922. Dawson's second exhibition in Milwaukee apparently went unnoticed by the press. Summarizing recent exhibitions in a subsequent issue of the museum's bulletin, however, Watson wrote that the exhibition had "aroused indignation and positive resentment; bursts of mirth and ecstatic joy . . . the younger art students came back again and again." Dudley Crafts Watson, "Recent Notable Exhibitions," *Art Bulletin* (Milwaukee Art Institute) 24 (February 1923): 2.

71. Dawson, journal, January 3, 1921.

72. Dawson, journal, January 8, 1921.

73. Dawson, journal, January 21, 1922.

74. Carl Sandburg to Mitchell Dawson, letter, February 21, 1922, Mitchell Dawson Papers, Newberry Library, Chicago.

75. According to his inventory, Dawson produced thirty Novoply sculptures between 1952 and 1962. See Manierre Dawson, "Inventory of Paintings and Sculptures," Archives of American Art, Smithsonian Institution, Washington, D.C. Novoply was first introduced in the United State by U.S. Plywood in 1951, and is still produced by Georgia-Pacific. (David Schmidt, sales manager, eastern region, Industrial Wood Products Division of Georgia-Pacific Corp., Atlanta, Ga. to author, telephone conversation, March 18, 1999).

76. Dawson, journal, January 2, 1910.

77. Karl Nickel to Richard T. Hirsch (special curator, James A. Michener Collection, University of Texas, Austin), letter, August 8, 1969, Ringling Museum of Art, Sarasota, Fla.

78. Dawson, journal, July 23, 1910.

P L A T E S

1 *View from Woods*, 1905
Oil on wood, 27½ × 23½ inches
Signed lower right: "Dawson"

2 *Ash Heap*, 1905
Oil on canvas, 16 × 22 inches
Signed lower right: "Dawson"

3 *Apidistra*, 1906
Oil on wood, 17 1/8 × 14 1/4 inches
Signed lower right: "M. Dawson"

4 *Flowers in a Yellow Vase*, 1906
Oil on cardboard, 21¼ × 14¼ inches
Signed and dated lower right: "Manierre '06"

Dawson '07

5 *Children and Ghosts*, 1907
Oil on canvas, $20\frac{1}{8} \times 26\frac{3}{8}$ inches
Signed and dated lower left: "Dawson '07"

6 *Steps*, 1907
Oil on canvas, $20\frac{1}{8} \times 28\frac{1}{8}$ inches
Signed and dated lower left: "Dawson '07"
Hirshhorn Museum and Sculpture Garden, Smithsonian Institution
Gift of Dr. and Mrs. John Gedo, 1978

7 *The Dreamer*, 1908
Oil on canvas, 26×22 inches
Signed and dated lower center: "M. Dawson '08"

8 *Scarp*, 1909
Oil on canvas, 34 × 22 inches
Signed and dated lower left: "M. Dawson '09"

9 *Germinal*, 1909
Oil on canvas, 34 × 22 inches
Signed and dated lower right: "M. Dawson '09"

10 *Figure in Glen*, 1909
Oil on canvas, 19¼ × 14¼ inches
Signed lower left: "M. Dawson"

11 *Red Bowl*, 1909
Oil on paper mounted on cardboard, 20 × 16 inches
Signed and dated lower left: "M. Dawson '09"

12 *Going into Mountains*, 1910
Oil on wood, 12 7/8 × 17 inches

13 *Wall of Arches*, 1910
Oil on canvas, $20\frac{1}{8} \times 14\frac{1}{4}$ inches
Signed and dated lower left: "M. Dawson '10"

14 *Discal Procession*, 1910
Oil on wood, 30½ × 24⅞ inches
Initialed and dated lower center: "MD '10"
National Museum of American Art, Smithsonian Institution
Gift of Lewis J. Obi, M.D.

15 *Differentials*, 1910
Oil on canvas, 12 × 16 inches
Curtis Galleries, Minneapolis, MN

16 *Prognostic* (left panel), 1910
Oil on canvas, 24¼ × 20 inches
Initialed and dated
lower left: "MD 10"
Private Collection

Prognostic (center panel), 1910
Oil on canvas, 33¾ × 35¾ inches
Initialed lower center: "MD"
Dated lower right: "10"
Milwaukee Art Museum

Prognostic (right panel), 1910
Oil on canvas, 24¼ × 20 inches
Initialed and dated
lower right: "—MD '10"
Private Collection

By painting a triptych, Dawson indicated that his message was essentially a spiritual or religious one, . . . we experience reality as a plan, as a diagram, as a possibility—as a prognostic of what will someday take place. . . . Rather than being bound to physical reality, and forced to literally transcribe it, the artist penetrates to underlying geometric principles and participates in the actual growth and vital flowering of the forms and shapes.
—H.A.

14 *Discal Procession*, 1910
Oil on wood, 30½ × 24⅞ inches
Initialed and dated lower center: "MD '10"
National Museum of American Art, Smithsonian Institution
Gift of Lewis J. Obi, M.D.

15 *Differentials*, 1910
Oil on canvas, 12 × 16 inches
Curtis Galleries, Minneapolis, MN

16 *Prognostic* (left panel), 1910
Oil on canvas, 24¼ × 20 inches
Initialed and dated
lower left: "MD 10"
Private Collection

Prognostic (center panel), 1910
Oil on canvas, 33¾ × 35¾ inches
Initialed lower center: "MD"
Dated lower right: "10"
Milwaukee Art Museum

Prognostic (right panel), 1910
Oil on canvas, 24¼ × 20 inches
Initialed and dated
lower right: "—MD '10"
Private Collection

By painting a triptych, Dawson indicated that his message was essentially a spiritual or religious one, . . . we experience reality as a plan, as a diagram, as a possibility—as a prognostic of what will someday take place. . . . Rather than being bound to physical reality, and forced to literally transcribe it, the artist penetrates to underlying geometric principles and participates in the actual growth and vital flowering of the forms and shapes.
—H.A.

14 *Discal Procession*, 1910
Oil on wood, 30½ × 24⅞ inches
Initialed and dated lower center: "MD '10"
National Museum of American Art, Smithsonian Institution
Gift of Lewis J. Obi, M.D.

15 *Differentials*, 1910
Oil on canvas, 12 × 16 inches
Curtis Galleries, Minneapolis, MN

16 *Prognostic* (left panel), 1910
Oil on canvas, 24¼ × 20 inches
Initialed and dated
lower left: "MD 10"
Private Collection

Prognostic (center panel), 1910
Oil on canvas, 33¾ × 35¾ inches
Initialed lower center: "MD"
Dated lower right: "10"
Milwaukee Art Museum

Prognostic (right panel), 1910
Oil on canvas, 24¼ × 20 inches
Initialed and dated
lower right: "—MD '10"
Private Collection

By painting a triptych, Dawson indicated that his message was essentially a spiritual or religious one, . . . we experience reality as a plan, as a diagram, as a possibility—as a prognostic of what will someday take place. . . . Rather than being bound to physical reality, and forced to literally transcribe it, the artist penetrates to underlying geometric principles and participates in the actual growth and vital flowering of the forms and shapes.
—H.A.

19 *Coordinate Escape*, 1910
Oil on paper mounted on cardboard, 19 × 14¼ inches
Signed and dated lower left: "M. Dawson '10"
Collection of Mr. and Mrs. Meyer P. Potamkin

20 *Urns*, 1911
Oil on canvas, 18 ½ × 23 ⅛ inches
Signed lower left: "M. Dawson"

In trying to answer the questions that are repeatedly thrown at me, "What does it mean?" "What does it represent?" I have to start with a statement that sometimes helps. "Art is a human invention. In nature there was no art except that all creations of the almighty are part of that almighty. "Art" as a word for us to use describes the invention of that part of creation that is man. All nature is bearing down on us day after day. We cannot avoid it. Every form that we could use is there. But away from nature and in the seclusion of the mind we can invent arrangements to be found no where else. One answer to the question, "What is it," is to point to the picture and say, "It is *that.*" "It exists nowhere else." —M.D.

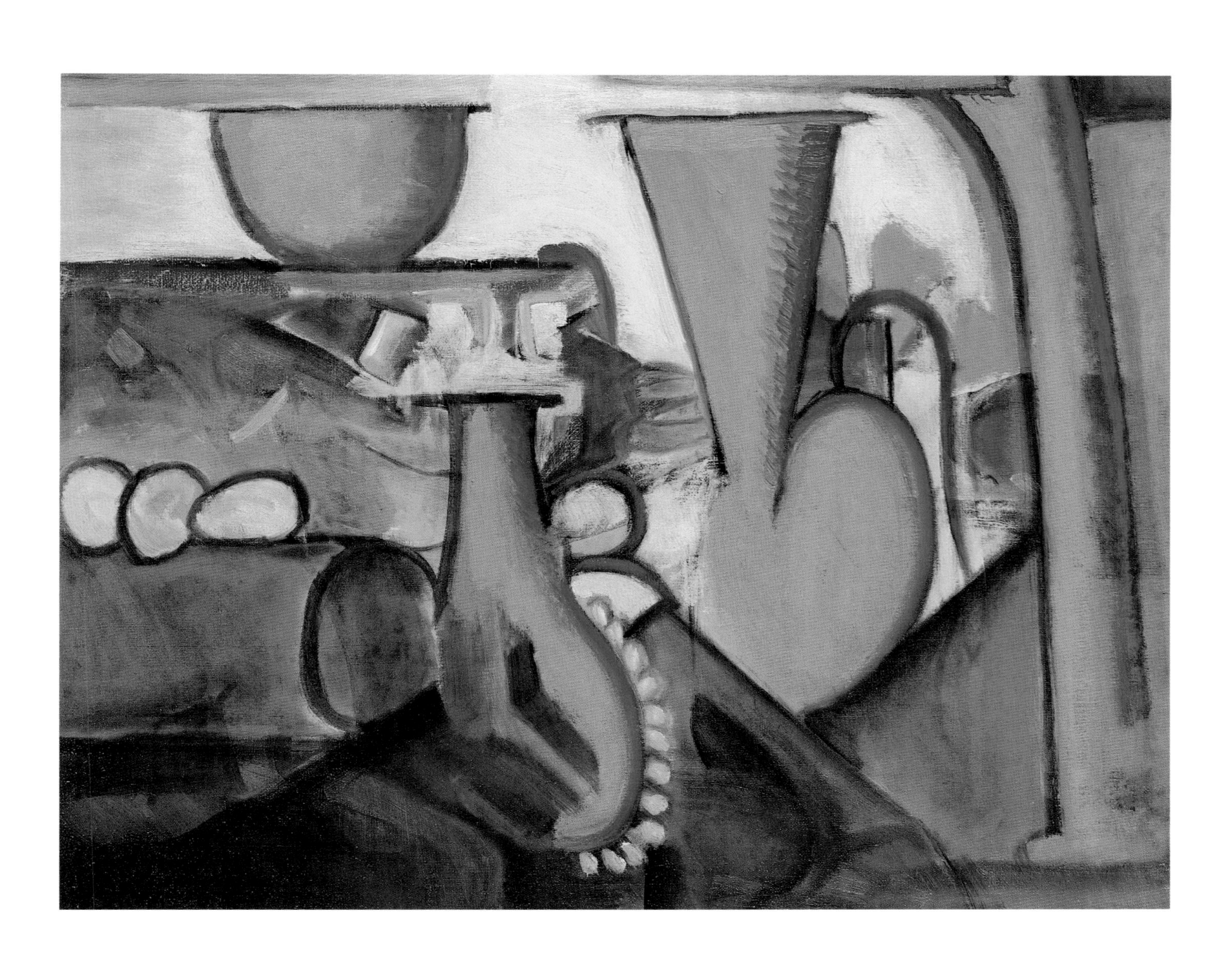

21 *Portrait*, 1910
Oil on canvas, 22 × 15 inches
Signed and dated lower left: "M. Dawson '10"

22 *Madonna*, 1911
Oil on wood, $32\frac{1}{4} \times 23\frac{3}{4}$ inches
Signed and dated lower right: "M. Dawson '11"

M.Dawson '11

23 *Lucia*, 1911
Oil on canvas, $32\frac{1}{8} \times 24$ inches
Signed and dated lower right: "M. Dawson '11"

24 *Cumaea*, 1911
Oil on wood, 32×23 inches
Signed and dated lower left: "M. Dawson '11"

25 *Cavalier*, 1911
Oil on canvas, $34\frac{1}{8} \times 28\frac{1}{8}$ inches
Signed and dated lower right: "Dawson 11"

26 *Scarp II*, 1912
Oil on canvas, 20¼ × 28¼ inches
Signed and dated lower right: "Dawson '12"

27 *Red Mur*, 1912
Oil on canvas, 16 × 24 inches
Signed and dated lower right: "Dawson '12"

28 *Meeting (The Three Graces)*, 1912
Oil on canvas, 58 × 48 inches
Signed and dated lower left: "Dawson '12"

Beginning in January 1911, through 1912 and part of 1913, many of his works employ motifs and sometimes complete compositions borrowed from the old masters but depicted in his own geometric style. . . . Through his study of their works he gained "insight into the artistry of invented shapes and composition." In the spring of 1911, while working on his old master-inspired compositions, he wrote, "Time and again I have had the thought that all artists in all times past and present are trying to do the same thing, to make a picture and make it right." —R.P.

Dawson '12

29 *Attack*, 1912
Oil on canvas, 58 × 48 inches
Signed and dated lower left: "Dawson '12"

30 *Birth of Venus*, 1912
Oil on canvas, 40 1/8 × 32 1/4 inches
Signed and dated lower left: "M. Dawson '12"

31 *Venus and Adonis*, 1912
Oil on canvas, 44 × 36 inches
Signed and dated lower left: "Dawson '12"

Dawson's painting between 1910 and 1913 has usually been referred to as Cubist, and in a very loose sense this is correct, but Dawson's "cubism" took a form that was rather different from what was happening in France. . . .

Viewed as pure abstractions, these paintings are generally quite pleasing, but to follow Dawson's thinking it is often helpful to juxtapose them with their sources. . . . To a large degree, Dawson was interested in using this source to create a purely arbitrary pattern of shapes, a kind of jigsaw puzzle arrangement that disguises and camouflages the underlying form rather than revealing it. —H.A.

32 *Abstraction of Figure*, 1912
Oil on wood, $32 \times 23\frac{3}{4}$ inches
Signed and dated lower left: "12 Dawson"

33 *Blue Boy*, 1912
Oil on wood, 33 × 24 inches
Signed and dated lower left: "Dawson '12"

34 *Untitled (Wharf under Mountain)*, 1913
Oil on canvas, 18 × 22 inches
Signed and dated lower left: "M. Dawson '13"
Norton Museum of Art, West Palm Beach, Florida
Purchased through the R. H. Norton Fund, 69.5

35 *Essenzee*, 1913
Oil on canvas, 26 × 18 inches
Signed and dated lower left: “Dawson ’13”

36 *Observation*, 1913
Oil on wood, 18 × 22 inches
Signed and dated lower right: "M. Dawson '13"

37 *Relations*, 1913
Oil on canvas, 22 × 32 inches
Signed and dated lower right: "M. Dawson '13"

38 *Hercules II*, 1913
Oil on canvas, 36 × 28 inches
Signed and dated lower right: "M. Dawson '13"

39 *Afternoon I*, 1913
Oil on canvas, $17\frac{1}{8} \times 22\frac{1}{4}$ inches
Signed and dated lower
center: "M. Dawson '13"

40 *Conversation*, 1913
Oil on canvas, 22×30 inches
Signed and dated lower
right: "M. Dawson '13"

41 *Sunstrike*, 1913
Oil on canvas, 18 × 22 inches
Signed and dated lower center: "M. Dawson '13"

42 *Figure Party-color*, 1913
Oil on wood, 44 × $35\frac{7}{8}$ inches
Signed and dated lower right: "M. Dawson '13"

43 *Passed Correlations*, 1913
Oil on canvas, 30 × 36 inches
Private Collection

44 *Letters and Numbers*, 1914
Oil on canvas, 12¼ × 16¼ inches
Signed and dated lower right: "Dawson 14"
Hirshhorn Museum and Sculpture Garden, Smithsonian Institution
Museum Purchase, 1978
(not included in this exhibition)

45 *White Face*, 1914
Oil on board, 32 1/8 × 24 inches
Signed and dated lower right: "Dawson '14"

46 *Red Scarf*, 1914
Oil on canvas, 32¼ × 24⅛ inches
Signed and dated lower center: "14 M. Dawson"

M. Dawson. '14

47 *Lucy*, 1914
Oil on wood, 14 × 10 inches
Signed and dated lower left: "Dawson '14"

48 *Imogen*, 1914
Oil on canvas, 26 ⅛ × 20 ⅛ inches
Signed and dated lower left: "M. Dawson '14"

49 *Three Trees at Culvert*, 1914
Oil on canvas, 16 × 24 inches
Signed and dated lower right: "M. Dawson '14"

DAWSON

50 *Pot and Green Leaves*, 1915
Oil on unfinished board, 16¼ × 12⅜ inches

51 *Profiles*, 1915
Oil on board, 22 × 14 inches
Signed and dated lower right: "Dawson '15"

52 *Two Figures*, 1915
Oil on board, 26 × 30 inches
Signed and dated lower right: "M. Dawson '15"

53 *Figure*, 1916
Concrete, 29¾ × 9½ × 6 inches

54 *658*, 1917
Oil on carved wood, 22 × 10 × 3 inches

55 *Gold Head*, 1917
Oil on canvas, 22 ¼ × 20 ⅛ inches
Signed and dated lower right: "Dawson '17"

56 *Monument by the Sea*, 1917
Oil on wood, 19⅞ × 23¾ inches

57 *Blue Trees and Red Rocks*, 1918
Oil on canvas, 17 × 12 inches
Signed and dated lower left: "Dawson '18"

58 *Brown Equation*, 1919
Oil on canvas, 20¼ × 18⅛ inches
Signed and dated lower right: "M. Dawson '19"

59 *Seen Under Veil*, c. 1920
Oil on masonite, 23⅝ × 23 inches

60 *Prayer Loft*, 1921
Oil on canvas, 25 1/2 × 17 1/4 inches
Signed and dated lower right: "M. Dawson '21"
Private collection

61 *Steps*, 1921
Oil on board, 14 3/8 × 20 1/4 inches
Signed and dated lower right: "M. Dawson '21"

62 *Deep Sea Flowers*, 1922
Oil on canvas, 14¼ × 22 inches
Signed and dated lower right: "Dawson '22"

63 *Equation*, 1923
Oil on canvas, 22 × 18 inches
Signed and dated lower left: "Dawson '23"

64 *Two Arms*, 1926
Oil on burlap, 22 × 26 inches
Illinois State Museum Collection
Gift of Dr. Lewis Obi, Frank McKeown and Lefferts Mabie, 1980.115.15

65 *Mex Theme*, 1933
Oil on carved wood, $22\frac{3}{8} \times 28\frac{3}{4}$ inches
Signed lower left: "Dawson"

66 *Argument*, 1946
Plywood, 33 × 40 × 1 inches

67 *Abstraction*, c. 1950
Oil on cardboard, 22 × 28 inches

68 *Elamite Woman*, 1953
Novoply (composite wood), 40 × 13 × 12 inches

69 *Hercules*, 1953
Novoply, 39 × 21½ × 12½ inches (with base)

70 *Crouch*, 1953
Oil on Novoply, 33 ½ × 14 ½ × 10 ½ inches

71 *Dayd*, 1958
Oil on Novoply, 66 × 23 × 12 inches

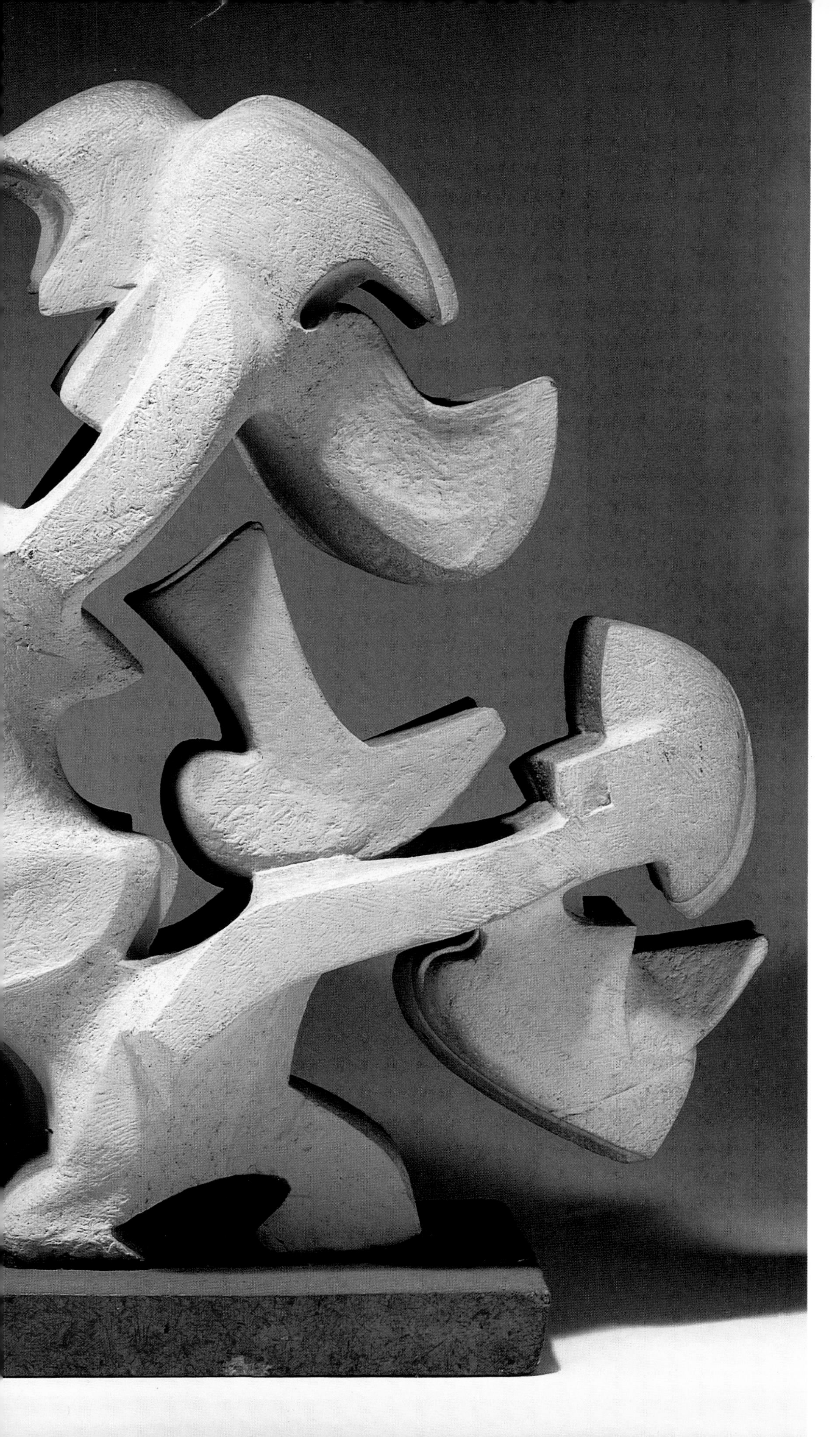

72 *Morning Figure*, 1959
Oil on Novoply, 30¼ × 44 × 11 inches

73 *Dark Word*, 1961
Oil on Novoply, 66½ × 26 × 12 inches (with base)

74 *Dairn of Keyr*, 1962
Oil on masonite, 39 × 47 inches
Signed lower right: "Dawson"
Illinois State Museum Collection
Gift of Dr. Lewis Obi, Frank McKeown and Lefferts Mabie, 1980.115.13

75 *Vision*, 1963
Oil on masonite, 39 × 47 inches

EXHIBITION CHECKLIST

Ash Heap, 1905
Oil on canvas, 16 × 22 inches
Signed lower right: "Dawson"
(Plate 2)

View from Woods, 1905
Oil on wood, 27½ × 23½ inches
Signed lower right: "Dawson"
(Plate 1)

Apidistra, 1906
Oil on wood, 17⅛ × 14¼ inches
Signed lower right: "M. Dawson"
(Plate 3)

Flowers in a Yellow Vase, 1906
Oil on cardboard, 21¼ × 14¼ inches
Signed and dated lower right: "Manierre '06"
(Plate 4)

Children and Ghosts, 1907
Oil on canvas, 20⅛ × 26⅜ inches
Signed and dated lower left: "Dawson '07"
(Plate 5)

Steps, 1907
Oil on canvas, 20⅛ × 28⅛ inches
Signed and dated lower left: "Dawson '07"
Hirshhorn Museum and Sculpture Garden, Smithsonian Institution
Gift of Dr. and Mrs. John Gedo, 1978
(Plate 6)

The Dreamer, 1908
Oil on canvas, 26 × 22 inches
Signed and dated lower center: "M. Dawson '08"
(Plate 7)

Figure in Glen, 1909
Oil on canvas, 19¼ × 14¼ inches
Signed lower left: "M. Dawson"
(Plate 10)

Germinal, 1909
Oil on canvas, 34 × 22 inches
Signed and dated lower right: "M. Dawson '09"
(Plate 9)

Red Bowl, 1909
Oil on paper mounted on cardboard, 20 × 16 inches
Signed and dated lower left: "M. Dawson '09"
(Plate 11)

Scarp, 1909
Oil on canvas, 34 × 22 inches
Signed and dated lower left: "M. Dawson '09"
(Plate 8)

Coordinate Escape, 1910
Oil on composition board, 19 × 14¼ inches
Signed and dated lower left: "M. Dawson '10"
Collection of Mr. and Mrs. Meyer P. Potamkin
(Plate 19)

Differential Complex (Study for Prognostic), 1910
Oil on wood, 16 × 12¼ inches
Collection of David and Mary Winton Green
(Plate 17)

Differentials, 1910
Oil on canvas, 12 × 16 inches
Curtis Galleries, Minneapolis, MN
(Plate 15)

Discal Procession, 1910
Oil on wood, 30½ × 24⅞ inches
Initialed and dated lower center: "MD '10"
National Museum of American Art, Smithsonian Institution
Gift of Lewis J. Obi, M.D.
(Plate 14)

Going into Mountains, 1910
Oil on wood, 12⅞ × 17 inches
(Plate 12)

Portrait, 1910
Oil on canvas, 22 × 15 inches
Signed and dated lower left: "M. Dawson '10"
(Plate 21)

Prognostic, 1910
(Triptych, Plate 16)

(left panel)
Oil on canvas, 24¼ × 20 inches
Initialed and dated lower left: "MD 10"
Private Collection

(center panel)
Oil on canvas, 33¾ × 35¾ inches
Initialed lower center: "MD"
Dated lower right: "10"
Milwaukee Art Museum

(right panel)
Oil on canvas, 24¼ × 20 inches
Initialed and dated lower right: "—MD '10"
Private Collection

Wall of Arches, 1910
Oil on canvas, 20⅛ × 14¼ inches
Signed and dated lower left: "M. Dawson '10"
(Plate 13)

Cavalier, 1911
Oil on canvas, 34⅛ × 28⅛ inches
Signed and dated lower right: "Dawson 11"
(Plate 25)

Cumaea, 1911
Oil on wood, 32 × 23 inches
Signed and dated lower left: "M. Dawson '11"
(Plate 24)

Lucia, 1911
Oil on canvas, 32⅛ × 24 inches
Signed and dated lower right: "M. Dawson '11"
(Plate 23)

Madonna, 1911
Oil on wood, 32¼ × 23¾ inches
Signed and dated lower right: "M. Dawson '11"
(Plate 22)

Urns, 1911
Oil on canvas, 18½ × 23⅛ inches
Signed lower left: "M. Dawson"
(Plate 20)

Abstraction of Figure, 1912
Oil on wood, 32 × 23¾ inches
Signed and dated lower left: "12 Dawson"
(Plate 32)

Attack, 1912
Oil on canvas, 58 × 48 inches
Signed and dated lower left: "Dawson '12"
(Plate 29)

Birth of Venus, 1912
Oil on canvas, 40⅛ × 32¼ inches
Signed and dated lower left: "M. Dawson '12"
(Plate 30)

Blue Boy, 1912
Oil on wood, 33 × 24 inches
Signed and dated lower left: "Dawson '12"
(Plate 33)

Meeting (The Three Graces), 1912
Oil on canvas, 58 × 48 inches
Signed and dated lower left: "Dawson '12"
(Plate 28)

Red Mur, 1912
Oil on canvas, 16 × 24 inches
Signed and dated lower right: "Dawson '12"
(Plate 27)

Scarp II, 1912
Oil on canvas, 20¼ × 28¼ inches
Signed and dated lower right: "Dawson '12"
(Plate 26)

Venus and Adonis, 1912
Oil on canvas, 44 × 36 inches
Signed and dated lower left: "Dawson '12"
(Plate 31)

Afternoon I, 1913
Oil on canvas, 17⅛ × 22¼ inches
Signed and dated lower center: "M. Dawson '13"
(Plate 39)

Conversation, 1913
Oil on canvas, 22 × 30 inches
Signed and dated lower right: "M. Dawson '13"
(Plate 40)

Essenzee, 1913
Oil on canvas, 26 × 18 inches
Signed and dated lower left: "Dawson '13"
(Plate 35)

Figure Party-color, 1913
Oil on wood, 44 × 35⅞ inches
Signed and dated lower right: "M. Dawson '13"
(Plate 42)

Hercules II, 1913
Oil on canvas, 36 × 28 inches
Signed and dated lower right: "M. Dawson '13"
(Plate 38)

Observation, 1913
Oil on wood, 18 × 22 inches
Signed and dated lower right: "M. Dawson '13"
(Plate 36)

Passed Correlations, 1913
Oil on canvas, 30 × 36 inches
Private Collection
(Plate 43)

Relations, 1913
Oil on canvas, 22 × 32 inches
Signed and dated lower right: "M. Dawson '13"
(Plate 37)

Sunstrike, 1913
Oil on canvas, 18 × 22 inches
Signed and dated lower center: "M. Dawson '13"
(Plate 41)

Untitled (Wharf under Mountain), 1913
Oil on canvas, 18 × 22 inches
Signed and dated lower left: "M. Dawson '13"
Norton Museum of Art, West Palm Beach, Florida
Purchased through the R.H. Norton Fund, 69.5
(Plate 34)

Imogen, 1914
Oil on canvas, 26⅛ × 20⅛ inches
Signed and dated lower left: "M. Dawson '14"
(Plate 48)

Lucy, 1914
Oil on wood, 14 × 10 inches
Signed and dated lower left: "Dawson '14"
(Plate 47)

Red Scarf, 1914
Oil on canvas, 32¼ × 24⅛ inches
Signed and dated lower center: "14 M. Dawson"
(Plate 46)

Three Trees at Culvert, 1914
Oil on canvas, 16 × 24 inches
Signed and dated lower right: "M. Dawson '14"
(Plate 49)

White Face, 1914
Oil on board, 32⅛ × 24 inches
Signed and dated lower right: "Dawson '14"
(Plate 45)

Pot and Green Leaves, 1915
Oil on unfinished board, 16¼ × 12⅜ inches
(Plate 50)

Profiles, 1915
Oil on board, 22 × 14 inches
Signed and dated lower right: "Dawson '15"
(Plate 51)

Two Figures, 1915
Oil on board, 26 × 30 inches
Signed and dated lower right: "M. Dawson '15"
(Plate 52)

Figure, 1916
Concrete, 29¾ × 9½ × 6 inches
(Plate 53)

658, 1917
Oil on carved wood, 22 × 10 × 3 inches
(Plate 54)

Gold Head, 1917
Oil on canvas, 22¼ × 20⅛ inches
Signed and dated lower right: "Dawson '17"
(Plate 55)

Monument by the Sea, 1917
Oil on wood, 19⅞ × 23¾ inches
(Plate 56)

Blue Trees and Red Rocks, 1918
Oil on canvas, 17 × 12 inches
Signed and dated lower left: "Dawson '18"
(Plate 57)

Brown Equation, 1919
Oil on canvas, 20¼ × 18⅛ inches
Signed and dated lower right: "M. Dawson '19"
(Plate 58)

Seen Under Veil, c. 1920
Oil on masonite, 23⅝ × 23 inches
(Plate 59)

Prayer Loft, 1921
Oil on canvas, 25½ × 17¼ inches
Signed and dated lower right: "M. Dawson '21"
Private collection
(Plate 60)

Steps, 1921
Oil on board, 14⅜ × 20¼ inches
Signed and dated lower right: "M. Dawson '21"
(Plate 61)

Deep Sea Flowers, 1922
Oil on canvas, 14¼ × 22 inches
Signed and dated lower right: "Dawson '22"
(Plate 62)

Equation, 1923
Oil on canvas, 22 × 18 inches
Signed and dated lower left: "Dawson '23"
(Plate 63)

Two Arms, 1926
Oil on burlap, 22 × 26 inches
Illinois State Museum Collection
Gift of Dr. Lewis Obi, Frank McKeown and Lefferts Mabie, 1980.115.15
(Plate 64)

Mex Theme, 1933
Oil on carved wood, 22⅜ × 28¾ inches
Signed lower left: "Dawson"
(Plate 65)

Argument, 1946
Plywood, 33 × 40 × 1 inches
(Plate 66)

Abstraction, c. 1950
Oil on cardboard, 22 × 28 inches
(Plate 67)

Crouch, 1953
Oil on Novoply, 33½ × 14½ × 10½ inches
(Plate 70)

Elamite Woman, 1953
Novoply (composite wood), 40 × 13 × 12 inches
(Plate 68)

Hercules, 1953
Novoply, 39 × 21½ × 12½ inches (with base)
(Plate 69)

Dayd, 1958
Oil on Novoply, 66 × 23 × 12 inches
(Plate 71)

Morning Figure, 1959
Oil on Novoply, 30¼ × 44 × 11 inches
(Plate 72)

Dark Word, 1961
Oil on Novoply, 66½ × 26 × 12 inches (with base)
(Plate 73)

Dairn of Keyr, 1962
Oil on masonite, 39 × 47 inches
Signed lower right: "Dawson"
Illinois State Museum Collection
Gift of Dr. Lewis Obi, Frank McKeown and Lefferts Mabie, 1980.115.13
(Plate 74)

Vision, 1963
Oil on masonite, 39 × 47 inches
(Plate 75)

APPENDIX 1

Transcription of Manierre Dawson's Journal, 1908–40

Several have suggested, and Father in particular, that I keep a journal. It doesn't seem likely that I could consistently report daily, but it might be to me of advantage to write down something intermittently.

This can hardly be called a journal.

The first pages are copied from my pocket note book with added commentary. Notes on European tour copied verbatim.

1908

DEC 26 All these days of hard study at Armour Tech, where I am taking a course in civil engineering, are brightened by continuing the making of pictures on weekends, in the past especially a delight during summer vacations. All the little paintings done while in high school, hobby works, had seemed not too important, but now I feel I am beginning to grasp something that may eventually be of worth, certainly to myself and maybe to others.

Engineering has some fascinations, but if I could choose a life work it would be the painting of pictures.

Early attempts were always an effort to copy most accurately what nature gives, particularly the gorgeous variety of sky effects. Now, however, there seem to be transcendent forms, shapes, relations that require the development of invented themes that can only be found in fancy, the inner mind.

The boys in the civil engineering department were asking me "What do you say art is?" I could say that it is an attempt to fix forms by painting or sculpture that have given me an emotion, hoping to find some who reacted as I did to these shapes and colors presented on canvas or in some plastic material. Music is an art which to many is easier to appreciate with some emotion. It has many means—comparative pitch, time, combinations and sequence. It can produce in most people some feeling that could be called an appreciation of art. A painting can be looked at as a whole. It stands still. The only movement is in the viewer whose eye rovers for detail.

Among the engineers I can get some interested responses by formulating mathematics bases, saying that the three most important qualities that art depends on are due to ratios (proportions, if you like): ratio of angle, ratio of intensity, ratio of scale.

I have a strong feeling, in looking at the masters, that the most recognisable communication is in the lines. Color may change, and some may be seen only in black and white reproductions. The lines are there. The subtle direction of a line and its relation to other lines can give excitement of great moment.

In early college days my paintings were somewhat cartoon-like, multi-figure, primitive arrangements which often amused the viewer, yet were painted in all seriousness. These paintings I gave such titles as: "Twilight," "Vista," "Figures on Pale Green," "Summer Evening," "Children and Ghosts," "Steps," "Indians," "Red Fort," "The Dreamer," "Adam and Eve," "Mother and Child."

This winter I am very hard at work Saturdays and Sundays on several arbitrarily constructed paintings of arranged figures, blocking things out without rhyme or reason other than to make the picture look *right.*

1909

FEB 7 Two fair sized paintings I have finished. Mitchell has named one of these "Germinal" and the other "Flowering Twilight." In these are many figures arbitrarily placed in some superimposed, building up to the top of the picture.

In between were several small paintings on wood. These are beautiful. It is distressing not to have more time for these things. Mother and Father have given the small things some praise, but I think they believe the larger ones (canvas) crazy.

MAY 21 Graduation will be next week. Father, knowing the chief engineer in the Chicago Sanitary District, wants to line up a job for me there. He also is a close friend of Atwood who might be of help. The Atwood Building was designed by Holabird and Roche who do more architectural business than anyone else in Chicago.

MAY 28 Last night we graduated with Batchelor of Arts degrees making us feel important. The caps and gowns made us a little too warm. The speeches weren't too bad. Gunsaulas is always an inspiring speaker. The others I have already forgotten.

MAY 29 Atwood arranged an appointment with Roche of Holabird and Roche. This might lead to something more interesting than hydraulic engineering with the Sanitary District.

JUN 1 I have met with Roche. The purpose of the interview as to convince Roche that I can help with my engineering training (experience lacking) in checking with the engineers and perhaps of doing a little of the engineering design myself.

JUN 3 Yesterday Roche has told me to report Monday to chief draftsman Long in the Monadnock roof Penthouse.

Monday—I have started with Holabird and Roche. I took with me two rules with assorted scales, my slide-rule, pencils, drawing tools, erasers, etc.—appearance 5 min. early. Long came in sharp 8:00 o'clock. I reported to his desk in front of the room and after two minutes of silence he asked me if I could trace accurately. I said, "Yes"

"Can you understand plans, "Yes."

"Can you relate plans to elevations," "Yes."

"Take the left table in the rear." "All Right."

I sat on a stool at the 4' × 8' slab drawing board. After 20 minutes laying out tools and examining points of dividers and compasses and maniplating slide-rule aimlessly, seniling in this direction and that as other draughtsmen looked myway, Mr. Long bruskly slapped down an elevation, on tracing paper, of the lobby of the Sherman Hotel being planned. "Get tracing cloth from Brodhag and trace as quickly as you can. All blueprints have to be out in *one month!*" "Can you work 4 hour each evening this week." "Yes." Some of us were to work Sunday too.

Sunday I have time to say that the week has been strenuous and very interesting. For relaxation I have painted a little wood panel—the theme: the corner of the table against the corner of the room.

Back in the draughting room I must laugh. It turns out that Long didn't know that Roche hired me as an engineer. He thought that because Roche was the designer of the firm, I should be a qualified designer. So far, my work has been tracing already formed designs and sometimes even scrubbing out with erasers for hours in order to alter ink drawings ready for blue printing. Later the surprise of the week has been the assignment to me of Banquet Hall No. 2 to be designed in Louis XVI style. I was too dumb founded to say anything. Long marched away and left me. A week's observation of designers who had booths along two sides of the corner draughting room (my room) indicated what to do. I went to Lebenbaum. "Have you a Louis XVI folio." "Sure thing, Here." I looked at the floor plan on the small ⅛" scale paper layout Long had given me, one wall shown with one door, I tacked down my tracing paper and stared at the elevation of Frenchplace room in the folio. Long didn't show up again til next afternoon. "How much have you finished." "Four elevations in ¼"." "Good," trace on cloth and send to printer."

After two weeks of tracing and getting pretty well acquainted with Lebenbaum, Smith, Suther and (both father & son) and others, I am drawing up full size details of hollow tile cornice section showing the steel hooks and heavier steel connections to the roof beams, learning much about construction detail and fire-proofing ordinances. I got hold of a copy of the building code, which I have read carefully.

At 5 minutes to 12:00 (quiting time at noon) a session with Lebenbaum, Jonck, and Smith. "Can't you get backing to go to the L'ecole des Beaux Arts," said Smith. "You should certainly make a European tour," said Lenbenbaum. "Study the buildings right here," said Jonck.

JUL 3 All evening to day talked with Father, whose concept of me as a civil engineer is fading, about my interest in architectural design, keeping in secret background all desires and wished about painting. Sculpture seems important but cooler.

AUG 7 Today the blue prints for Hotel Sherman are all completed and bound together—copies sent to contractors for bids. It is hoped the Sherman will be ready to open next year.

We are given a days vacation. I have painted two little wood panels.

AUG 14 Adjustment to office work is pretty well made. I am lucky that Long has not understood me to be a civil engineer, but has placed me among the designers although I am not given much designing to do—there are so many of us and so much to do besides designing. Only two or three of the men have been starting plans and elevations from scratch after ideas have been stated by Roche. The rest of us work on details and some rush work tracing. Long has found me useful as a checker of the work of Purdy & Henderson, our consulting engineers It is necessary to see that our designers don't cut doorways where steel columns or windbracing exist.

SEP 5 Smith, Lebenbaum and others have told me I must go to Europe to get the most experience in art appreciation. I have believed that. In contemplation of a possible trip next year I am saving every penny I can. I carry a sandwich in my pocket for lunch. Noons give me library time. I am boning up on Europe. Father gets next to nothing for giving me living at home. The Art Inst. costs little (25 cents entry)

I can't buy any more canvas for a while and only a minimum of paint.

After the Sherman Hotel there is leftover work on the LaSalle, the Court House, and the City Hall. More buildings are coming up. Holabird is a good jobgetter. Likely it will be a very busy fall and winter.

Its a great help to be able to walk to work 2⅗ mi. and walk home to 24th St. At noon there is sometime to go to the Art Institute or the Crenor Library. What world of ideas can be got from the masters of painting or architecture.

It is a great joy to have lots of music. Father sings to Mother's accompaniment. We always have two front row balcony seats at Orchestra Hall. At each symphony program either Father and I or Mother and I, or Mitchell and I, or Aunt Kate and I use the tickets.

SEP 17 Lebenbaum whose parents are well-to-do was given a few years in Paris. He has told me many things about European travel. I am now just about certain that I shall travel next year. The main question is where the funds. Father has plenty of load on his shoulders. Can I save enough even with the $6.00 raise Long has given me.

SEP 26 I am definitely aiming toward Europe. Though it will ostensibly be a tour for architectural study, I am thinking of the opportunities to see museums and maybe have chances to paint—at least to sketch. I am looking these days at traveling—kits for water color painting or for oil painting. How very simple to carry an outfit for water color painting. A block of paper and a very small box for color and brushes. I am making a slight frame that will hold oil paintings right after painting. I am allotting one wall of my suit case to store the thin wood panels I expect to use. The water colors could almost be carried in a pocket.

DEC 25 I have announced that I shall sail late May or early June depending on when I can book passage. Ads suggest one of the one-class boats. Father had spent two years in Europe in the 1870's. He thinks it will take $5.00 a day to stay in Europe. I am hoping to get by on less by much walking and staying only at small inns and pensions. How easy it would be to travel like Henry James Americans who never have the necessity of thinking about expense.

1910

JAN 2 I am painting Saturday afternoons and Sundays and many times starting a painting on a weekday evening.

Many times in the D-room we discuss what is good or bad in architecture. Sometimes I have mentioned my paintings and what I am trying to do. All the boys agree that architecture is a human invention and is artificial. They can all understand how inventive music is. But when I say that great art in painting does not represent or copy nature, some say that the closer to nature the greater the art. That is not my understanding. We are influenced by nature because we are born into it, but great art must come from within oneself and is thus from nature only in that one is part of nature. Spinoza seems to say that all things, all thoughts, all actions are part of nature or of the almighty cause or what you may call it. That seems a very proper philosophy for the artist.

One dictum of Christ's, "Blessed are the pure in heart for they shall see God," is very appropriate for the artist. This purity can mean keeping clear of copying, clear of following fad or custom. And by all means keep out sobbing sentimentality. The artist *is* trying to see God. He is trying to make things *right*.

MAR 1 Today, confirmation of a booking on the "Canada." I will be in an outside room with three others. I am saving every penny I can.

APR 3 This spring has been a prolific one. Paintings mainly on wood. Canvas from last year almost run out. The basswood sheets from the crate factory and a little of the Meteer chicken sheathing is still on hand. Some of the paintings are far out and viewers laugh at them, but I am dead serious about every picture. Hoskins from the D-room has been the only one of the designers who seems to get my ideas. Aunt Kate, too, indicate understanding. She finished a course at the Chicago Art Inst. A few years ago so has had considerable exposure to design. She has been helpful in putting canvas on stretchers for me. She knows how to do it better than I had been doing it. Mother is sympathetic and, without knowing why, gets some emotional feeling on looking. She had spent 2 yrs in Vienna studying piano. Music is a good base for understanding painting. Father hasn't said a word about the painting I set above the library shelves (8" high)

MAY 1 I hope no one will call this a monthly. It is hard to find time to write.

Beside my own savings I have had generous contributions to my fund: Father $100.00, Uncle Charlie $100.00, Uncle John $10.00, Aunt Kate has given me a good travel book that should be a great help. This with Baedekers for each country which I will buy as I go along will keep me from too many mistakes. I am told that Baedeker maps are excellent.

My passport has been received.

Some very helpful surprises as I get near the time to go. Lebenbaum has given me a very complete list of pensions in the cities I expect to visit. These he says he has tried and found very good places for Americans, very clean, with good beds and good meals and low prices. How more fortunate could a traveler be! He has given me a letter to a Mrs. Stein in Paris and tells me I must visit her.

Kate Kellogg tells me she has written to her sister Hattie, (Mrs. Hal Foster) in Troy New York who sometimes visits New York and know their old friend Arthur Davies. I haven't seen his latest work but, as a former flame of sister Alice, he had left some small dream-like sketches with the Kelloggs. I have seen them.

It turns out that Miss Dimock, the friendly Art teacher at our high school (I had a crush on her at one time altho she was twice my age) will be in London about the time I reach it. She has frequently spent summers in London or Paris and will be helpful in telling me what is worth seeing.

As it nears time to go abroad, Mother and Aunt Kate seem more excited than I am. They worry about my going alone. I tell them I am a great walker and know a little German. I have enough smattering of French to be able to ask the way. One advantage of traveling alone is that the itinerary can be changed at a moments notice and stays can be cut short or lengthened according to may own pleasure.

JUN 4 Holabird and Roche have given me two weeks vacation with pay and have virtually promised to have a place with them for me when I get back from Europe, back to Chicago.

I have come up to the farm for a few days before entraining for Montreal. There is no time to paint because I committed myself to start a vegetable garden. There has been time, however, to put all my paintings and sketches safely away in the loghouse where I hope they will be undisturbed. Several of these I would like to have on 24th St. Here no one sees them. But making boxes and packing is beyond me. It seems so dry here every spring and summer, I think there is no better place for storage. Things accumulate. I wonder if the pictures will ever sell.

JUN 17 Leaving to-day for Montreal. The train leaves Chicago at 3:02 A.M. arriving in Montreal 6:00 P.M.

This pocket notebook will be handy. Several on board are bound for "Canada," one-class S.S. With some I have become acquainted. I have met John & Anna Stacey, artists whose work I have seen frequently at Arts Inst. shows. John is a very capable craftsman in a pointillist manner. Anna is more free and more original though her work might be lost in the local shows. The Arnolds, teachers at the Chicago Kindergarten College, and the Staceys joined at dinner in Montreal (dutch, of course). We didn't see much of the city—railroads and docks are rather dismal. We boarded the "Canada" at 7:00 P.M. Sometime at night the ship was underweigh.

One of my roommates is undersecretary of the Canadian Treasury. He is old but vigorous. He is the only one of us who takes a cold bath on arising. The other roommates are Fulcher, Ph.D. an instructor at the U. of Wisconsin, and an inoffensive M.D. from Milwaukee, who never had much to say.

The approach to Quebec from the river gives a marvellous view of the fort and town on the hill. We stopped at Quebec from 1:00 P.M.–7:00 P.M. Visited the town, then ran to the ship when it rained at 3:30. There is nothing American or English about Quebec. Everybody talks French. The streets are narrow and hilly. Signs are in French. My smattering of French was helpful.

After leaving Quebec I saw mountains for the first time, blue and dim in the north. Our route will be north of Newfoundland and south of Anti Costi—then north of Ireland to Liverpool.

There is a lot of walking on shipboard; for exercise, to pass the time, and meet people. One can spend a lot of time in conversation in a walk, which can't be too long, interrupted by 5 meals a day. Some time passes in chess with Fulcher. This has added a little to my pocket book, as he insists on playing for money. Miss Chase and her pupil Miss Burton are Aboard.

7:00 P.M. Sunday sighted a whale. In straits of Belle Isle passed an iceberg in the fog. There was an eery staring and stopping of the engines and much blowing of the horn.

JUN 21 My sketchbook opened these days on ship board, gives my impressions of some of those on board. Sitting with my back to the outside of the cabin wall, no one can look over my shoulders, but some noticing me sketching ask to see the sketch. If I were writing no one would think of looking over my shoulder. I have pretty good portraits of Fulchers', Arnolds', and Staceys', I want to get to drawing Miss Scott, Miss Jones, Miss Chase, and Miss Burton.

The florid gentleman with the foreign accent, that I supposed to be German—American, turns out to be English from Yorkshire. The young man from Alabama is a masher, if I ever saw one, but is jolly company. He is going for Miss Scott (I never heard her first name) but she is becoming sea-sick and probably wont be on deck much.

Some have been sick even when the sea was calm. I think they are the ones who went to the prow and looked down.

Last day I have made a sketch of Miss, the girl with the beautiful figure, whose face needs improvement. Then just before closing my sketch book I made an arbitrary arrangement of shadows and triangles conceived while looking at miss Scott in the sunshine. I'll make that into a painting later.

JUN 26 The first day in England I can feel the floors and sidewalks still moving. Liverpool is not as foreign looking as Quebec, but has what I hope I shall not encounter again—the most depressing sights of poverty imaginable. In a section of the city women and children are literally dressed in rags. Clothing is a most indescribable covering of patchwork and the young people are never seen walking—always jog—touting and speaking an unintelligible jibberish.

It is hard to get use to traffic passing on the left and hard to get accustomed to counting in English money. Tomorrow to Chester.

JUN 29 I came here by train because of rain and stayed longer than intended (3 days). In Chester there is a great quantity of carved stonework in red sandstone. Rain has prevented outdoor sketching. At Liverpool I forwarded by suitcase, so I am traveling light. I get about on rainy days in my mackintosh.

Walking around the walls of Chester I was hailed by the Fulchers who had hired a carriage bound for Hawarden (pronounced Harden). They invited me to join them. We drove to

Hawarden church, then back thru the park and Chester. I am staying at the "Northlands," (Miss Perry) 6/o a day,—a very good place. At dinner we had some enormous gooseberries some 1½" in diam.

I have mapped out the general route to see the cathedrals and colleges. I shall make a digression to Chatsworth neighborhood and must visit the Adsheads, cousins of good friends of Fathers at Winterton in Lincolnshire.

The nice thing about traveling alone is that no fixed schedule has to be adhered to. Changes can be made for any of my own reasons. I expect to go from Chester to the area around Buxton (Chatsworth, Matlock Haddon Hall); then to Lichfield, Durham (long rail trip) York, Winterton, Lincoln, Peterborough, Ely, Cambridge, Leamington, Oxford, Winchester, Salisbury, and then to London.

Before leaving Chester I walked out to Eaton Hall (4½ mi.), a good example of the best-modern (1870–82). It was well worth seeing.

Railway to Bakewell—then on foot to Over Haddon.

JUL 1 At Over Haddon, a village of a dozen houses. I am at the "Lathkill View" a typical small stone cottage overlooking the Lathkill and Haddon Fields. Hundreds of rabbits seem to run wild on the hillsides. "Lathkill View" is kept by "Annie Wildgoose, licensed Retailer of Beek, foreign, and British Wines and dealer in Tobacco." This place is very rural, primitive, clean, and charming.

Fri. I have walked over to Haddon Hall, went thru it , up on the tower, and out in the garden. From the Hall I walked up into Chatsworth Wood but didn't go to the House because it is only open on Tues, Weds, & Thurs. I saw several tracts thickly reforested to pine and spruce. It made me very want to plant more pine on our hill in Michigan. Back to Over Haddon for the night.
From Over Haddon I walked to Matlock along roads lined with stone walls, most of the way about a rod apart. Arrived at Matlock Bridge Saturday and stayed over till Monday. Plenty of time to see the tors, etc. This was a charming dale at one time, but now a rat-race for tourists. I am disappointed with Matlock.

JUL 4 A long railride to Durham. This a fine place. The Wear at Durham I like better than the Derwent and Durham has its cathedral, a grand structure, perched on a height at a detour of the river. As I came from the station an old man came down the street singing a hymn. At dinner another man walked up and down in front of the hotel playing jigs, marches, and Scotch airs on a flagiolet, stopping at intervals to harrang passers-by. To me it will all go with Durham.

JUL 5 The cathedral is tremendous. The massiveness of the piers in the nave is very impressive. This interior gives clues to what might be done in modern churches for the more transcendent feeling of those who need churches. At 10:30 A.M. this morning I attended a service in which many hymns, responses, and chants by the choir, and prayers, etc. from the pulpit. The acoustics are such that the sounds from the choirs traveling along the nave, which is of great length reverberate in the aisles and echo from the west front to the alter and back giving the whole thing a stirring weirdness. The priests voice on account of the accoustics sounded at times like one of the bells in the tower.

To York by rail and then to Lincoln detouring to Winterton to visit the Adsheads. York minster is grand and extremely informative in detail. Some very find windows

A diary is impossible. It would take time at the fag end of the day. After a day or two the real emotions felt at the occurance of an event cool off before they can be set in writing. Architectural presentations give daily excitement, but I have to judge things in the light of subsequent comparisons.

Separate notes on architectural detail wont be copied out here. I have enjoyed trying to analyse the chief structures in the cities I have pass thru, not dwelling on them as long as I wished because my projected itinerary would never be completed unless I had more money to go on. It will be interesting, as I go along, to determine the changes in style in the churches and in the manor houses. I am not digging very deeply into history—there isn't time enough. I can judge, what to me, is good or bad (good to excellent can be said of most things looked at) A superficial study of features does happen, showing the Romanesque, Transitions, Early & Later English, Flowing, Geometric, Continuous, Decorated, Perpendicular, Collegiate, etc. I expect to find several Tudor. Renaissance, Jacabean, Georgina, Palladian country manors and places worth standing before and sketching.

Downtown York is surprising in the number of names encountered on the main street that show me the base of the Dawson name in England. Here I have seen Dawson, Fawson, Hawson, Lawson, Mawson, Pawson, Rawson, and Sawson. I am told these derive from the Danish invasions.

In York I heard a suffragette speak to a crowd in the street. She handled the hecklers with great skill.

Although I have walked and expect to walk many miles, it is necessary to take the railway for the greater distances. Trains are very much on time and fares are moderate so I have been able to keep average daily expenses within 10s.

I am at the Adsheads in Winterton, Lincolnshire. Mrs. Adshead is a fine old lady, a wonderful hostess, and sweet to her afflicted husband who sits paralysed, in a wheelchair. It is hard to guess what he says but after an hour or two I have gotten to understand his particular sounds so we get along very well. He is eager to hear about his relatives in Oak Park, Ill. and any features of life or scene in America. The Adsheads have arranged a meeting with the vicar and we are all going to picnic on the river.

The vicar has one of the most perfectly kept gardens behind the vicarage. Also, he has a very pretty niece. My sketchbook is about one third full of English types. I shall make a portrait of this niece. When the vicar went into the house to attend a visitor, the girl and I had a rapid fire conversation. Finally she advanced so I thought we were about to kiss. The vicar at that moment returned.

She was much fun going to the picnic next day, plopping down in the carriage between the vicar and me. I enjoyed the close fit.

Sunday I attended services at All Saint's church, Winterton. Mrs. Adshead lent me gloves so I wouldn't be undressed. Later, the vicar walked with me to a quaint old church at Burton.

On walks thru the country-side, here and there, one encounters delightful surprises in the way of rural living and residential architecture. The gardens are amazing, from the simple door yard to the large formal gardens. The most pleasing gardens are those exhibiting mild regularity. Some carefully planned arrangements of color and texture using a great number of varieties of plants make compositions showing amaging artistry. The most successful can be accidental. There is evidence of great design.

I have seen some fine country churches. Always showing up are unique place names. What a variety!

I am gradually getting used to the money. In a little slotted purse I carry gold coins and silver shillings. All other coins are carried loosely in left pants pocket. It is necessary to note carefully the sliver half crowns and florins. They are so similar yet quite different in value.

Lincoln: I am not going to describe the cathedral. That has been done in the books. With its false front and mixed styles, it, yet is extremely powerful in position, and in size and detail very worthy. It can be looked at inside and out with great interest in the detail.

By train to Peterborough. The west front of the cathedral with its three great arches is strikingly unusual. The interior is Norman. The later design of the front is deceiving.

I enjoyed Peterborough. It will be well remembered because of my overnight experience. Though I try, for safety, to carry as little money as possible, here my little purse was more loaded with gold coin than usual. Since the hotels were full up I finally went to a pub recommended by the Grand Hotel and was given a room up a narrow stairway behind the bar. This seemed to be a square upstairs hall. It had seven doors. The bed stood against the only wall long enough between two of the doors. Here I slept with my purse under my pillow. I woke in the morning perfectly safe in spite of the feeling, at the start of the night, of almost certain robbery, the whole atmosphere seeming so villainous. Breakfast at the Grand was one of the best so far.

Over to Ely. The cathedral is large, old, and imposing and very individual in appearance due to the turreted towers. This is the longest nave and choir that I have seen and very varied in structure and ornament—marvellous Octagon.

Cambridge had been a doubtful point. I am glad I trained down to Cambridge. In the Fitz Williams Museum I saw some Turner water colors and paintings by Rosette and Burns-Jones—Fine College buildings.

Leamington is a great clearing-yards for American tourist traffic. There is a different crowd each day going to Warwick, or Kenilworth or Stratford. There are usually more than 100 around Kenilworth ruins all the time. At Warwick Castle every party going in meets a party going out and all going out meet some coming in. At Stratford I can get no feeling of connection with Shakspere. Fine country all around.

JUL 19 Arrival in Oxford. I shall stay two days.

Much has been written about the colleges and the town. It is very collegiate and ivy-covered and worth more than two days stay. I have nothing very important to say. Weighing the importance of the stops is difficult. A short run to Woodstock and a walk to Iffley (Norman church at Iffley).

Reading the last few pages comments seem trite and common place but do recall to me the circumstances of my journey. The word "circumstances" brings to mind how circumstances govern what we do, what happens to us and to our thinking. Accidentals, too, can bring things to mind unexpectedly. The second day in Oxford, rain brought me in before the end of the day. Strange light from across the way filtered thru my window making a picture alongside the bed head. This started a drawing which is going to be a beautiful painting.

From Oxford to Winchester, in my compartment on the train was a suffragette who wanted me to be an anti-suffrage man so she could argue for suffrage. When I agreed with her first few statements she was at a loss to continue. After a silence I made a few comments on art. When I spoke of introducing in my paintings, inventions and personal shapings of forms, she became violently dictatorial insisting that only the faithful copy of what one saw was real art.

Winchester: the cathedral is very long with nave, choir, transcepts and lady chapel laid out in very regular plan. The exterior was disappointing because of the comparison of the pinnacles at the front with the stumpy, truncated central tower, but the interior is very beautiful and impressive. There is a tablet in memory of Jane Austen. She was buried below it. Her "Pride and Prejudice" is, to me, one of the wittiest and most romantic novels ever written.

I didn't dwell on the many interesting historical events connected with this small city. To get to London and have time and money left I must on to Salisbury.

Salisbury cathedral is the most beautifully, proportioned, and with its extremely tall central spire, is the most successful composition of mass I have yet seen. It is called purely early English. I can see it is. The walk to Stonehenge is worthwhile and arrival put me almost in a state of feeling great antiquity. The mystery of the layout and origins and the questions of purpose, and engineering add intriguing thoughts dwelt on a long time after. One spoiler!—Souvenir shacks.

JUL 23 Arrived in London today, after my rush thru Winchester and Salisbury each of which was worth more time than I gave it. As far as enjoyment goes I could stay here all summer. Paris is ahead and Rome is ahead—and a long list of other places.

Pension very modest, comfortable, and cheap—meals plain with plenty of beef, mutton, cheese, and orange marmalade. I am not far from the British Museum and not far from omnibuses on Oxford St., which I only use for farther points. I walk and walk, seeing much but, of course, not everything I had planned to see. Time can run out. Miss Dimock is very helpful in choosing places of interest. We had a fine day in Kensington—palace and park. Above all I shall remember the National Galleries and the Tate. The sculptures at the British Museum I have looked at again and again. I am not spending much time in architectural observation although there is plenty to see, but I am dwelling intensely on the masters of painting who have much to say and were able to say it.

I am getting from the masters some insight into the artistry of invented shapes and composition. The great painters remind me of Beethoven, who as he goes along in a composition, gives the unexpected turn in theme variation, giving out heavy strikes where needed and small melodic hints for decoration.

Rubens certainly know what he was doing!

The National Gallery, National Portrait Gallery, the Tate, New Gallery, Dore' Houses of Parliament, Westminster, Trafalgar, Wallace, British Museum, St. Paul's, etc. etc.

Enumeration of places is not very informative, yet taking each, when read here, it again brings back views and happenings, excitements, and beautiful people, things and persons that were pleasures to look at. The agregate facade of London sometimes seems common place till a striking presentation of something extra ordinary like St. Paul's (certain views) Westminster, Parliament Buildings with tower, even the dry London Tower, accents the rambling scene. I was too busy to sketch much. I made one of my best portraits sketching a fleeting recollection of Miss Dimock.

The route to Paris was necessary to get there, but unpleasant. I can't recommend cross-channel boats. They are designed for the purpose and drained with gutters and outlets so deck boys can flush away the vomit. It is a stinky voyage, fortunately not long.

I wanted to see Amiens, Rouen, and Beauvais not far from Paris. I stopped at Amiens on the way to Paris. I shall make separate trips to other places. Amiens cathedral is my first experience of the marvels of French Gothic which presents the most nearly perfect structural logic to be found anywhere. Our skyscrapers are sound in interior bones and plan but our elevations are fraudulent and conceal that sound interior. The faces of our buildings are imitative in design, and imitative of material and the ornamentation bears no relation to the steel and concrete behind it. The early French Gothic Building started on a solid foundation, laid stone on stone, rising on piers to the hips of the intended arches. Flying buttresses started on outside piers and pressed against the start of the arches so that the vaulted roof weight couldn't push the haunches out. Then the arches and roof vaulting was completed. Pinnacles added extra weight for the security of the buttresses. There must have been a great amount of scaffolding used in construction and much labor. The visible forms of the churches reveal the structural necessities.

At Paris, on exit from the station, a porter carried my suitcase to customs. It passed quickly without inspection, merely a glance as I laid the case open. Then to cab. I had the address of the Lebenbaum recommended pension of Mlle L. Guillier. When I told the driver (his horse could barely trot) in my best attempt at French, "Vingt-et-un, Rue Valette—a gauche le' Pantheon," he started right off turned left as we drove straight at the Pantheon and stopped at the 21. My room is top floor, very clean, pleasant, but small, with meals only 6 fcs. per day, so cheap I wondered if I hadn't misunderstood. The meals are excellent served on a long table, wine adlibitum, several courses; Mlle Guillier at the head speaking French only and to only a few who were studying French. For the American part of us, conversation is brisk and sometimes informative, but rarely touches on art. Mention of pictures or artists usually hushes the conversation temporarily. The theatres and eat spots raise the most talk.

Here I am with the intention of staying at least two weeks and intending to make side trip to Versailles and Fontaineblean, perhaps Rouen & Beauvais.

It enters my mind that after Italy, if I have any money left I must return here. Two weeks is not enough of Paris. The Louvre is inexhauslible—buildings galore can be looked at and looked at.

My room has an outlook on the garden and on the street toward St. Etienne. Every morning I hear the piper and can see him driving his goats to stop, mil, and deliver at this and that doorway. The neighbor church chimes have a fascinating tune hard to remember. The chamber maid represents many french women thin arms, heavy legs, charming face without prettiness, sometimes very bad teeth.

I have returned from Rouen, Beauvais, and Fontaineblean. I gave a whole day to Versailles, a magnificent place. At the palace at Fontaineblean I surprisingly chanced on the Arnolds. We went thru the place together and then to the Gros Fonteau and Mid d'Aigle in the forest. *There* are the biggest beech trees one is ever likely to see and under foot the longest fattest slugs I could ever have imagined.

Beauvais is a remarkable cathedral structure, fine example of the perfection of the French Gothic, and the stained glass very worth seeing.

I am getting in a little more sketching this week. I am happy when a theme thought of becomes a reality. One must trust ones own inventions. It is certainly not necessary to paint something this or that way because a master has done so well doing such a thing.

I am deriving great pleasure from the little oils on wood that this raining spell has given time to finish. It is surprising how natural these far out constructions seem. It would be good to be able to tell here as a matter of record, just why these certain shapes and forms and relations mean something so significant of the emotions of surprise, elation, joy, or what not, that registered at the time of conception. Only the pictures can tell. It is my intention when doing these arrangements to make a *fix* of what was seen to produce the aesthetic feeling. Later there is always some hope that others will see that I have done something *right!*

Paris stay is at an end. Train to-day (16th) to Coln. I will stay over the next day.

The cathedral is a beautiful copy of French Gothic. It doesn't display as skilful construction as Beauvais, but it is solid.

AUG 22 Arrived in Mainz yesterday. I had taken the boat from Coln to Bonn then set out to walk among the Siebengebirge. Big dinners at country inns cost only 1m. each. I took boat again from Unkel to Andernach. I walked into the country around Laacher See. All along the Rhine I have noticed the planted forests. The trees are set close together so as to shade off the lower limbs to make more clear lumber. The most beautiful part of the river is between Bonn and Mainz—castles and vineyards all along.

By boat again from Mayen to Coblenz—express steamer then to Mainz. I helps to know some of the German language. At country inns big dinners cost only 1m. While the English stop business for tea, the German stop everything for noon dinner. Here is a long work in the newspaper on the table before me; "Bundesratsbevollmachtigter." A bottle of wine is too much to drink alone. I have entertained a German lady at dinner—Frau Braurig, on her way home to Basel. She was much amused by my language mistakes. She knows no English. She gave some travel hints that I hope will be useful.

AUG 26 Basel. South of Mainz I stopped briefly at Heidelberg and Strassburg. Saw the sights of each. Here in Basel the "Hotel des Balances is the finest yet. I arrived in Basel on the day of the celebration of the battle of St. Jacques. There is a lot of French to the cities of Strassburg and Basel. Tomorrow train to Zurich.

Here at Zurich I am comfortably located. I can't understand Schweizersprache. I am taken to be a German.

The lake is beautiful. Villages around the lake are neat. Orchards and vineyards are meticulously cared for—everything in order. The back ground is striking. Yesterday coming toward Switzerland the hills began to give a sense of mountains and then looking above the apparent skyline, up in the sky snow clad peeks were startlingly revealed. Tomorrow I start to cross Switzerland on foot. I'll be headed first for Luzern, then study the map deciding the best route after that.

AUG 27 This afternoon I walked along the lake to Horgen, then up over the hills and across the Sihl at Sihlbrugg and arrived here at Baar near Zug. The Hotel St. Gotthard is clean; supper: unlimited ham, cheese, bread, honey, milk, and a glass of beer. This beer is mild and equal to any along the Rhine.

From Baar next day I walked around L. Zug to Arth. In approach I was much reminded of Turner's "Arth from the Lake Zug" which I had seen reproduced several times. Dinner at Arth with others. At the table were guests speaking English, German, French, Schweis, and Italian. From Arth I walked along the foot of the Rigi to Immensee. The nostalgia from so many of the names of places comes from romances in the books read sometime ago.

Immensee is all that the name suggests. It commands a fine view of the Rigi and Arth lying between the Rigi and Rossberg. I spent Sunday night at Immensee and Monday morning started on foot up the Rigi. It is a tiresome three hour climb on a good but steep path. I put up for the night on the Rigi-Staffel, which is 15 min. Below the Kulm. I intended to see the "Sonnenitergang" and the "Sonnenaufgang," but saw neither. Clouds gathered just before sunset and it rained all night into the morning. But before that, I had the view, a panorama under good light conditions, of the various Alps and Lakes making the climb worthwhile. Large numbers of tourists with alpenstocks came riding up on the funiculaire. I had walked up with my umbrella and met no one. Going down doesn't demand so much wind but is hard on the muscles and heels. The path down is steeper than that going up and is full of sharp stones which soon took both soles and heels off my shoes. I went down to Weggis on the Vierwaldstatter See.

I came to Luzern from Weggis by boat. Here in Luzern I shall stay a day for shoe repair. These are the best shoes I ever had. Tomorrow I go to Brienz weather permitting.

I reached Brienz at 7:30 P.M. From Luzern, walking mostly in the rain (I had my raincoat and umbrella) minding nothing but the mind. I crossed the Brunig and debouched into the Aare valley in the evening as the rain stopped. My eyes and ears took in; the sights of sunlit peaks in the clouds, the charming Aare valley with its waterfalls and mists in motion, and sounds of cow-bell, squawking children, waterfalls and the dripping of water from the rocks overhanging the road.

An idle day on account of rain. Made one water color.

SEP 11 Lugano after 8 days. On the 3rd I took boat to Interlaken and walked to Grindlewald, tried to find our friend Mrs. Lovell but was unable to locate Chalet "Aufder Hohe." I had time to walk to the upper Glacier. Next day walked over the Gr. Scheidegg to Meiringen and on up the Aare valley to Guttaneu. That was Sunday. Then it rained Monday and Tuesday. A dreary time at the hotel highlighted by excellent meals and three sketches. It was a heavy rain. A little above the village it was snowing. The mountains were getting whiter and the white came father down the mountain sides. The diligence from Gletsch was covered with snow. The next day the road over the Grimsel was so bad the diligence couldn't go at all.

When it cleared (third day) I set out to the pass. At Handeck Falls I was surprised to meet two of the fellows I had seen on the Canada "they had just turned back on account of snow. A little further along I came to snow—a little at first, then deeper then, at the Grimsel Hospice, 6" deep. Further, in snow up to my knees I followed a path over Grimsel. The path was tramped down a little by shovelers who were trying to clear the road. Miniature avalanches were descending now and then. Larger ones had already piled snow 6–7 ft. deep. I was in snow 3 hours before coming down far enough to get below the snow line. The sun on the snow made me see purple for hours afterward. I put up at Gletsch for the night.

The next day I crossed the Furka in more snow but was soon over and down by short cuts to avoid the windings of the road. A free ride from Realp to Hospenthal in a cab returning empty cost me 50cm. tip. That little ride helped because I entended on making the St. Gotthard pass the same day. I did so. On the St. Gotthard I was halted where others had gathered. A uniformed sentry told us we would have to descend into the valley and follow the right bank of the Reuss to get out of cannon practice range. We waded the river and walked to where we could climb up to the road again. There was a constant echoing of cannon firing.

It is quite sudden to descend from the barren St. Gotthard to the Valle Leventina and find the so different Italian Swiss country. Travelers were now saying "buon' giorno." I shall remember Faido in particular on account of Hotel Francioli where dinner was 2½ fr., breakfast 1 fr., and room 2 francs. The best hotels so far have been in Switzerland.

SEP 11 I am resting up here at Lagano two days. This is a fine hotel with a broad terrace extending across the rear and out to the lake with easy garden furniture, meals outdoors, delicious wine—8 lira a day.

A few hours of Como, another beautiful lake a—and then three days at Milano. Of course, out to Certosa di Pavia—an hour with Leonardo's "Last Supper"—a short time at the Ospedale Maggiore—a visit to the Brera. The cathedral is marvellous but overworked. It is necessary to tie some of it together with steel rods, many, many, man hours of carving.

Over night in Pisa, I am one of two guests at the "Grand Hotel. The leaning tower leans only slightly further than at first.

SEP 19 Siena's the place! A most curious labyrinth of streets, all crooked. Most of the buildings are four or more stories high. The common houses, the university, the warehouses, factories, and barns are so much alike, one doesn't know what sort of building one is looking at. No two fronts are parallel. The public buildings and churches are architecturally good.

One can't imagine a more unprepossessing entrance than that at 319 via Sallustio Bandini which I entered coming to Mme Saccaro's pension. The building across the street is the university. The front looks like a small Chicago factory. The street, 16 ft. Wide, looks like a Chicago alley except that here there is never any accumulation of rubbish or even of dust. "Most extraordinary" to use the favorite expression of the English guests. I am the only American.

Pension Saccaro is the most thoroly satisfactory pension I have struck yet. I occupies a rambling 2nd story running thru adjacent houses. Corridor floors change levels as they go from one house to the next. It has a roof garden commanding a fine view to the northeast. It is clean and my room and meals are only 5 lira day—and such cooking! I look at architectural detail and have visited many churches and public buildings. The Accademia di Belle Arti is a pleasure to roam thru. The city has a wealth of detail at which to look again & again.

At sunset everyday a disjointed jangling of all the bells in town starts the braying of all the asses and the howling of all the dogs.

SEP 21 The distinguished looking man sitting across from me at the dinner table is John S. Sargent. Sitting next to him is his sister. They are formal and very polite and seem interested in my tales of wild west Chicago.

I have now been sketching in places where I run into Sargent. Without being obtrusive I've had chances to see him work. I realize how little I know about the mechanics of painting. Above all Sargent's painting looks masterfully easy. But I notice one thing. At the start of a painting he is very careful and then as it develops he lays on the paint with more freedom. When about done he looks at it with piercing eye and making a stroke *here* and another *there*, gives the whole a look of spontaneous dash. Although nine-tenth of the work is very careful indeed, there is a look of bold virtuosity when the thing is done. But with all the good things he does there are occasional lapses into something very common-place.

Sargent has more than once asked if he could see what I was doing. It pleased me that he should take any notice at all. Casual meetings have sometimes led to discussions. He is in favor of portrayals of sunlight. He says "like Sorolla" (who ever that is) and I try to point out the value of invention, novelty, originality, the intensive effort to compose. I suppose I am influenced by admiration of composers of music. Of the masters of painting, Sargent brings up Hals and Titian. I suggested to him: VerMeer as the most conscious as well as the most intuitive painter. I wish that in my paintings I could place everything in the right spot, and position, and attitude, and relation to every other thing in the picture.

Sargent today looked long at my small wood panel. "What is it," he asked. "It is from a theme suggested by the corner of the fountain, and the jar below it, but is not an attempt to make a copy of either," I said. When I was about to take back the little panel of wood, he said "No, let me look at it." This pleased me beyond any praise I had received at any other time from anyone. He never said at any of these meetings that I was on the wrong track.

S's piercing, slightly protruding eyes seem to see like some physics instrument, but he is blind to some of the things I see. When I pointed out a particularly determined slant in the painting at the Museum, he considered it the product of ignorance. I thought that Micharino definitely made it because the picture required it.

SEP 30 I broke away from attractions of sunny days, the harvest moon passing out, the sketching weather, the country sights, the children and old men who sang in the evenings, all the things associated with Siena and the pension Saccaro.

Siena is so compact that a few minutes takes one out into the country, so a part of several days was spent outside the city walls. My pieces of wood are getting filled. Much sketching was done under the stimulous of explanation to Sargent.

From now on I shall be mostly in the larger cities: Rome, Florence, Bologna, Venice, Paris (again), Munich, Dresden, and Berlin.

OCT 1 In Rome I am staying at pension "Marley," a very comfortable place—marble floor in my bedroom with velvet fringe on the walls below an elaborate cornice. If the ceiling and floor above is constructed as I have seen such in recent houses, above me are heavy timbers with space between ceiling and floor above me loaded with sand for fire protection.

I am better located here for sight seeing than I was in any other big city. My window faces the buildings of the Chamber of Deputies on the Piazza Monte Citorio which is at one side of Piazza Colonna. The "Corso" cuts the Piazza in two. Around the Colonna are a dozen cafes all active. Tables and chairs are set all over the sidewalks and the street. The whole piazza seems like one big open air restaurant. On certain evenings a band plays good music. That is the time to go out and eat "Cassatta." The Corso is quite full in the evening, both sidewalks and street. All the girls are on parade. You still see survivals of the wasp waist as well as the no-waist-all hat style. The Roman "sports" are out too. Their favorite gesture is the twirl, the twist of moustache ends with two-fingers. An average Italian looks a little worn in dress. The fine dressers are the army officers. By the way, Italian battleships (seen elsewhere) painted dark grey, look more menacing than our white navy.

There's an endless quantity of stuff to look at in and out of galleries. There are so many galleries! It is the sculptures that are outstanding, indescribably beautiful. No words can give an idea of the exquisite quality of some of the cream colored marbles.

The Sistine Chapel and the neighboring galleries of the Vatican, with St. Peter's alongside are the great places to visit and revisit. Rome raises appreciation of Rafaello, and Michel Angelo to higher levels.

There are fine examples of architecture, both fragments and well preserved buildings and the many sculptures, for art or history, show the considerable glory of ancient Greek and Roman times. There are a number of, probably accurate, portrait busts of Roman Emperors that probably give a true picture of those grim personalities.

There are here as fellow guests two American Rhodes scholars from Oxford. They are wearing moustaches, of course, as do every Italian boy or man from 16 yrs up. I had started one after entering Italy and now look like a native, but am classed as a German, away from the pension, because of my use of German for the purpose of economy.

When in the Forum or Palatine I do not feel the atmosphere of ancient Rome. One can reconstruct the form of the site of the Forum but reality is that of the present since it is surrounded with modern buildings, and one is pestered to death with post card salesmen and beggars.

There's a time after museums close and dinner is ready, when it is too dark to sketch and one has had enough of sight seeing of the day. That is the time when these not very important words get written down.

Two more young Rhodes scholars arrived four days ago after the others had left. One day we walked out to the Appian Way. At the beginning of the most interesting part the others got tired. I went on alone. The Via Appia is different from other Roman ruins hereabouts in the way it does give genuine impression of age. There are no modern buildings around and no modern human beings in sight. In the Forum I can't associate the ruins with ancient Rome but the Via Appia I find easy to line up again with the "rotting corses of the six thousand slaves," and it would be no shock if one met St. Paul coming to Rome. I wonder whether I should really consider 2000 years any considerable duration of time in view of eternity before and after.

Rome is a dirty city. Defecations line the rough ramp to the Pincio and a particularly bad odor comes repeatedly, as carts pass loaded with jars of household waste. Urinals are simply the gutter along side buildings.

The guides do a great business with the tourists. The guided are misinformed and hurried along. And very noticeable it is that tourists see but seldom look at anything.

OCT 8 Today was a free day at the Vatican and Lateran. I have given many sights a first look and to some I have returned again and again. I know of the Vatican and other places now and can stop before the most, to me, important features. Rome has given me in the Sistine Chapel and St. Peter's my first real acquaintance with Michel Angelo.

Rome is a great city for churches. Priests and monks are always in sight. Tonsures are a great variety. Now and then troops of boys or girls from some monastic or convent school go by. Each group has its own uniform. All except the youngest children appear leaden and stupid. They have been regimented and little is left but superstition.

There is a fine view of Rome from the park on the Pincio and the grounds of the Villa Borghese. Things are showing autumn colors under the clear skies.

The magnitude of Rome is not in area or population. It is in the wealth of stuff to see. My words haven't said much, but if I ever reread this brief account, it will recall, to me, stops and turns, the views, the time spent looking, and the ever present realization of the tremendous amount of work done, the many hours, the many years given to working on things that have endured and on things now lost.

One very unpleasant fact ever present in Italy is the trickery of the natives in all money deals. I have never received correct change from railway ticket clerks, always having to ask for the balance, always eventually getting it with a smile, though the intention was to beat me. Coins have to be inspected. There are a multitude of counterfeits. The only bad lira I came away with not having inspected it, was received at the main post office in Rome. This atmosphere of trickery, necessitating such constant vigilance, is oppressive.

I must now say, but not because of the same feeling Whistler had, "I'm going."

OCT 16 Nothing has been written here as I toured Naples with its important collections, then to Viterbo, Orvieto, and Perugia. So much moving and so much looking has kept me from writing. The museum at Naples must not be skipped and Pompeii—impressive—and glowering Vesuvius. Some superlative carvings at Perugia, where I stopped a few hours, made me want to linger. I began to wish that I would be late to the train and would have to stay overnight. I was late to the station but the train was late. So I got out of Perugia.

Florence I saw first in the evening. In the dark the tall buildings and towers loomed up and hinted what was coming later. I like things in Florence. It's art has been the finest expression of the Renaissance in Italy. I say I *like* all this but I have no desire to extend it into the present. Many are making repetitions of the past and digging back without understanding. This is particularly true in architecture, and so true back at draughting room of Holabird & Roche.

I am at a pension with some fifty guests. We have a full dining room—very good meals—clean bed room—guests going and coming every day. There are about a dozen each of English, Americans, and Australians. A very good example of Henpeck and family—a pretty girl across the table and an interesting fellow alongside at meals.

I shall never be able to detail the multitude of sights and pleasures of view. Many, many masters are housed in the Uffrzi, the Pitti, and the Accademia. Michel Angelo's finest sculptures are here in the Medici Tomb Chapel. These grand sculptures are delicately fine yet overpowering. Where can six greater sculptures can be found?

The constant rambling in this delightful city, the returning exhausted to my 3rd floor room, leave little time to write. It is, however, a good thing to write here, for it gives me always a starter when I write a letter home. Writing home I do in chapters in succession to: Father, Mother, Grandma, Aunt Kaye, Mitchell & Lovell. I shall write too, to Kate Kellogg who will keep Mary, Gertrude, Hattie, and Orno informed. Father and Mother always let Edward Darrow read these letters.

The soprano studing singing, arriving toward opera, living on the 2nd floor, pretends to be enthusiastic about my sketches, but observing her, I see she is not looking at them, is only tring to pose to gain attention. How far might I go! Having so little money to spend I am not taking her anywhere. The tenor next to me at the table is most valuable in giving rise to conversations which give opportunity to formulate opinions on sights seen. He is fluent, talkative, and yet will pause to give any of us a chance to say what he thinks. The little girl across the table would be fun to spark, but she is a non-wit, seems interested in nothing beyond clothes changing and eating. She and her mother spend the greater part of meal time recalling the eating places in other cities and the specialties that pleased. I am wasting time writing about them.

Florence is a place to keep going and doing. Many extraordinary things are free for the looking. Where entrance is charged it has never been more than 1 lira. One can't escape the Duomo with its Ghiberti doors and the Giotto tower nearby, the Palazzo

Vecchio, the out door sculptures, the unique Uffizi-Pitti corridor crossing the river on the Ponte-Vecchio, shops galore, and best of all the Medici Tomb Chapel. If the Medicis lived now-a-days, one wouldn't grudge them their wealth if they patronized art as they did in the Renaissance.

This pension makes my stay pleasant. Every bit of food tastes fresh. Desserts are marvels. Today—roast sweet chesnuts in brandy set afire. I am taking it easy before going to Venice. I have switched from watercolors to architectural creations (inventions) I shall show these to Roche this coming winter. It is hard to tell how far my money will take me. Paris has to be next after Venice and then I have to cross to Germany.

English and American newspapers are encountered here and there, so I have some general information of happenings. Aeroplaning is brisk in America, the French are taking all speed records with their monoplanes. These certainly beat our bi-planes. The Germans are experimenting with ponderous balloons.

One walk out of town—to Fiesole—picturesque villas on a traced hill- gnarled olive trees abound many over 100 years old.

Mrs. Mason says Sargent is in town, but doesn't know where he can be found. I must look him up. He was very cordial when we said good by in Siena.

A bright morning, an unusually decent cab driver, and a nice lunch put up by the pension, all combined to give me a very nostalgic parting impression of Florence.

Venice is totally different from all other cities. *That* I expected. My many previous views of the city and its canals seen in paintings and in magazine illustrations, and a previous study of the map that placed everything where it was, must have been what produced a feeling of having been here before. My mental pictures—of the various buildings lay so clearly in mind and turned out so accurate, and the plan of the city so expected, that it all seemed I remembered it. I couldn't realize I hadn't been on these canals and the Piazza before. To begin with, the points of the compass seem all right. From the station I took stamer to the Rialto, and then walked thru the tortuous Merceria (only a few feet wide) to the Piazza San Marco coming out under the celebrated clock. I hunted up my pension—all this from the station without consulting my map or Baedeker. I went from one place to another without making a false turn and never asking the way. This and following rambles were remarkable because Venice seems such a hopeless labyrinth with streets where there are many, only 4–8 ft wide, often leading into blind alleys.

On going into my room on the first night on turning on the light I saw a most terrifying sight. On the net hanging around my bed was an army of wicked mosquitoes. I killed the two that had gotten inside the net. It wasn't easy. All this mosquitoe business was on the first night. Last night was cooler and from now on the weather is expected to end the mosquito season. The slovenly Russian countess and her maid appearing at breakfast that first morning, were terribly bitten in the night and mostly scratched thruout the meal. They seemed to have arrived at night. I saw them only at breakfast.

Venice is full of pictures. The event of the day right now is the International Art Exhibition. Most represented are Venetian painters. The style of the present seems to be realism with nature copied in a careless manner. The prize winner was a local teacher. His painting, to me, was bad. It makes me want to take more care in my own work—producing quality rather than quantity. But it is necessary to do as many things as time permits in order to learn more of line and color.

There are many towers throughout the city, each leaning in a different direction. Familiar are the cathedral, the palace, the library, Santa Maria della Salute, S. Georgio; and what's this! no campanile! The tower had fallen a few months ago. Now, a new foundation is completed and work has started to build a facsimile,—same-looking brick, similar stone.

There are many gorgeous paintings in the public buildings. I have been looking in all accessible palaces, churches, and galleries, learning a lot. One strange Titian, said to have been painted in his 99th year, called unfinished, is a perfect example of pointillism.

Piazza S. Marco is a wonderful place. It not only is surrounded by fine buildings but is a gathering place for all Venice, particularly on the three evenings when the band plays. The piazza is some 180 yds long and 60 yds wide, yet the square is crowded so it is not easy to walk about. Among the boys and girls it is the custom to pretend accidental bumping. This leads to many a pick-up. The act is especially good when made to look entirely unintentional. It appears that the girls do more bumping than the boys. Some of the girls are strikingly pretty.

The thousands of pigeons are scary on first encounter. After that they are nothing but a nuisance. The pigeon population should be reduced. I have made one stunning sketch. I feel like carrying it on my person for fear of losing it.

NEXT STOP PARIS!

NOV 2 At great expense and tedious riding I have returned to Paris. *Here* is the Louvre. With Italian experience I can now get more benefit from this enormous collection.

I am again at Mlle Goullier's. It is still a solidly clean comfortable place. I do not plan a long stay here because money is running out. I shall look up Mrs. Stein. That will please Lebenbaum.

An Englishman here, Whitley, is a good companion. We did the Louvre together. He is full of information on recent art trends. He speaks of "cubists" attracting attention.

I do not know much about Miss Stein. Whitley has told me she is becoming known to a few as a writer having a novel style and as being a collector of many things being talked about in Paris. I shall call on her with Lebenbaum's letter for I am sure he will want to know I did so.

I have called at Miss Stein's on Rue de Fleurus, showed my letter to the long-skirted woman who answered the bell. She spoke English like an American, didn't bother to read the letter and informed me that Miss Gertrude was busy that afternoon, but would be at home Saturday evening. Telling Whitley about it, he suggested we call together and also suggested I take along a wood panel to show. He said Saturdays brought a mixture of nationalities to Miss Stein's, but, while there was much confusion and the light was not good, one could see an extraordinary jumble of paintings, a few of them remarkable and well worth examining.

Whitley introduced me to the hostess, a fat woman sitting in a very large chair. A brief conversation with Miss Stein let her know that I was a fellow draughtsman of Lebenbaum's, but that I was more interested in painting than architecture. I told her that I had been in Paris earlier this year and that I was glad to be here again; could not stay long because money was running out, and I was afraid of not getting home without making a desparate call to the U.S. for funds. After some time she beckoned me to her chair. With some diffidence I showed her my little painting which I had carried under my arm. Looking at it for a while steadily she passed it to a bearded Frenchman who said a few words in comment, raised his eyebrows and with just a suggestion of a bow returned it to me. Than came the surprise. "Can I have this," said Miss S. "Do you mean buy it," I asked smiling, and thinking I would gladly give it to her. "Yes," she said "Would 200 fcs. be right." "Yes." This is the first painting I ever sold. I told her it had no title. But I had called it, to myself, "Statement." She turned to the long-skirted woman who had met me at the door and said "Wouldn't this be nice for Christmas for __________. I did not know who that was.

The following Monday, due to my interest in the Cezannes at Miss Stein's, Whitley took me to a dealer on Rue Laffitte to see some of Cezanne's paintings. Whitley was a walker so we walked to the shop which had nothing about it that seemed to advertise its purpose. The window was empty. The dealer was polite, but as the conversation was in French, I got very little of it. The few paintings he showed impressed me extremely. I wanted to see more, but he was very slow bring each out. Finally he told Whitley of a coming appointment so we left, myself thrilling as we went. My mind has been full of the few things I saw. One painting I cannot forget, a late one and apparently unfinished. The arbitrary black lines, the tying of knots, the emphasis these made in showing where the parts were important to the composition, and the great variety of altered forms were very instructive to an understanding of inventive pictures, and gave me a big lift in support of what I was trying to do in my own work. One thing I noticed was the invariable success of Cezanne's color.

I have bought return from Bremen to N.Y. on S.S. "Friederich der Grosse." Now it is going to be "watch expenses" at Munich, Dresden and Berlin. The $40.00 is going to be a big help.

NOV 14 Nothing written but brief letter at Munich. A few days now in Berlin.

There was tedious riding via Strassburg to Munich.

I found Munchen a clean, well arranged city, somewhat drab and mixed in architecture—much bizarre, distorted copying of Italian Renaissance. Much walking and looking took me thru the extensive collections of the old Pina Kothek—some magnificent Rubens there and more walking at the new Pina Kothek across the way. I like Rubens more and more beginning to see him as in innovator, a master of arrangement. He has an almost unlimited compositional power. The Glyptothek is interesting especially in the more antique items in the collection.

I have found the best beers are made in Munich.

Dresden—a beautiful city—why couldn't I stay? I had to do and do and get further, so as to meet the boat.

The city has a great deal of style. It is one of the neatest of the large cities and where the architecture is mixed it is mixed with logical design and understanding. I spent two days with the pictures in the museum—a multi-collection. It was impossible to digest properly. The much mentioned feature, the Sistine Madonna is large, but not one of Rafael's best. Tho leg weary I received priceless instruction from this great collection—almost all the masters. Museums are really places for learning art—learning what it is all about.

I spent an hour at the Austellung d. Kunstler verein. Not much is being done in the academies.

I am beginning to settle on favorites: Tintoretto, Rubens, Poussin, Delacroix, Turner, Constable. I think I have been most affected by Cezanne who, in the few works of his I have seen, doesn't take the scene at face value but digs into the bones and shows them. He isn't afraid of bold lines in landscape or figure and he makes the color what it should be.

From the train one sees on any line in Germany, plantings of pine or spruce—many thousands of acres. They have really gone in for reforestation.

Before I was long in Germany it had turned into winter. Berlin weather has been terrible. Snow and slush prevail and there has been no daylight. Street lights are on all day.

This pension has been good as others have been. Some of the guests are Germans. Two of these wear monocles, speak excellent high German and perfect Oxford English, but when speaking to each other speak a gibberish which I am told is popular in the universities.

These men say I should have looked up the new stuff being done around Munchen. In looking at some of my sketches they tell me these are "right in line." By their description of what is going on in Germany in art circles, in the groups that are far out, there is something being done akin to some of the work I saw at Gertrude Stein's.

In painting a great picture inventive organization is essential, and those transcendental feelings about shapes, attitudes and relations—must be signified by the form given out by the artist. Accidentals sometimes happen good or bad. But the important thing is design. Art is a human invention. I am realizing the universality of fine art in all peoples in all parts of the world, and there is a continuity so that apparent new departures are not as much breaking away from the past as some would suppose.

Everywhere as in all Germany are troops tramping or training—there must be millions in the army. That is the season that all street cleaners, rubbish collectors, and switchmen are women. You see them along the R.R.s doing track repair work.

Unter den hinden to the museums—more acres to cover and yards of canvas to inspect.

I called on our old friend Mrs Stiles who is now living the year-round here.

Tuesday we went to a performance of "La Boheme" at the Komische Oper. It was well given—a perfect balance between the singers and between singers and orchestra. The singers subordinated themselves to Puccini, none trying to be the star of the show. The acting was good—no Ibalian arm waving. The whole was beautifully done. The Komische Oper is of convenient size for seeing—good proportions—good accoustics. The audience was still throughout each act—clapping only at the end of each—no break for applause after each aria.

I have seen more monocles in Berlin than in London.

This is poor weather to see Berlin. I want to see more but the S.S. leaves Bremerhaven on the 19th.

NOV 30 Shipboard: We left on schedule. My ticket was 2nd class but that class was so large some of us were pushed forward into 1st class rooms. This put me with two Germans in a large room amidships which is in the position having the least pitching and rolling. The meals are fair but ship smells are bad.

First days were calm. Porpoises are chasing the ship and giving us a good close look. After Monday still winds whipped up tremendous waves so racks had to be placed on all dining tables to hold the dishes from sliding off. Through the portholes, as the ship rolled, we saw, at intervals, either only water or only sky. A worry, as the ship rolled till water met the port holes—would we ever roll back the other way! I was nearly seasick Weds. and Thursday—Thanksgiving Day—after that big American style turkey dinner. Since Thurs. I have enjoyed myself exploring the 1st class, chatting with some of the stuffed shirts; and at other times overlooking the rear deck watching the steerage people playing the accordion and dancing folk dances. Most of those in the steerage have that look—inexpressible happiness—they are going to America.

Second Sunday was sparkling with sunshine. Monday (No. 2) was cloudy and cold, turning warm and sunny the same day. This last day is cold and rainy clearing when in sight of N.Y. Harbor entering is thrilling. Passing the statue of Liberty there was cheering and weeping. The weeping never stopped until the dock was in sight.

On approach to N.Y. ones sees for a while a cliff of buildings 10, 12, or 15 stories high and then after getting used to that, suddenly up in the sky appear the towering skyscrapers. New York has its building code prescribing certain building limits, but nothing like Chicago where the present height limit is 260 ft. which makes only at most 22 stories.

The landing was easy (at Hoboken) through customs in two or three minutes on declaration of nothing dutiable. Time yet to get across to New York. The last part of this written in my room in St. Denis Hotel. Broadway at Eleventh.

Next day: Looked up Arthur Davies, the Kellogg's friend. He gave me some time in his studio, said he had seen my little sketch for the larger "Germinal," and really gave a good look at my little wood panels and the snap shots of "Flowering Twilight." He was complimentary—wanted to know if a move to New York were possible. His own work is dreamlike and very original. After an hour (how I wish I had a studio like his) we visited Albert Ryder—a very exhilerating time there. He is a great artist. I felt extremely elated when he looked lengthily at my paintings and photos.

Other studios of men about whom I had known nothing, but whose work showed the most clever craftsmanship and made me sad to think how little I had done so far. One of them showed me Califano's copy of a Courbet. I would have thought it our original, a beautiful seated nude in a woodland. Courbet and Ingres seemed the most frequently mentioned in the talk of these men. One discussion was about the "wild men" of Paris. I may have seen something of those mentioned, without having thought of them as wild.

On my tour the masters had impressed me. Ingres I think is like VerMeer in one way; the careful composition and construction of the forms, where everything had line and value put *right*.

I can't get over thinking of Ryder. He is a great inventor of shapes, haunting impressions of those inner feelings which he has and which I can feel with him. He seems, however, close to his end, doing little except repainting, touching, and burnishing. His studio was a picture of awful disorder.

I can't linger in New York. Fosters have invited me to visit them in Troy. Nothing is left in my pocket except enough for hotel bill, trip, and R.R. fare to Troy. I have wired Father to send money order to Foster's address and shall go to Troy.

Hattie Foster is disturbed by my kind of paintings. Hal Foster says he knows nothing whatever about art. He is a manufacturer of small handy things, little metal inventions, hangers, clips, whatnot. Daughter Helen took me out to the little lake nearby to skate. She is a beautiful skater. I am a dub on skates.

DEC 5 Money arrived and I take off for Chicago Tomorrow morning.

DEC 15 Meeting Davies was a great stimulant. I am sketching for projects, thinking much about Rubens and Tintoretto, and the Cezannes in Paris. And Ryder's paintings haunt me.

Settled with Holabird and Roche again, sparetime is spent on painting some boards to cover the other unused fireplace opening close to the piano.

1911

JAN 2 Back in the draughting room grind, thankful for the four extra days in Christmas week. Sketches are developing plans for "museum" paintings. These rely somewhat on those last themes that came from so much looking at paintings in the galleries, and on conversations about new trends.

I have stretched canvas (I wish it were better grade) for a picture of a lolling woman with almost the most important interest: the lines surrounding the figure. Davies would be pleased to think that I haven't forgotten his advice to do figure painting. But I haven't been thinking of that advice. The urge had causes before that.

I am in the downstairs D-room with Hoskins, LeBar, Reed, et al.

Mr. Cooper, Father's carpenter client brought me some wide boards, which I intend to try to split with a hand saw. That will give lighter weight and double the area.

Dudley Watson who had studied at the Chicago Art Institute has seen some of my late sketches. He suggests joining one of the special life classes at the Institute. Where would I have time away from my job and my desperate try to use every spare hour to get important works finished? To get me coming he has taken me to look in on some of the groups sketching away before the nude model. I think this has been useful to me. The figure I am working on begins to look like one of those models. I have been arranging the pose and must confess that it looks like anyone of the dozens seen in the museums. At a loss to choose the proper angle for the arm at the left of the picture, I am getting the idea of presenting two or three positions and leaving these all in the picture. This does not look unreasonable and I think adds motion, though I usually think of motion, in a static picture, as belonging to that produced by directional relations of lines.

FEB 12 I think I have finished my painting 36 × 32 done mostly at night. It looks better in the daytime, best in bright sun light. I shall call it *"Lucrece,"* just to give a title for my record.

I have cut up the wide boards into 32" lengths and have split one. When primed I shall draw from my pencil sketch a beautiful woman in full dress which I think will be brown.

I am working on two projects—the one on wood and a canvas "portrait" 36 × 28 of a woman in a blue dress. This last is getting to look like a Rembrandt.

APR 2 It takes so long to complete anything in night working and on Sundays, but I have now completed the wood panel. Aunt Kate says it looks like Helen Darrow. I don't see much resemblance but it might be O.K. for a title to call it *"Mrs. Darrow."*

Why are titles necessary? Only for identification. My little record book should give, without title identification by date, size and ground material. It might be best to put the title only on the back. All those words sometimes used "Theme," Symphony," "Nocturn," "Impression," etc., do not describe the emotional content which is peculiar to painting and any visual art. It is not musical, poetic, or story telling, but is found in the depth of the picture, described by line, comparative intensity, scale, and color; by the significant attitudes of the forms which are there. Color is that necessary aid to giving the eye an assist in realizing the meaning of the shaped and the correctness of the lines in giving the feeling.

Time and again I have had the thought that all artists in all times past and present are trying to do the same thing, to make a picture and make it right. Sculptures are pictures. All buildings are pictures, that is, visual presentation of feelings about form. While architecture concerns itself with utility and the mechanics of construction, to be right it must also make a picture. I use the word; "picture," to mean the rightness of view of a thought. Maybe I am babbling.

In trying to answer the questions that are repeatedly thrown at me, "What does it mean?" "What does it represent?" I have to start with a statement that sometimes helps "Art is a human invention. In nature there was no art except that all creations of the almighty are part of that almighty. "Art" as a word for us to use describes the invention of that part of creation that is man. All nature is bearing down on us day after day. We cannot avoid it. Every form that we could use is there. But away from nature and in the seclusion of the mind we can invent arrangements to be found nowhere else. One answer to the question, "What is it," is to point to the picture and say, "It is *that.*" "It exists no where else."

My efforts to convince Roche that a style can be developed for the elevations of our present day skyscrapers, that would indicate the true structure of these buildings, are not meeting with any success. In fact he will not spend more than a few seconds either looking at designs or discussing the idea that a breakaway from the accepted conventions would be progressive. Once he said "Progress! Holabird will get a new job for the firm, that's progress."

It is easy to see that the heavy impact of all the schools and traditions, based on the beauties of the past, keep our designers glued to classic examples so much admired by all who have seen the palaces and churches of Europe.

It is discouraging, to me, to think of a life as an architect trying to convince the public to accept an expression of the fact that current construction is of steel column, beam, and wind bracing enclosed for fireproofing and habitation and mounted on bed-rock for security. Decoration could be unlimitedly varied, but external appearance should definitely express the structure just as much as the northern French Gothic expresses the stone on stone buildup, the absolute necessity of the flying buttresses for bracing, and the pinnacles for weighing down the piers.

The artist painter has an advantage in that he can conceive, start in, and complete a design without having a client already backing the production. The architect can make all the designs he chooses but is foiled in completing his work by lack of a client.

The whole question of my activites is an economic one. What can I do to make a living? I am thoroughly convinced that architecture will eventually come into the proper line for our modern society. But what can I do in the meantime.

MAY 7 I have completed the Rembrandt esque portrait. It hasn't yet been named. Over past weeks—a small wood and a canvas "the Trees," 15 × 22 which I love. It is simple but has a lot of stuff in it. I am starting on other 32 × 24 boards and one card board larger.

I wont get a vacation this summer because vacations are only due after a year's work. That makes no great time for painting. I am flirting with the idea of retiring to the farm and being able to paint at intervals and really get something done. It probably wouldn't work. There is discouragement in an architectural future because I am a poor salesman and in this profession it is necessary to get out and hustle-in the jobs. There are no wealthy members in our family and no wealthy friends to start on for clients.

The paintings I am now projecting make-one sad to think I can't exclusively make a daily work of them. What other job can I get that will not be a knuckling down to the past and at the same time give more time to the paints and brushes.

It is a dull season—department stores and office buildings—double hung windows strictly standard—hollow tile or brick spandrels—L'Ecole des Beaux Arts doorways—the same for cornices.

So far, each skyscraper in the Loop has had one or two deaths from choke-damp in the wells dug for the concrete posts to bed rock.

SEP 24 Nearly completed are four paintings on the wide boards, one cardboard 36 × 28, and one 30 × 24 canvas. This past month I have done three small woods.

I have started on canvas a picture of a woman, a hybrid between a nun and Mary Kellogg. Another "abstraction" of a woman at her bath. These don't seem to come along very fast.

DEC 29 Tomorrow we have the day off as we had Sat. A week ago. These extra days will have made starts for the New Year. I am resolved then to get more paintings *done*. This past autumn, sketches and sketches have laid up a pile of work that at the first opportunity I can plunge into.

1912

JAN 1 I have finished all the incomplete paintings except the woman in brown and the woman bathing. For their completion I have only to emphasize a line or two. They can't get by the next week end.

FEB 25 More things are finished and more underweigh than for a long time. I am following a pretty regular schedule. Opera nights and symphony nights the only planned breaks. I can get 3 hrs work in the evenings of 4 out of the week day and sometimes as much as 12 hours on Sundays

JUN 2 Having worked 1½ yrs without a vacation Holabird & Roche are giving me 3 weeks this summer, so very soon I'll away to the "Humps" as Mitchell calls it. I have crated all the unfinished boards and canvasses and will ship them to Michigan. There is still a clutter of things in my studio room. All that stuff I can finish on vacation and maybe do some other pictures. I plan 7 days work every week.

SEP 29 Today, Father's and Mother's anniversary brings suddenly the realization of time flight. I open this book after months of neglect. It has been lying under my bed. Many things have been done, many have not been done. Slaving in the D-room—the ridiculous Monroe building—who wants a medieval, Italian building on Michigan Ave?

OCT 25 Lunch with cousin Jack Manierre at the University Club. That building is collegiate gothic designed by Holabird and Roche. We met two who invited us to sit at their table. One was from N.Y. the other, Mr. Ryerson had just come across the street from the Art Institute. When Jack mentioned that I was an artist painter Mr. Ryerson became quite interested and asked many questions. I asked the N. Yorker if he knew Arthur Davies or Albert Ryder. He knew them both. Ryerson had met Davies and liked his work but didn't feel sure of Ryder. I asked him if Davies had mentioned me, because he might have knowing that I was a Chicagoan. The answer "No," makes me think Davies may have forgotten me.

DEC 16 I was wrong about Davies forgetting. He has invited me to send some of my things, what I consider the most novel, to him. He has promoted and gathered a great show to be presented this winter by the Association of American Painters and Sculptors. What can I send? My "Three Graces" is like a Pompeiian wall painting. The other large paintings are too much like what I've read about in the "Manchester Guardian." All my good stuff is at "the Humps." What I have here are small paintings that would be lost in the assemblage Davies intends. The string of paintings I am working on is of middle sized paintings but very non-objective. The subjective themes are working out beautifully, but I can't send unfinished, unframed pictures. I will have to select from among these to decide what to finish and then make boxes. Where am I going to get time?

Thank goodness for Christmas vacation days, four of them. These Sunday works begun in November after I had finished "Figures in Action," a dozen or so, are incomplete, unframed, no boxes made. The show, I believe is to be in February. I think I can stand working evenings till mid-night. Strangely night painted colors seem beautifully bright in daytime.

Bennett has just sent me a newspaper clipping which announces the "Armory Show." The paper mentions several names unknown to me, mostly French. I recall talk at Miss Stein's. The name Matisse sounds familiar and I think that Picasso was in the talk, too. With all the great quantity the promoters would not particularly want me from way out here in Chicago.

It seems all my time is taken to stretch canvas, run downtown to buy paint, copy sketches. I seems a desparate time, but if I can finish that string of pictures, they are bound to come out some time. I have written to Davies.

1913

JAN 26 Nothing on hand that I can send. Two pictures I like, both very "abstract" (that is a word I hear more and more now adays) I hope to finish soon. A dozen others are almost ready. These are themes and elaborations making shapes that seem to give out those peculiar feelings: what are they—awe, mystery, reverie (I can't find the words). Whatever they are, these feelings are produced entirely by the shapes and colors that are not those of any visible or external objects.

Long says we will move into the Monroe Building.

The water-color "rendering" I had made, some time ago, of the Monroe Building, not as big as Buck's, but I think a better job and my co-workers think so too. I took in to Roche trying to interest him in giving me one of any coming rendering jobs. If he would do that, I might set up shop and get into that line for jobs to keep me going by myself.

MAR 16 The Armory Show will be here in Chicago next week. I have painted abstractions since November. Aunt Kate asked me how I was progressing. I told here I had twelve new ones backed against the wall. She asked if she could see the twelfth. I brought it out. "So that is Twelve." "Twelve" I shall call it. The others haven't received a title. I have little liking for my titles. They are only for identification and go in my record book for that purpose.

There is no canvas left but I have some wood and card board. I have the notion that some wood is not too safe to stand thru humidity, temperature changes, or hard freezing. The little pieces of bass wood, if kept dry, will be very durable. I am not familiar with redwood though I have used it two years.

MAR 25 The Armory Show opened yesterday at the Art Inst. Today I have had a good look. I stayed long and looked and looked. It was with great difficulty that on coming out I could convince myself that I hadn't been thru a dream.

The man with the moustache and tremulous hands who seemed in constant attendance saw me as the most lingering of spectators. Engaging me in conversation I found him most interesting and informative. His name is Walter Pach. I asked him about prices and was amazed to find how low prices are, except of course the Cezannes and the paintings of one or two others now dead. He says he is a close friend of Arthur Davies and on hearing my name said that Davies had told him to be sure to look me up. I have invited Pach to come to our house tomorrow to dinner. I want to show him my things.

MAR 27 Walter Pach called on us yesterday evening. He said he was tired and hadn't expected the visit to be anything but tiresome, but that Davies insisted that a major project in Chicago was to see what Dawson was doing. Pach was, he said, amazed. The fireplace board in the living room caught his eye. When I brought out "Germinal" and "Flowering Twilight" he seemed fascinated. He said he was not a "complimenteur," but the compliments he gave the things I showed him gave me great pleasure. I brought out the one I had just varnished. This should have gone to the Armory in N.Y. It wasn't titled. He gave it "Wharf under Mountain." *That* I had not seen in it.

I go to the Art. Inst. everyday. This is the most important exhibition ever presented in Chicago. It is having terrific impact on the public. The turnstile count has never been so great. The whole show is producing in me a great excitement. It is an eye opener because I had begun to think of my own work as an exception. But here I am, knowing now that many are thinking and expressing the same ideas that I am growing into. Again I am impressed by the universality of art expression.

The Chicago newspapers are putting out the strangest headings and the silliest comments. The articles in the newspapers sound far more crazy than are the pictures which they are shouting about "Crazy-quilt," "lumber factory," "Nasty," "Lude," Indecent" are the common descriptions. Such terrible misunderstanding when, to me, there isn't an insincere work shown and almost everyone is fitting into the stream of progression that in art has never stopped, nor broken away at anytime to discard the qualities that make fine art.

These are without question the most exciting days of my life. The works of Matisse and Kandinsky are extremely important in breaking open the avenues of freedom of expression. I am feeling elated. I had thought of myself as an anomaly and had to defend myself, many times, as not crazy; and here now at the Art Institute many artists are presented showing these very inventive departures from the academies.

Pach has visited us now and then. He said McRae had been in town and out again. He was so busy with dinners and meetings that I didn't get to see him.

APR 4 Walter has taken the "Wharf under Mountain" with him and said that when no one was looking he would have the men hang it. He said he had met a young man Giddings who might be of help.

I wish the show could stay longer. Thinking only of the Cubist room, and forgetting just then, coming through the south galleries on the way and just before my destined beginning of looking, I stuck my head through the doorway of the S.E. room, and startled, saw my painting, above the line, of course, and with a slight reflected spot on it. But what joy to have a picture in that company.

The French paintings are more entrancing than ever. I have $220.00. I have begged Father to lend enough so I can buy Picasso's "Woman with a pot of Mustard." $324.00 Father is disgusted with the idea of taking such a thing home. I said it would look marvelous over the mantel in the library. That, to him, was a horrible thought. I may have to settle for the Duchamp "NuEscisse." $162.00 which is larger, almost as large as the "Nude descending Staircase."

I have learned more from this exhibition than at any previous view of old masters who had already taught me a great deal. I look back to my discussion with Sargent and wish he could see this exhibition. Maybe he would see what I meant.

Walter said he had no trouble getting the painting hung, but if any of the staff should notice it, it might have to come down. He said that so far none of the boss men had come anywhere near the show. I bought every newspaper everyday and searched thoroughly for any mention of the added item. I could find none.

The "external" blacks of Roualt and Leger made strong figures The "internal" blacks of Cezanne are more what I have in mind to use. This exhibition will in all probability have an effect on my painting as well as on thousands of painters throughout U.S.

Pach promised to write. I promised, too.

Since I left Holabird & Roche I've had a glorious time painting. Hanging over the mantel in the library is the Duchamp. I am having a good look at it. These three paintings I am doing now Hercules I, II, III may show D's influence. I am contemplating more colorful things to come.

A Mr. Arney, who had stopped several times at my table in H.&R.'s D-room in the past year, phoned me a few days ago to ask to call on me. He had admired a "rendering" on my table. Maybe he has a rendering job for me, which I would be glad to get as I have run out of money. I am very short on stretchers, paint, and canvas. I seems my paintings are very thin because of this shortage.

Answered Arney as he rang the bell, invited him up to the little studio 11' × 14; south light, miserable. He is still a salesman for W.K. Cowan—furniture. Arney has made a proposition. His firm is branching out into the business of remodeling offices and shops and will need some one with architectural experience and the ability to make watercolor renderings of designs, reconstructing, and decorating. Will I work for them. "Yes."

APR 13 Started with W.K. Cowan last Monday. Office on Mich. Ave three blocks nearer home than H.&R., in the neighborhood of the Art Inst. (across the street) nearer the Public Library and the Crerar than before, working with congenial aids and on speaking terms with the private secretary Miss McGary, sweet to look at and think about. Others take her to lunch. I am saving my money.

This new employer is less demanding than H.&R. whose frequent requests for four hours overtime some evenings interrupted the completion of an important painting. However, one of the distresses in Cowan's business is Arney's attempts to get cheaper material and labor.

The material Arney buys and the labor he employs is not always first class. If he employs any scabs, Cowan is going to have trouble.

It is interesting to note that steel lathers, ornamental iron workers, and structural steel workers are in 3 separate unions. The lines are sharply drawn. No one but carpenters can drive a nail into wood or saw a stick in two.

I have been at Cowan's 4 weeks. Yesterday he called me in and said he wanted to ask me a question. "What do you think of this business?" I said I had begun with enthusiasum but now thought it was headed for trouble. I told him about the electricians who had to remove the lights put up by scabs at the Cowan offices on

Madison (his brother's) and how the carpenters had had to sit on their thumbs while this was done. I told him of several violations of the building code. "Who is responsible"? "I don't know." "It is all right and clear on the plans, elevations, and specifications."

MAY 25 Cowan has abandoned the remodeling business and is keeping only the furniture sales. Now out of a job, I actually hope this will last awhile. It will give time to attack my paintings furiously and maybe get something done.

At lunch with Father at the City Club I met a young architect, McArthur who has been working with Frank Lloyd Wright and wants to strike out for himself. He wants to do houses like Wright's. He is enthusiastic and made the proposition to me that I work for him with the prospect of eventually becoming his partner. It didn't seem possible to leave the pictures I was working on, yet I promised to show up next Monday at this office on Randolph.

Here I am working for an architect who knows practically nothing about construction or specifications. I had had a lot of experience checking Purdy and Hendersons steel designs and had many contacts with the superintendents of construction talking about materials, and when I left H. & R. I had fished out of waste baskets copies of specifications for various buildings. I could therefor do everything that was to be done to make McArthur a practical architect.

It is distressing to work with McArthur—his designs have no merit whatever and I have to draw up details of construction of houses that I wish would never get built.

I have made crude crates for some of my paintings with 2 × 4 around the edge and boards nailed across just enough to hold together. Father is crossing to Ludington on the boat after Jones delivers to the dock in his one horse wagon. He'll be able to watch the carrying of these crates aboard and will be on hand when they unload. Bradshaw is to meet him with wagon. I think Father is much relieved to know that the clutter of paintings will clear up a little.

Pach writes reminiscing about the Armory Show and asking how I'm doing. He is enthusiastic about a current notion of some painters that emulsifying our paints in milk makes the most satisfactory paint. I have tried it and after a few trails have given it up. It is much work to make a smooth and useable emulsion and I am not convienced that it makes more durable paintings.

JUL 2 Arney was breezing down Boul Mich this noon. He is working for the Nachtegal Mfg. Co. in Grand Rapids. They make counters and cages for small banks. He says they want to branch out and build or remodel bank buildings. Arney says if I want he will suggest me for head of the building department. My engineering training plus architectural experience would be just what they want. We walked a block together. "You may get a letter from them." Office will be closed 4th until Monday.

JUL 5 Letter arrived from Nachtegal. I wrote back I would take the job $75.00 per week to start. Office was closed, so I phoned McArthur that I was leaving at end of two weeks and that I wouldn't ask for the pay he owed me. So far he hadn't paid me a penny. I had been doing nearly all his draughting and writing all his specifications—everything except the preliminary sketches which he copied from designs Wright had used, which again were very much like Louis Sullivan's prairie style houses. Because of the lack of originality it was tiresome work. I will be glad to get out of it. When I told McArthur I was leaving him he didn't seem distrubed and looked relieved that I didn't ask for money. Surprisingly he asked me to his home for dinner—a farewell dinner day after tomorrow.

Surprised again by the excellent dinner cooked and served by a maid, one of the prettiest of women and presided over by McArthur's beautiful Austrian wife. He'll be lucky if he can keep it that way.

JUL 21 I am now established as head of the building department. My desk is nothing but a 4' × 8' draughting board on collapsible legs in a corner of the draughting room, and so far, I am the only designer and draughtsman in this department.

I am well fixed with a good room at Mrs. Benjamin's on Lexington Ave. S.W. I have meals at Mrs. Simpson's half a block away. Mrs. Benjamin and daughter, a spinster piano teacher are formal but gracious. I have the free run of their parlor and use of the one bathroom. I seem to be the only one to use the tub. The rain water smells mousy. I use only the city tap water.

AUG 3 Mrs. Benjamin was in raptures to think that they were housing an artist painter, but, after I showed her one of my little fancies, has looked at me as though I might be a little crazy.

Dot Benjamin has gotten over the horror of my paintings and has consented to attend the county fair with me one of the evenings when it gets going.

I have a card for the Public Library. I took out Marcus Clarke's "His Natural Life" which is quite as Hyndman says of it,, a horrible story of convict life in Australia.

I have an invitation to dinner Sunday 17th with the Gaylord Holts and some other Sunday I am likely going out to Cascade to see the Holts there. They must be old by this time.

Picinic at Spring Lake with boys from the D-room. We cooked and ate and after a dinner of frankfurters all wanted to sit at cards and drink beer. I lost at cards, then won it back pitching horseshoes.

We have a job at Logansport, Ind. I will have to go there.

AUG 23 A week ago Wednesday I spent in Logansport, Ind. The staying was better than the going and coming back. This is the first job of my department. I took measurements and examined the old building which we are remodeling with a terra cotta and bronze front and new cages and counters inside. The old building has a serious crack in the sidewall so I am taking no chances, designing the front with proper steel posts and an I-beam and metal framed plate glass windows

On the way back to G.R. it was necessary to stop-over in Niles. The stop-over was blessed with time to make a sketch of a theme and elaborate it. I must paint it the first chance I get. I saw this face-like figure upside down in the polished lobby floor. It made a mysterious connection with neighboring table leg. Very peculiar—I may lose it if I have to wait too long for completion. The time to finish a thing is when one is strong for it.

I must pick up again my correspondence with Walter Pach. He wrote several letters after reminiscing about the International and I wrote back. Each of us had the prime feeling of turmoil and the great question of what to do. Each has the grave problem of making a living. Walter with his continued compliments on what he saw on 24th St. gives me encouragement to continue thinking of art as my life.

Many of the best things I've done are conceived at that time, when awaking from sleep I lie thinking of possible pictures. Compositions and colors are then seen at their clearest. It is also a time when words seem most definite and well organized.

The Benjamins are pleasant people. The haven't objected to the muss I make at my drawing or painting. Yesterday Dot and I went to the fair and enjoyed the shows; very briefly the undressed girls at the side show (Dot blushes easily) but lingered long at the races and the fireworks. The specialty circus acts continued so late we missed the last street car and had to walk home across town. It was a tiresome walk. Dot will have lame feet for a week.

AUG 30 I could see this coming. I have quit Nachtegal. The past week we have had a continuous argument on construction. Nachtegal said the bank front must be less expensive. He offers the idea that the piers (posts) in the front can be of the old brick laid up no thicker than the plans show and yet can omit the steel. I tell him the building is likely to collapse if that is done. I had figured the very least factor of safety. He knows better. I can see that if this policy continues in future building jobs it will be no place for me. I should get to the farm Labor Day.

This September goes down as one of the glorious times of my life. Weather is perfect and after an hours work at grass cutting tree trimming, or garden cultivating, for setting-up exercise, I can fall to and paint out doors or indoors, sunshine or shade.

With all this fine hill country around and our family ever present, it is yet necessary for an artist to live in a private world. It must have no confines and no restricted views of nature. It is not necessary to know sources, which are probably unlimited. Blessed are the pure in heart for they shall give from subjective fancies, quick revelations, or what not.

At the farm with a box of nearly squeezed out paints and only pieces of canvas left from cutting larger pieces. It is not easy to get canvas, stretchers, or paint. There is no store within fifty miles

I am going to see if the Ludington Lumber Co. still has some of the thick card board. Ostwald, the German, in his little book "Letters to a Painter" recommends paper and cardboard as more durable than canvas. I have more confidence in canvas, and, while I have painted dozens of times on wood I can't say I trust any wood except basswood. Yellow poplar (button wood) might be very dependable, but where can one get it. I can remember painting on thin cardboard almost paper thin. Those paintings some day, will have to be glued on wood or canvas to give permanence. At present it is distressing to be so short of paint that sometimes it is necessary to paint thinly. Turpentine will spread colors but it should have added some oil or varnish to make the film hold together.

SEP 25 All canvas, cardboard, wood pieces are used up. I leave here next week. Looking around, I saw that part sack of portland cement. Without more than an hours delay, I had a narrow box made and was soon mixing screened sand and cement to make a block of artificial stone which I will carve before going home. I am not intending to become a sculptor, although a piece has advantages having a number of views from which to regard it—higher, lower, and from all points of the compass.

These last days several small pieces of warped pine catch my eye. Put together on the lines of a composition these can make a ground to paint on. I have no tool that would plane these down to a level, so what I shall do is make a flat carving like on the two pieces I put together last year.

With the balance of that cement, I have cast a flat slab and am carving two dancing figures.

Walking past that knarly old plum stump makes me think of chopping and sawing something out of it some day. I leave for Chi. tomorrow.

OCT 5 Back in Chicago. All the way on shipboard I couldn't keep from thinking of making something out of Fathers lumber pile. Thinking of it, it could be gruesomely elegant with the cutout boards fastened to a back with color applied to emphasize the shapes to make the thing stand stark but rough.

Mitchell is writing poetry and some of it has gotten into print. There are a dozen or so writers here who are making the east take notice of the individuality of the separate men in the group. Each one is acquiring style and none are dull. Keith Preston our schoolmate at Moseley and South Division is witty as all get out in his newspaper column. A few of the Chicagoans have appeared in several magazines and are about to have books published. I must get my things out on exhibition. Some come to look at what I have in the studio and all over the parlor and library at home. Some seem fascinated but many just come, see and go.

This literary atmosphere is in contrast with the situation among painters. A very few are feeling around for something more than academic. However, the Art Institute is still hide bound and even more so than before the Armory Show. Criticism was so severe last winter that those running the galleries are scared to death. Art stores along Michigan Avenue (dealers) are dead set against anything resembling cubism. One of the trustees of the Art Institute who thought of buying a Cezanne was talked out of it by ridicule of the examples shown in the International.

NOV 29 Smith appeared in the Lobby of Orchestra Hall as I was stretching my legs at intermission. He too has left H.&R. and now is established as an architect on his own. He wants me to join him and partner to fill that end of the business that will keep the construction details in safe design. I told Smith I could join him Monday.

I have been having a fine time since returning from the farm in Sept. doing on every kind of project for which I can find the time. Some of these new paints are very rich in color.

DEC 6 A surprise letter from Pach to say that Davies is choosing thirteen men to join him in a traveling show. These are painters and one sculptor that he thinks are significant of the best things being done in a variety of ways. He thinks Stella and I are the most abstract. He himself has done some "cubist" things. I certainly will join up. Davies is asking for that old "Steps" and the "Wharf" and "Humps." That's where "Wharf" is now. I have written to Pach.

I have written another to say I would some how get the "Wharf."

DEC 12 I have received directions for shipping. I will get right to it.

It is too bad to miss the Pittsburgh stop but I shall make all the other appearances. Next is Montross in New York. My only chance to see the exhibition will be in Detroit.

Having mislaid it twice, I must write here Arther B. Davies address: 337 East 57th St. Pach says he doesn't like to have it in too many peoples hands, for fear of bores who might encroach on his time.

It is distressing to endure the dullness of Smith's D-room. His partner seems to take lots of time off.

I have Wing's letter virtually giving me the bank mural to do.

Weather report from Ludington—Lots of snow and cold.

Smith says, "Take a week-off" (without pay) "Come back Monday after New Year."

Dudley Watson came in to look over my things. I had the two big canvases to show him as well as several smaller ones. He showed great enthusiasm for the "Meeting" (three Graces) and especially the little "Beech Tree." My studio is so much clearer after the shipment Father took with him to the farm. Two of the big ones "Attack" and "Figures at Cliff" went to the Humps. Christmas was as usual—commercial.

Dudley has accepted directorship of the Milwaukee Art Society. This may be a chance for some showing of my work. Of course, till well established he can't be definite about anything.

1914

JAN 10 I have returned from the Humps with "Wharf." At Pentwater, the end of the P. Marquette line snow was a foot deep. Never have I put in such a gruelling day of walking thru snow, deeper, and deeper as I walked into the hills. My cold wet feet kept from freezing by the steady tramp. This was an eighteen mile walk. It took 8 hrs. There wasn't anything to fix as a cover for the painting without make it heavy and bulky, so, with it wrapped in newspapers I carried till, dead tired, I reached the train 5 min. before it took off in the evening. I have shipped it by express today. Too late for the catalog but it will be in the show at the Montross in February.

Florence Bradley called. She had been to Jerome Blum's studio and he had told her about me. She has brought some of Marsden

Hartley's paintings to Chicago to show at a warehouse of her father's, unused at present. She suggests I show there. She seems much affected by Hartley's work but seemed to consider my abstractions as having gone further. I believe she is sincere. She is an atttractive person though a terrific cigarette smoker, constantly in an Aura of smoke. She is enthusiastic about Margaret Anderson's project "The Little Review."

I haven't met Margaret Anderson. Mitchell introduced me to Jane Heap collaborator. She is unusual in appearance, very interesting to listen to, very positive, a person feminine, but on first appearance masculine. Short hair and tailored suit give that first impression—handsome with prettiness.

Wing briefly in town to get me to review bank plans. He says he knows nothing about architectural design, but that the front doesn't look right.

Very true, now that I have seen the elevations, the picture of the bank is the product of ignorance. It is extremely bad. I told him if he wants a Greek design with two story columns, so popluar in banks, the order should be followed faithfully. If it is to be Doric he must follow Doric order and have the proportions true. I showed the wall that should be kept clear for the mural and he said he would see to it that it would be there.

Have had letter from Wing—bank is proceeding. Davies very much concerned that I ask real pay for the mural. Wing, I feel, is hedging a bit.

Harriet Monroe, who is "art editor" for the Chicago Tribune, came to the house to see my pictures. She doesn't seem interested in painting. She said only that she didn't understand the new things and that she hadn't seen anything good in the Armory Show last winter. In the Tribune the only mention she made was that the paintings could be seen at 216 E. 24th St.

The only artists I am intimate with at this time are Frank Dillon, Dudley Watson, both students with me at South Division (1901–1905) and Jerome Blum. I have not known Blum long. He is the most French-like of the post impressionists and a novel character. He raves about my things and can't understand why the jury turned down my abstraction submitted for the Chicago Show at the Art Inst. This is the first time I have tried out a jury.

I was asked to explain my work to the manager at Thurber's. In talking about art, correctness of words is difficult and the choice of a word may confuse rather than explain. Showing a picture tells more.

FEB 8 Dudley has written that he is projecting an exhibition of paintings in "the modern spirit" and wants me to show most of the things I have here at home. With this exhibition coming up the same thing is true again—so many good things are at the farm. He wants me to send particularly "Meeting," "Figures in Action," "Germinal," and then a selection of what I think would show a progression from naturalism to abstraction. The "Prognostic" will be somewhat by itself—so early, so non-objective, so definitely made up. All together I can give him a good show.

FEB 12 Another Dudley, Mitchell's friend, visits almost everyday now, and is fascinated with one of my brown abstractions of last year. I know he is penniless. He wants me to keep that one for him till he has enough money to buy it. I am very pleased that he likes it, so I have offered it to him for $5.00 which I told him will almost cover the cost of canvas, stretcher, and paint.

FEB 15 Dudley has written that the show will be about April 15 to May 15. I have made boxes and packed a large number of paintings enough to cover two walls of Milwaukee's big room and an overflow to the basement since Dudley wants some of my very realistic early water colors which he says he will frame for me, if I send them right away.

MAR 1 Today was opening day for the "fourteen" at the Detroit Art Museum. I had looked up trains and found I could get there toward noon and go in with the crowd at 1: P.M., stay till closing and catch an evening train back to Chi.

It was almost inconceivable that so many in Detroit would visit a museum. Sunday was a free day. Families attended. Comments by the children were frequently more appreciative than those of their parents who had been longer under the impact of standardization. The news from Chicago and New York the previous year had had some effect and an intelligent commentator in Detroit had told people to look and try to get something out of the works to be presented. The crowd was really curious and not at all jeering. It was especially thrilling to stand some 10 feet away from my paintings and pretend to be looking at something else while eaves dropping on comments made by viewers. Every looker seemed pleased with "Steps." A frequent comment from a visitor looking at "Wharf" was "I don't see any wharf but I believe I could get to like it." Stella's "Coney Island" being the biggest canvas was the most noticed.

Davies heads the shows. He has five beautiful entires. I have only three. Glackens, Kuhn, McRae, Of, Pach, Prendergast, Schamberg, Sheeler, Stella, Taylor, Tucker, and Coluzzi were the others, all painters. I liked something about each except Taylor's. I didn't think he had much. I stood around for four hours—never had more fun in my life. The gallery was just as full of people as the Chicago Art Institute on a free day at the "Armory Show."

Being in a dull rut at Smith's and wanting to give more time to painting especially if I should have a chance at the mural at the bank, I quit Smith. I gave two weeks notice and got everything in the office all caught up even making a watercolor elevation on my own time as a gift.

I have tried to interest Davies, Pach and others to send something to Milwaukee. They seem to recall an obnoxious former director and don't seem likely to join up. I have told Dudley about Blum, and Dove, and Hartley, and Sheeler. Of course, several of the men are busy with the traveling fourteen.

I wish I didn't have so many things hidden at the farm. It seems everytime I want some of my best stuff it is there. And when I am there and want to send something somewhere, it is back on 24th St.

Blum says he will send 28 paintings and 20 or so etchings. The opening date is set for April 16.

Grimbel's will lend from their collection of Frechmen. Eddy will lend a Picabia. I will lend my Duchamp. I plan to go to Milwaukee the day before opening to help with hanging. That will give two days before the evening opening reception.

I've been having many friends and some strangers come in to see what I have at home. What I have is now very limited because so much stuff is already packed. Father says with the pictures gone from the parlor and library the place looks decent again. What I have remaining, besides some small oils and some charcoal sketches, are the paintings I am now finishing, very colorfull paintings which at least give visitors the knowledge that I am not color blind.

APR 12 Walter has sent statement of the expenses of the traveling show. There was no printing bill except at the Montross. The whole is remarkably low—each one of us $26.00.

APR 17 This will be the third night in Milwaukee. First day had all boxes unpacked and paintings sorted along the wall. Blum didn't a painting that suggested itself as a center piece. He lined them up next to each other in position that didn't clash. In the center of one long wall I place "Meeting." In the center of the other wall we put "Germinal." That wall had otherwise only larger paintings so we stepped up from the center and then down to the corners. Just a few of my pictures satisfied the spaces between the door and the stairway, and the door and open hallway. The hallway took nice care of Charlotte Pollak's ten drawings. Eddy seems to set highstore on these drawings as though he couldn't ever bear to part with them, yet he offered to sell me some.

Second day: finished hanging by 1:00 P.M., then went around viewing and discussing. Dudley, Lucille, Jerry, and I with about a half hour look-in by Buckner decided on only one small change.

The walls were ready for the evening. The reception was a society event. Almost all, but Lucille, Jerry , and I were in evening clothes. Everyone noticeably perplexed yet intent on reaching an explanation. The paintings were diverse and the people in looks were of every kind. I had many exciting conversations and especially enjoyed the beautiful art teacher who tried her best to "bring me out of it." Giving my best effort I tried to show the desperate seriousness of every painting.

We had a few of the French painters. Picasso is missing. Why couldn't I have raised that $324.00 and had that painting. It would have made this exhibition. But I know it would have generated a storm of protest and much snorting in the newspapers.

Decided to give Milwaukee another day. So did the Blums.

Friday afternoon, after Dud had told me that the exhibition committee had ordered the "Garden" (Adam & Eve) taken down before the regular school-children's tour of the galleries and that his job depended on it, Blum and I threatened to take everything down (of course we wouldn't). We got Dudley appeal to the committee to meet with us determined to explain the total innocense of that particular painting. The meeting took place delayed by Buckner, president, and the doctor, leading obstetrician, and the third an immovable lorgnetted woman, delayed long enough so that in the midst of heated discussion, with the door to the gallery ajar, we saw a troop of children being guided past the pictures by their teacher. None paused before the obnoxious painting anymore than before any other. No child giggled and non stared. The painting is to remain. To remove it would attract attention. It is one of the 1908 play paintings: a bright yellow man walks unaware of a yellow woman standing behind a light green tree trunk, topped by four dark green leaves; perched on a branch is a black bird, the tree standing in front of red rocks, the whole against a grey foreground and pink sky.

APR 26 Dud has sent me a clipping from the Milwaukee Free Press of April 17 showing "Prognostic," and calling it a Portrait of Dudley Crafts Watson. They are having great fun with it.

I shall go, as has happened almost every May, to the farm to plant more pine trees. This time probably two thousand which are likely to be the last planting. Open areas on the hill are about taken up. Father orders the trees from D. Hill nurseries in Illinois. After coming back to take care of the end of the show, I'll go to the farm for a long, long time.

All possibility of wanting to follow any line in the profession of architecture is certainly done with. The dream of a trail of country life is ever present. The library table always has a book or two, all the way from Thoreau's "Walden" to the most recent expositions of how to make a living on a farm. None belittle the hard work and endurance necessary to succeed against the forces of weather, fungi, insects, and the mortgages. Wing, as president of the Ludington State Bank might be able to tell me just how possible or impossible farm life is.

My equipment is several summers (since 1903) in this wild hill land with every kind of tree, shrub, or vegetable planting experience. One specialty, at which I believe I am an expert, is in pruning fruit trees. We have a few of every kind of fruit that can be grown in Michigan. Each has its own requirement in pruning for fruit production and structure. Grafting is an interesting proceedure in changing variety or in repairing wounds or weather damage. All these proceedures I have practiced until perfectly familiar with the processes. Work in all kinds of different fruit picking has been done enough to know what the grower has to do at harvest. One thing only is missing. I am a wretched salesman. I think I could develop into an expert producer but disposal of products has yet to be learned.

I know there is work to be done on a farm in winter, yet I have the hope that if the bridge is crossed I can find painting or carving time in that season.

MAY 18 Eddy has called up to ask me to bring "Rotor" and the "Loop" to his home on the northside and then in afterthought says "No I'll call you and Blum soon to come to dinner. Bring them then."

MAY 25 Bennett, whom I met in 1910, who has written me twice since then, writes asking about "Flowering Twilight"—how much do I want for it. I write to him $200.00

He sends check and asks me to ship it to him. Shall do right away. With Grant and Eddy that is the third purchaser (4 pictures)

Have been to Eddy's and have seen his big collection of paintings which he has hung in nearly every room in the house. It is somewhat indiscriminate. The newspapers had made a big notice of his having bought the "Dance at the Spring" by Picobia and two or three Sousa—Cardoza. Cezanne is strangely missing and Picasso is represented only by a small, early, pointillist picture of an old Spanish woman. What a fine collection he could have with his money. One would think he would have something of Cezanne, or Van Gogh, or De Gas, or Gaugin. There is a little feeling as you look at the paintings with Eddy, of the possibility of the collection being to him a practical joke. His remark, with a leer, that my two paintings would be excellent for Christmas presents, mentioning two of his friends he said "That will shock him."

Eddy asks me to let him keep the paintings for a while—no word about buying. He knows that they are for sale and he knows the prices. If he has them a while they may be seen by some and bring about a little publicity.

MAY 31 At the farm for I hope a long, long stay. The first thing is my obligation to the vegetable garden and the fruit trees, then a solid stretch of painting. How can that be when so many interruptions occur through demands to fix this or that. Why aren't there more mechanics in our family? I am the mason, carpenter, plasterer, jack-of-all-trades.

JUN 10 Jerry Blums letter says maybe they will be able to come for a visit to the farm. I had urged this before I left Chi. It might be helpful to each of us to paint together. We are miles apart in approach to a picture but that shouldn't stand in the way. I must look up some clay for Lucille, and maybe I can find a stone or two. There will always be portland cement on hand—we do so much laying up of stone and pointing. Here I am reminded I must get out to the log house and fill some of the gaps between the logs. The original chinking of lime and cow dung mixture has fallen out in some places, and I must screen the upstairs windows if Blums are to be made safe against mosquitos.

JUN 15 Wings letter indicates delay in the bank mural till money is available. I have half a mind to offer to wait for the money or even to do it free. I shall be in Ludington Weds. and can talk with him.

Wing tells me that the most dependable farmers he deals with are the fruit growers. The dairy farmer makes his money out of his labor. The beef grower makes by marketing his roughage—the acres of cheap wild pasture he can acquire. The fruit farmer makes what he can by the Grace of God. He operates a factory without walls or roof and makes a good return on certain years when his weather is good while other fruit sections have frost, high winds, or hail making the market give him a price for his crops.

JUN 25 Blum writes that they may be able to come up in July. A project with a man, Wright, who wants to prepare a vaudeville act for his daughter, was to design a setting. I was supposed to be associated in this work, but I almost dead certain it is only a dream of Wright's.

July 4, '14 Last night was fun. I attended an ice-cream social at the local school house. Sitting two desks in front of me was the prettiest girl in the room. I couldn't keep from glancing that way again and again. It was fascinating to see her turn a profile and once or twice a full face in speaking to someone. At the end of the party every one started home at the same time, every one on foot. When I saw three of the girls (one was Lily Boucher) start down the road, I decided, without a second thought, that they needed an escort. It was a good chance for a pick-up. The Boucher girls lived further away than Stella W., whose parents I have met so, when Ester stopped to chat with Stella, I went on ahead with Lily. This was a turning point for me; not only was this girl-beautiful but she spoke grammatically which is a rarity in the country. We made a date for sunday afternoon. She timidly admitted that her folks may look askance at me, she is only 17, for they are rigidly churchy. She had never been permitted to talk to any but schoolmates and church goers.

I am in love with Lily Boucher. This is the first time I have thought seriously of married life. May be she is too young and, too, how can I support two or even one.

If I were subsidized, how many years would it take to arrive at a stage where I could sell enough paintings to bring in the bread and butter. I would hate to fall into a position of teaching for a living, and anyway I am not an expert in craftsmanship. I could teach engineering with my degrees of B.S. and C.E. but that would be going backwards. I am convinced that there is something great urging the neccessity of producing paintings. So I keep on doing. Satisfaction of accomplishment can be—but no money. What to do?

The happiness of the marriage thought is countered by the knowing that it would mean hardship, privation, struggle.

Here enters the thought again. Why not stay here on the farm, add a few acres of level land (these hills are hardly arable) and earn a living from the soil, with every spare hour devoted, at times to the pleasures of married life, or at time to the pleasures of painting, sketching, or carving. The course of my life is troubled by my poverty.

AUG 14 Jerry and Luci get such a bang out of the wild fruit which they come across.

We went to the woods with easels, paint, and canvas, to see what painting from nature would produce. When I told Jerry to ignore what he did see and imagine how it could look, he said he couldn't. I know his work. It bears his individual hand-in no matter what he does. Luci does no sculpture even with all this time on her hands. She says she is enjoying the country too much to put work into it. I had gone to Claybanks to get clay. It is still unused.

We were invited Saturday evening to the meeting of the "Young Peoples Society" of the Epworth League, a party at Levi McClatchie's. Jerry had a cracking good time and couldn't take his eyes off Maggie Stickney, Ester Boucher, or my girl Lily Boucher. A good time was had by all.

On the Lake Michigan beach, a fine swimming afternoon, Jerry stared and left us to go 100 yds away to look at Florence French, of the local French family, a physical education teacher in Chicago schools, whose figure would be outstanding anywhere. In any situation Jerry is never self conscious or timid about looking at anything. I don't know whether she was embarrassed or indignant. She moved away from there in a hurry.

AUG 31 I have talked with Levi McClatchie, whose 50 acres adjoins us on the south about buying his place. I had looked at two other farms, 40 acres each, nearer town and somewhat heavier soil, and find that Levi, too, has been looking at these same farms. These farms are nearer his church. He told me about them before he knew I was at all interested in his layout. His thoughts run more to provision for his cows than to fruit which is present farm is loaded with.

Our small alfalfa field was mowed in June by Bradshaw. Now I am busy with a scythe giving it a second cut. This is a hard job, but a little everyday gives the necessary setting-up so I can relax between sessions at the easel.

I had talked with Jerry pro and con becoming a farmer. He was for it for me but against it for himself. I've had a good letter from him recalling their visit. He had contemplated a jaunt to Tahiti but the war has chased that thought away. Here on the farm we hadn't thought too much about the war, just kept reading the papers. Not having any stock of any company I paid little attention to the break on the exchange. I've been hearing some concern from Wing and others.

SEP 6 I have written to Father that if he will buy the McClatchie farm with the bank's help, he can have half the gross annual fruit sales to go toward my purchase with 6% added interest.

OCT 5 I have closed with McClatchie. Everything is running well. By color it is autumn, but most ways it is like summer. Migrating birds appear now and then—birds that we don't have in summer. I enjoy my Saturday evenings at Boucher's, two miles away, spending hours with Lily.

The McClatchies will be able to get away this fall. McChas almost closed a deal for the Cribbs place, a 40 acre general farm which has a good 8 acre apple orchard.

We had several brush fires going this week. If Jack Frost, the big man, who is working for me, doesn't get tired there will be 8 acres cleared this fall on the north 40. Then there is the east patch of stumps to clear on the 30, and scattered stumps here and there to dynamite.

OCT 15 It was a pleasure to receive a money order from Eddy for the paintings I had almost forgotten. I remember them well, but so many things are now foremost on my mind. I have been depending on Father for almost all my capital money. This picture money will just about buy that team of horses at the Sander's Auction. Wing assures me that the bank will take my notes if I want to buy at that sale.

The team and a disc are bought. I already have a plow. Omar Kistler has fashioned me a new point for new land plowing.

NOV 5 McC's have begun to move part of their belongings. Till now I have been living at the summer house, only going to McC's for meals. A room at McC's will be ready for me tomorrow. The weather has turned cooler, so it will be well to spend nights in a warm house. I am not certain about plans for the winter. It has been taken for granted that I shall be in Chicago Christmas.

I have decided to stay here as long as the land is open to work. There is an awful lot of clearing to be done. There is much to do in shaping new ground; there is piling of the brush, trimming poles for firewood sawing, getting out stumps, picking up stone, all has to be before plowing which is hard on man & horses, and, after plowing, picking up all the roots torn up by the plow.

Frost started a fire running toward the woods. If I hadn't noticed it, before going to bed, the whole forest would have been burned over—our ten acres of young pines would have been wiped out. The fire was caught in time: It was good because it warned Frost, and Bradsaw and me.

NOV 20 Charles Sibley and wife Blanche are about ready, I think, to agree to come and work for me. Blanche would keep house. Charlie would bring his team to work for its keep.

McClatchie has closed the deal for the George Cribb's place and will move in about 3 weeks.

Sibleys have agreed to come when McC's move out.

Tonight there is a pie social and entertainment at the school house. I am going and Lily is going. She will take a pie.

DEC 9 Things wont be exactly convenient till McCs move out and Sibleys move in. The barn is crowded—Levi's horses and cows and my team.

Thurs. and Fri. comes the Farmer's Institute to Scottville. I'll attend one day.

This week ushered in a revival meeting in a specially built temporary wooden tabernacle. Stevens will commit his rantings there. Daily News say 1000 have been converted already. I think the next revival will re-convert most of the same thousand. I have bought a buggy so I can get around to these things. Sibley has a wagon, not very good. Before spring I'll have to buy a wagon. Charlie has a sled, so I can postpone buying one. Snow is coming—I'll have to buy a cutter. Hardware and farm machinery dealers are always ready to take my note.

DEC 18 Levi finished moving today. I've started to board at Bradshaws. The bed is comfortable—the room is cold, unplastered, and uncarpeted. When Sibleys move into my house I'll be back.

There is no suitable place to paint though stormy weather gives time. A few sketches are ready to transfer to canvas or cardboard. Canvas would have to be shipped parcel post which limits size or by express (the office is 11 miles away) But for the time being I can't afford to buy anything. These art stores wont send on account.

Between storms I have done some land clearing. I'll be swamped in the spring with clearing, plowing, planting, and spraying all coming about at once.

In a year or two I shall have to build a kitchen addition. It is not very satisfactory to have kitchen, dining room, washroom, stable clothes, boots, etc all in one room.

DEC 23 A big box of nuts and candy arrived for birthday and Christmas. I wont get to Chi., there is too much to do. Christmas dinner will be at Bradshaws. On my last trip to town I bought something for the Bs. Albert is growing a beard. He will need the razor I bought for him. Small articles of clothing for the rest, except old Mrs. Ray, the glutton, a big box of candy.

Nothing but sleds travel now. The team pulls the big bob-sled that Hansen made for me. Going to town I sit in the straw filled wagon box covered with a blanket and handling the lines with double gloves. The best footware is 4-buckle arctic over shoes over high topped work shores. My horse Jim gets plenty of work daily and then some evenings taking me to visit Lily. The mail-carrier has hard work getting around with horse and cutter.

1915

FEB 4 Sibleys are here and everything is going smoothly except Blanche is on the party line phone too much. Monday and Tuesday I attended the Farmers Institute at the court house, stayed over night on the second night at Wing's just east of town. C.G. Wing, classmate of Fathers at V. of M. has a sly wit and is an accomplished conversationalist. The evening with him was better than the insititue.

Sunday night came rain that froze on every branch, and twig, and weed. Hundreds of tree branches might have broken down if there had been wind.

I have ordered 300 sour cherry trees and 150 apple trees from the Monroe Hawley nursery. That will plant 3 acres of cherries and about 6 acres of apples. Next year I must plant some more.

FEB 14 We have taken down Levi's log shed. Six of the logs are large, clear white pine. Charlie will haul them to the Kistler Mill and have them sawed into planks and 2 × 4s.

Everybody who has not had measles is now having them. There are at least 150 cases in Summit and Riverton. Bradshaw's 2 kids, Bender's 2, Gillette's 5, and Charlie Fitch's 6—all these in our neighborhood are sick at the same time. None stay home, going to school, church, or town before entirely well, so, spreading it to an epidemic.

FEB 25 At the Stull auction sale I bought a nice looking Jersey cow. She is giving 12 quarts of milk a day. We can make her give more when she gets used to her new quarters. Tomorrow Charlie and I must go to the woods to cut down an old crooked tree, saw it up into short bolts, and bring in to cut up for firewood.

MAR 20 Three weeks of tree triming in cold weather have passed. It looks like another five would bring the orchards into pretty good shape. We use a lot of milk and make 7 pounds of butter every week.

The Hardie sprayer arrived. It has a one-cylinder engine, fairly simple in design. There don't seem to be any working parts that we can't fathom.

MAR 21 We have sprayed all the peaches and gave the apples a strong lime-sulphur spray. Later more lime-sulphur and some arsenate of lead. Cherries will be sprayed after petal fall. Spray has to go on fruit trees before any trouble (curl leaf, scab, leaf spot) shows up.

MAY 9 Judging by the bloom, all varieties of fruit will bear heavily if there are bees enough. The weather has been fine bee weather. In the case of the sour cherries which are self-fertile the may flies can be very useful to knock the pollen down on the pistils.

MAY 24 Mitchell has sent me a copy of Margaret Anderson's "Little Review" in which his poem is placed on the first page. The "Little Review" is a queer combination of bright new effort and some very usual stuff. It may get better as it goes along.

Lillian Boucher and I expect to marry some time in June or July when there is a break in orchard care. That might come just after cherry harvest.

JUL 28 Tomorrow Lily and I expect to go to Hart. Mich.—to breakfast then marry before the Probate Judge, then in the buggy behind faithful Jim to Lake Michigan beach. Lily is preparing a picnic lunch. After swimming and lolling and eating we go to the log house at the Humps where Mother has been fixing a room for us. Lily has so much appeal, it is hard to wait.

AUG 30 Lili and I are now moved into our own house. All the furniture is Sibleys except stove in front room. The house looks spic and span since Lili has had her hand in the cleaning.

OCT 22 Nothing written here since August. Time goes with the joys of married life and the hard farm work hastening it.

Mitchell has sent copy of the "Little Review" within it his smart little piece. The writers and editors are having a lot of fun with this magazine. It is a fine outlet. It makes me want to get back to painting. I expect soon to make two or three sharp line compositions, figures may be in them, but they are entirely geometric and made up. I am also thinking in terms of sculpture. Sculpture takes longer per piece, so why not paint pictures of imaginary sculptures such pictures would take less time and would be not so heavy. All these diversions don't show that my main line is to go ahead with the abstract ideas of 1913. Farming interrupts. It is forcing an interlude. I must get back when I can.

Writers have their little magazines such as "Poetry," "Little Review," and others. Why can't we painters and sculptors have a "Little Gallery." Where can we find an angel?

DEC 1 Lili is enceinte. She takes it quietly. I am elated. We are planning on spending a week or more with my family in Chicago. We'll take in Christmas and New Year on 24th St. and see a bit of the Loop and Jackson Park and Lincoln Park, ride street cars and elevated trains, and the speedy I.C. Michigan Ave ("automobile row") has changed in late years and will be further changed. How can so many car manufacturers make good?

DEC 31 A busy week:—It was one of our good old Christmas gatherings. All were present (except brother George) with Lili added. Everyone is good to her. They should be. A clean, intelligent girl would be welcome in any family.

Christmas morning passed in traditional manner. As was the custom, Uncle Charlie and Aunt Fan, Uncle John and Aunt Mary, Uncle Robert and Aunt Ollie, Uncle Walter and Aunt Emily, Jack Manierre, Julia and George Short, Charlie Martin, and Helen Dawson, All came-in in the afternoon. Ruth & Aunt Elva were unable to come in from Hinsdale. There was the usual singing, chatter, and eating of Grandma's big animal cookies.

On two days this week Lil and I roamed the Loop with Luci and Jerry Blum. Novelty restaurants were tried out, Russian, French, Italian, and plain American cafeterias. Mitchell has been much engaged with Harriet Monroe's "Poetry" magazine and Margaret Anderson's "Little Review." I was asked to write something on art. I am no writer—maybe someday, if I'm able to do a little work on it. Mitchell is in the midst of the writers who are coming to the front: Carl Sandburg, Sherwood Anderson, Ben Hecht, Max Bodenheim, and others, quite an exhilarating crowd. Max is barging in at anytime to use Mitchell's typewriter. He manages to stay for lunch after work, or come to lunch to work afterward. Max's writing is "advanced."

A great deal of attention is given the paintings here on 24th St. and especially to those Mitchell shows occasionally downtown. The art salesrooms don't want anything like these. There is scoffing, ridicule, and love in the criticism, sometimes even raving appreciation. All the paintings here are small ones. The larger ones are are at the farm in barn and attic. I must plan part of an addition to the house to have a studio room. If built as a lean-to it could have a balcony for storage space. I need it.

1916

JAN 4 The city is full of excitement for Lili. I am sometimes out alone when much walking and standing is necessary as at the Art Inst. or the Field Museum. Lili was pretty tired but astounded after a viewing of the Field Mus. I dropped in for a few minutes in the D-room at H.&R's in the Monroe Bldg. All gave me a warm welcome. I was pleasantly surprised that some of the men had made the trip to Milwaukee to see my show in April last.

JAN 30 Back on the farm with my nose on the grindstone:—I am carving a white oak figure about 2 ft. high and have cast a block and slab of portland cement-sandstone. I can pick up and leave work on a sculpture easier than paintings which sometimes have to dry, and anyway chisels don't have to be cleaned.

I am projecting, for the first stormy weather when I won't feel guilty to be away from farm work; some paintings of imaginary sculptures standing up in realism, the sculpture's designs being not like any human figures. These things wont jibe with my previous work, but in the shapes, the lines and curves, I think one can see the similarity of the forms with those I have put into the paintings. Those three paintings I finish last fall may be hard-lined and cartoon-like, they, too, fit in.

FEB 22 I finish three sculptures during the blizzard of last week, one, a wood 26", a stone 30" and a relief of knobby shapes 13 × 24 cast twice from a carved wooden form. This suggests a possible way to duplicate if I happen to make a more attractive design. I just got started on picture of a sculpture (abstract).

I remember what a hard week we had last spring planting those trees. We must get ground ready early this spring, whatever way I can do it. Charlie tells me he is going on a farm for himself this spring. He is living on me without doing much work, and feeding his team on my hay till they are nice and fat. I've seen to it that my team is well cared for. They looked shabby after we came back from our vacation. Charlie and Blanche had had two weeks off in January.

John Jamerson has promised to come work for me at $1.50/day. This is the common rate around here.

MAR 17 Just a few degrees above zero everynight. John J. is working energetically, more than earning his wages. Charlie is working better on account of the example shown him by John.

I finished just one painting this month.

JUL 11 The Stearns Hospital called up this morning to say a fine boy arrived to Lili at 5:00 AM. We are in the midst of berry and cherry picking. I can drive Jim downtown evenings. The pickers come only during the day, so I can leave safely. None live close by.

AUG 12 The baby is a fine boy, eats well, sleeps well, and talks a bluestreak in his own language. It is remarkable what a great variety of sounds he can make, almost all the sounds that are made in English, French, or German. He has good eyes and good ears, and a vigorous kick.

OCT 16 A daily hasstle with harvest hasn't been recorded. All fruit is picked and hauled, except a few crates of apples and pears to our own cellar. The poor horses have had to work in the orchard and then plod to town with loads in the evenings, getting home around midnight. I stood it because I know it was not endless. Maybe the income from fruit will carry us thru to spring. Maybe it will pay for a hired man and for material to do a little work around the house. And during winter I must not neglet the orchards. Can I have a little time, too, for painting or carving.

NOV 30 Painted three pictures this month—pictures of sculptures. Instead of going off to Chicago this winter, it behooves me to get forward with the pruning, to have a less strenuous spring.

If the daily life were recorded it would, a large part of it, be of engagement with Lili and the baby in every kind of family association and chore. Watching a child grow is a succession of events to fix in memory. Each period will bring changes to something never the same.

DEC 21 Two barrels of apples went to the folks in Chicago last week. Those should last all winter if the attic stays cool. For my birthday and Christmas, Mother and Father sent me a generous check. Instead of spending this on a visit at Xmas we should buy blankets and babyshoes. Lil is tremendously pleased with the purse, ear rings, hand kerchiefs, and addition to her silverware.

1917

JAN 6 Snow deep and wind howling. Gerard looks out the window and says loudly "Hot day!" He'll be talking English soon. His own language is very expressive, almost to our understanding. I am carving pieces of birch lumber in a design using the numbers 6, 5, and 8. After supper I can work on the kitchen table. For sometime this month I have a sketch of a painting of a sculpture on a pedestal as though this were standing in a city square. For lack of a better name, I call this "Ring Figure." Another sketch is for a "Torso," cut up a bit. Another, I don't know what to call it.

FEB 11 Saturday eve received Mitchell's letter telling of the awful death of Aunt Kate. She had only one eye and couldn't see, while she was burning waste paper in the furnance in the basement, that her clothing on the blind side had caught fire. In panic rapidly ablaze, she rushed out into the yard and rolled till flames were gone. She died two days later. It was horrible to think about.

MAR 31 Not having any steady hired man, I am having to get along with any day labor I can get. The war work coming is luring men to the cities. I don't know how I am doing it. We are not behind in our work, yet, outside of chores, I work only 10 hrs a day—that's all the horses can stand and is all that men who work for me expect to give. The days are getting longer. In another month I can work outside in the evenings.

APR 19 Lili is pregnant, expecting in November. A strong, young girl neighbor Bethel Morton is working for us. Lili has had to keep house, make the butter, sometimes help with the milking, care for Gerard, and cook for workmen, who, living 2 or 3 miles away, have to be fed a big meal at noon.

All planting is done. This the earliest spring start yet. Gerard says a few words: Papa, Mama, bed, butter, raining, bird, outdoors, and pud (for pudding). We have nourishing puddings: rice, oatmeal, bread, or tapioca. Lili bakes excellent pie and cake but not often. She bakes all our bread, using whole wheat flour mixed with the white.

We had to entertain Laidlaw the well-man and his white horse for two days. In that time we drove our well-screen, by hand, seven feet deeper getting down to coarser sand and thus Clearer water. We had been getting a little fine sediment from the higher layer.

JUL 11 Everything according to its need is sprayed up to the hour. Several weeks ago ten of us formed the Pere Marquette Land Loan Association in order to borrow from the Federal Land Bank. We have applied for mortgage loans and should receive money in about a month. This will put all debts into one note. The appraiser was here last week. He expressed himself well pleased with our layout. He praised the alfalfa and the soil which produced it so well. The county agent with him admired the crop and Frank Warner from the U.S. Forest Service said it was the finest alfalfa he had seen. The alfalfa grows well because our soil is neutral and at 4 to 5 feet deep it is alkaline. The trees don't go that deep but alfalfa roots go down a dozen or more feet.

Warner looked at Father's pines—found no disease. He says it is the largest plantation in the state. The oldest is the 3 acres at the Ag. College in East Lansing.

JUL 23 The Ford dealer brought out a car last Saturday. The dealer put me at the wheel and levers, told me how to start and stop and told me to drive him back to town. After I stopped in front of his place of business without running into the curb, he considered I had learned to drive. So I drove home. The state speed limit is 35 mi/hr. The car was $360.00, freight 12.10, delivery 2.50, gas and oil included. 9.25 additional for license, total $383.85 The car is new. We all keep going out to look at it.

The car will save hours on the 10 mi. trips to town. It can carry more than the buggy and will save many wagon trips. Hansen has made me a fruit rack with a brake. The brake will save the horses many grievious strains holding back down hill. With this rack I can take more to a load.

AUG 17 One of the pleasures of this between harvests is the going out to the Michigan beach, taking supper with us, going swimming. Gerard has been walking for many weeks. He now runs. He loves bathing and likes to duck under water. He'll learn to swim in no time.

There is a fine crop of pears and applies in the offing. Peaches are a beautiful crop. We thinned early, so the fruit is large and going to be highly colored. I have never seen finer looking peaches. All the trees (that is, peaches) we have were on the land when we bought it. I never had a hankering to plant peach trees. My favorites are cherries, pears, and apples.

Labor Day—Two varieties of peaches are picked. We begin on the pears tomorrow. Looking over the peach orchard I saw a fine picture. Then over to look at the Spys. Finer yet. I am glad I planted lots of Spys. They are a good apple and the tree is long lived and makes a good grafting stock for other varieties.

OCT 17 Applies are all off the trees, sold, or put away in the cellar. We keep about 20 bushels in the cellar, and send 2 or 3 barrels to 24th St.

Jim Brickley, Bradshaw's step son, has indicated he will consider working for me. He can move into the Bradsaw-house now that Father has that 20. It will be a better place for him and family. He will have a wage to depend on if he comes. His trial of farming for himself failed for lack of capital.

Jim says he come as soon as he pulls his beans and gets his potatoes out of the ground. I will supply him with milk and firewood. Jim has had experience of all kinds in fruit farming. I have known him since before he married. He has a good reputation. He has four daughters, oldest about 14 I am counting on this help to let me catch up on my picture painting.

Dreams of pictures are still of pictures of sculpture. These are easier to see in the minds eye and remember.

NOV 20 As winter's warnings appear Lili and I are wondering how close to her time she dare stay at home. Esther is married to Everett Gillespie and lives in Ludington. Perhaps Lili can stay a day or two at Esther's till time comes to go to the hospital.

NOV 27 —drove Lili in the car to Esther's. The road was passable. We wondered what would happen suppose her pains began at home during a blizzard with no way of getting to town. Would a doctor brave the storm with horse and buggy or would I have to help Lili with no experience other than as witness to calving or foaling and with the dangers ever present in child birth, what would we do.

NOV 29 Lili lonesome wanted to come home. She thought she might have to wait days yet. I brought her home. I, too, find it hard to be separated. At 8:00 in the evening Lili began to feel her time coming, so in great haste, back again to town, this time to the hospital.

DEC 1 —Yesterday I called the hospital at 6:00 A.M. a fine baby girl was there.

DEC 8 Lili is home again, bringing little Hope with her. What would we do without a car? Hope is bright and a good sleeper. It's a bigger family. Bethel is more necessary than ever.

DEC 24 A happy Christmas morning it will be for our family. Bethel will go home for Christmas. Except for chores which are plenty, we take most of the day off. Gerard wont understand the holiday as anything special, but he'll have fun with new toys and a candy cane. Hope won't give a hoot if the bottle comes at the right time. For her, all kinds of baby clothes had come ten days ago. We have asked Brickleys to come in the afternoon—tea, coffee, and conversation. Gerard talks in sentences a yard long. That will keep things going.

With Jim working, I am going to have more time to pursue the phantoms of imagination, the dreams filled with shapes that fixing will preserve.

I am going to let Jim trim all the peach trees, all 3200 of them. If he hurts them, no matter, they are not going to be part of my farm scheme for long.

1918

JAN 30 This month I painted 3 sculptures. I shall title them when I can think of something suitable and not misleading.

I have had to join Jim in the orchard to show him the reasons for certain proceedures especially those that lead to strong not weak structure. Narrow crotches are weak Wide angles never break. Equal Ys are likely to break Unequal Ys get stronger.

Done:—a little sketch in green.

FEB 5 Jim's help, which I thought would give a few daylight hours for painting, can't quite keep up the the pruning. It is necessary for me to put in nearly full days in the orchards. Painting is neglected. However, one of the best things I've tackled is going ahead these evenings. The gouge, the half-inch chisel, the rubber mallet and sometimes the sharp jack-knife are carving an old pine board into what I call "Loft." I have a sneaking suspicion that the theme included a door ajar and a crest which might have originated from a hat Lili was making up and had hung up there to be out of Gerard's reach.

One thought has occurred; that if the house were burning down I'd rescue "Wharf" and "Loft" first as soon as the family was safe. Thinking along that line I begin to think of the paintings in the attic that would be impossible to save. Several of those I love and selection would be hard to make. I remember how hard it was to pick and choose for the Milwaukee Show. The saddest thing that time, though, was not to be able to reach the paintings at the Humps. I'm sure Eddy would have a different thought of my work if it had all been presented.

Since seeing here and there in magazines and books repros of current art products, I become amazed at some of my early doings. I am thankful, as I look back, for the chance meetings with Sargent and Davies. I realize there was a wealth of directing stimulus from each.

A little dream idea of a line drawing I shall later paint on canvas. As an engineer, I'll call it "Equations." I can already hear, "what does that mean." I have already used that title before and shall probably us it again.

I have hung a few paintings that Lili likes, and I will change to others periodically. These, the children can grow up with. Children whose minds haven't yet been tarnished by standardization and convention seem always to get something out of the pictures I show.

Father is dickering with a prospective purchaser of the house on 24th St. so I have written to him to start right away shipping my stuff that stands in the attic. He can't do it all at once, but he can take time and make successive shipments by boat when the lake opens in the spring. There are a few boxes. Some of the canvases can be rolled on 8" stove pipe face out. If covered with paper and gunny sack they will ship safely, being on board only over night. I can be waiting at the dock to receive them so they wont be slapped down on the jumble of other shipments.

1919

FEB 12 Over a year has gone by without entering anything here. Plenty of activity has been going on, but this activity has been muscle work. Last summer on account of war needs, the government persuaded me to grow grain. We had to harvest from the south 20, oats, wheat and rye, and I even grew some corn in the younger orchards. Of course, I had been triply exempted from the draft—age, children, 100 acres.

Only one painting finished—"Equation" 20" × 24"

MAR 20 We and our neighbors have just finished 1 mi. of electric power line, buying all material and doing all the work. ½ mi. is at my expense because it is that far beyond nearest neighbor. Power Co. wouldn't build but will now send electric power. It will be great to have elctric light, gadgets, and especially electric pump instead of unreliable wind-mill.

1920

JAN 30 A harrowing year has passed. Heart rending because so little has been accomplished. Apples take so many years to come into bearing. The trees look fine but bring no income. The banks have been easy on me, they like my layout, but my line of notes is getting longer and heavier.

Jim left in the fall to go to town to work as a carpenter. He must have a bruised thumb by now. His in-laws in the country say that rent and food takes all his wages, so the family is getting threadbare.

This winter I'm without help. I have painted another "Loft" and another "Equation." Maybe before spring something more.

Last year I bought 35 more acres—Federal Land Bank loan will be coming. This I planted partly to apples. There was winter wheat and oats and hay on it, which Jim and I harvested. I find myself, now, having a new mower, drill and harvester bought last year but not paid for. At one of the coming auction sales I shall offer these and a few other tools for sale. They should sell well, being nearly new and the price of grain being high. I should never have gone into grain even for a year. I am a fruit grower only, yet think of myself as an artist painter.

I contracted to buy 20 acres from Asa Williams, to be paid for in 10 years. This, I fall planted to apples. I'll be getting land poor with 135 acres.

MAR 15 The search for hired help must be intensified. I have an ad in the paper and have had two calls. One I ruled out—a man, wife, and 6 children. I'd be afraid of that crew. The other I have an appointment to interview. I mentioned his name to our bank cashier and he said, "Oh, I know his father, Swanson is a most reputable and creditable farmer.

MAR 20 Stuart Swanson and wife (18 yrs old) are moving into the Bradshaw house to work for me. He is a very clean, muscular man and his wife looks neat. They have a child almost a year old. He is a war veteran. I have promised him to let him work on the B. house to close up for better warmth. This work with some plumbing to be done next winter. I have already torn out the partitions up stairs in my house and have completed foundations for an addition to the back. I also sank a foundation to the depth of the cellar floor which will carry a chimney for basement furnace and flue for the kitchen stove in the new kitchen, to be. A lot of work on both houses will start next fall. Being a pretty good stone mason, and having plenty of field stones gathered over the years, the plan is to extend our basement south, build a stone limed stairway at the rear, starting inside the house, build a stone chimney and surround the rear of the house with 10" of stone. There will be one stone arch over one doorway. Stone arches are always fun to build. The stone work vill all have more or less horizontal coursing to look functional. While all this is going on, we might as well build, or at least rough in, a stone foundation for a sun-room. With a lot of rough plumbing to do, soil pipe, wastepipe, sewer pipe, water supply pipe, elevated cement tank, septic tank, tile drains, it will be at least a two year job.

JUN 1 All fruit crops look good. Stuart is a hardworker. We have never had the orchards in better shape, have even been hoeing out the grass around tree trunks. The young cherry trees are now of bearing age and we shall have a considerable crop, more than ten tons of sours and a ton of sweets. In apples only Levi's old trees are bearing. Young apple trees have only a scattering. But peaches! There's the bumper crop. How to get the cherries picked, the peaches thinned and finally harvested!

I have bought a Ford Model T truck. These long tedious haulings with horses are over, I hope. Neighbors say "You'll be sorry. The truck will jounce your fruit till its bruised beyond sale." They don't know I have ordered pneumatic tires with special rims that can be bolted on (the truck came with solid tires). And, too, the springs are soft under a load.

Lili is expecting again probably in January.

Father has had an ad in Chicago Tribune and has engaged for me four girls who like the idea of a vacation doing outdoor work. Two of these are college students, two are teachers. A week later two college boys are coming. They can all work in the cherry picking and the peach thinning and in hay time the boys can take a little of the hard work off our hands. We have a big hay crop. Many loads will come from the 35 acres I call the "Lee" farm, it being on an eastern slope away from the wind.

JUL 2 Every chance we get we pile onto the fruit-rack, and drawn by the horses, the whole crew, family with children, pickers, go to the beach after the days work. The girls fix up a picnic supper. We get back by 10 o'clock. Our breakfast bell rings at 7:00

JUL 30 This years cherry crop has really been a good one. It has brought in $2448. Expenses have been high, but if we get something from peaches I may be able to pay for the truck, and the car, and tools, fertilizer, spray chemical bills, etc. I don't expect to reduce the mortgage or the long line of old notes, but will be able to pay all interest, taxes, and insurance. Farming is a hell of a thing to get into. But what can I switch to? One aim now is to get out of debt and be able to look at a bank balance big enough to feel safe against a bad year or two.

AUG 18 We are lucky in our hired girls. The men quit after hay time. Both strong young fellows spent a great deal of time talking about sunburn and sore muscles. Birdie and Esther are becoming our good friends. Gladys Parnham is a striking, muscular, severly handsome, dark skinned, good natured girl with a light hint of the Maori blood coming from her mother who was born in New Zealand.

Mitchell vacationing at the Humps is quite taken by Gladys Parnham. Gladys Swanson is a pretty woman but my Lili outshines them all. Mitchell still unmarried says I'm lucky. I think so too.

SEP 3 The girls have gone back to school. The peach thinning was all done. This last week was more or less a loaf.

Stuart and I, with the help of Gladys Swanson's uncle, can handle the peach crop. Pears and apples wont take long.

OCT 25 All fruit is off, all money due is collected, all bills have been paid. Tomorrow Stuart and I become masons, carpenters, and plumbers. I shall hire an electrician. I wont study up in that trade

DEC 26 We had a grand Christmas yesterday. A feeling of security is with us if we can forget the mortgage and the long gruelling task ahead. Financial security visible sometime in the future does not remove the feeling of being sunk here in farming when art should be my life and the excuse for being.

Never the less, building will be fun. We have every partition removed in the first story and are camping within the house. It will be a long time before the house is put to rights. The plan has long been made. From the living room we can go to sunroom, hall, or dining room without passing thru any other room. From the dinning room we can go to hall, living room, or kitchen, without passing thru any other room. From kitchen we can go to stair hall, dinning room, or laundry without passing thru any room. The down- stairs bathroom is accessible from corridor connecting hall and studio room. Kitchen opens into that corridor.

I am helping Stuart on his house, so it can become comfortable. He can then get back to work on the farm. I expect to prune the permanent trees. Stuart can work on the peaches. The first year that pears and apples amount to anything I'll cut down the peach trees. Peach raising is not for me. We are the last county to get to market, so most years demand has about been satisfied by the time our peaches are ripe.

1921

JAN 3 With all this work going on I can't paint much. However, I am determined before the winter is over to finish this last "Loft" which will be in sequence with some of my recent things which reduce design to the bones of the theme and its related surroundings.

I must write to Walter Pach. He has been so good about writing and did so much for me in 1913 & 14 to get me out into view. Dudley Watson is also being neglected. With all his dispersed enthusiasm he did all he could to bring me notice.

It's a big laugh how I ever got onto a farm. The thought was developing over a good many months and was clinched after I met Lili. Here was a farm girl and here was a prospective farmer. This much is certain; farm life has its pleasures, but they are not the intense pleasure that art can bring. As to work, the two don't mix.

JAN 31 Yesterday the sweetest little girl was born to us—Carolyn. She is the strongest and most precocious of all three.

"Goodness gracious, for pity sakes, God dammit," as my Lithuanian neighbor says. I haven't written here for months, and yet notable things happen right along.

This hiatus has covered a dark period as far as painting went. The "Loft" was completed. One viewer calls it the most spiritual of my paintings. They are all spiritual!

DEC 7 Building, farming, sleeping, and eating kept me away from recording affairs either important or inconsequential.

We have made progress in building, the addition roofed temporarily with sheet roofing. It is difficult to lay tile in the kitchen without heat. Outside it is 15 degrees. After the floor is in, the range can be moved out into the new kitchen. With the space heater in the dining room we shall keep warm. At present we are sleeping in the living room. Partitions up-stairs are not complete.

Writing back and forth, the folks think it would be nice to spend Christmas and part of the winter with them at 4909 Dorchester Ave. They are renting a 3 story house there. It has two extra bed rooms that we can use.

1922

JAN 8 Here, we are at 4909 three weeks. Stuart driving the sled and team with tarpaulin rigged over the straw filled box had delivered us to the train. The children kept warm under the blankets. Evelyn Birdsall is with us. She has been a very necessary helper. All stood the trip well except Carolyn who is teething. The Chicago visit is an eye opener for all.

After getting settled the first thing I asked Father about was my carton of sketches and letters in the attic on 24th St. which ever since Father had moved, I had forgotten about. "What Carton?" It had been utterly overlooked. The house has been sold and torn down. I don't mind losing the sketches and small paintings but I'm sick about Davies letters and some of Pach's, and one very gracious letter of Prendergast's.

JAN 12 Walter says he would like to buy the Duchamp, but mentions a price that isn't tempting whatever. I would ask that much for one of my own. I am painting furiously up here on the top floor, accomplishing little.

JAN 21 Last week with 3 paintings under my arm, I showed these to Thurber's and to Anderson's—nothing doing. I wish I could have shown "Loft" either the carving or the painting. Both are at the farm. At Mitchell's office Carl Sandburg looked at them, one was the sketch for "Loft," and attached a word to "Loft." It has become "Prayer Loft." When I told him the title "Compaqes" for another, he said "Whatever that is, that's it."

While in the past year we were about breaking even, funds are low by winter time. I have sent Stuart his wages. I am tempted to sell the Duchamp "Nude." The larger family could well use the amount it would bring. Mitchell has not found anyone in Chi. who did not scoff at it and de- value it. Walter Pach still wants it. I'll ask more for it.

Lili and I have gone to two concerts and have attended a performance of LaBoheme at the Auditorium. What a wonderful theatre that is! Louis Sullivan somehow got perfect accoustics. We were in the balcony. I remember in the old days even a pin-drop could be heard in the second gallery.

FEB 12 Back on the farm. I had to leave my paintings in Father's den.

MAR 10 "Prayer Loft" and the Duchamp are in Pach's hands. "Prayer Loft" will be hung in the Waldorf in the "Independents." I have failed to get into catalogs at some shows, but this time was early enough to be listed.

MAR 29 Walter can't quite get the stark simplicity of my picture, but does say, "it has the indefinable air of being the work of an artist." "That is the most important thing."

Walter has met Jerry Blum at an exhibition he gave. He has written a few paragraphs on it for the "Freeman." He writes often for the "Freeman." In the April "Shadowland" he has an article on Maurice Prendergast and is almost thru the translation of the 2nd Vol. of Elie Faure's History of Art that Harpers is publishing

MAY 3 Walter has been in Chicago and had a chance to see some of my work at Father's house and at Mitchell's. He say he was delighted with it. He says "It was a big pleasure to see that work irrespective of who did it. *** There is the right inspirational quality, the right aloofness from dead matter, fine color, fine line, a personal note that rises above all reminiscences."

NOV 27 Dudley has written asking for another show at the Milwaukee Art Inst. on or about Jan 2. I start getting boxes ready right away.

DEC 25 Another fine day, with the day off between chores. Last week I shipped twenty seven paintings to Milwaukee. Some were old but not shown in Milwaukee before, some were new, only two of them within the year. I let Dudley take some liberties with the titles. In some cases these were not appropriate.

The show in Milwaukee can only have small things. I can't make large boxes. The family has to be fed and I am almost out of money. I can't say "no" to Dudley, yet I can't present my best stuff. I'm afraid the show will be a flop.

1939

JUL 23 So long out of mind it was a shock to see this book again. Though not forgotten, it has been lying in a stack of wood and card board sketches in back of paintings on the balcony. I had gone to fetch something to show cousin Martin and his friend Satula (?) I am stirred almost to rush to paint. But one of our biggest fruit crops is calling.

To look at the "Record," over these blank years, titles seem to be the only fun I was having. Very little painting or carving was done for more than a dozen years. Hi Simons didn't know when he objected to my titles that I didn't like them either. I can see that since 1922 titles don't mean anything. I guess they never did, but some of them bring back the feeling of satisfaction when a particular superb work was finished. I can remember the winter evenings with the children away from home, Lili sewing, myself chiseling, working on themes suggested by those pictures of Mexican sculpture that Mitchell sent with his last letter. (1933)

OCT 20 The last load of apples was hauled to Jebavy to-day. What a relief! This is early and I am already planning an unusual winter. The pruning was so thoro last winter that November's light trimming will see the orchard work done. This is the first time on the farm that I don't have to look forward to a long stretch of 7 day weeks working on tree tops.

Lili and I farmed this year with no help except pickers. She drove the tractor when we sprayed just as she many times drove the team during spraying or haying in former days.

A little repairing has been necessary in the barn. At the lumber yard I have seen some left over scraps of masonite which might be useful to paint on.

OCT 26 I have bought some 19" strips of masonite which I will cut up and prime for a winter of painting. It will be hard to begin but the many drawings on hand give a starting point and once lately I had a mental flash so clear and so right in color that I am itching to fix it in durable paint.

DEC 26 The kids are home for the holidays. Much joyous celebration more for family reunion than for X-mas took place. Gerard took out his violin and to-day with Carolyn at the piano played Beethovens violin concerto arranged for the piano. How they read such things by sight I don't know. Music is a great love of my life, but I can't play anything.

Mitchell and Rose have sent me Walter Pach's "Queer Thing Painting." He mentions me briefly but doesn't say a word about my painting although he has had such a series of views of my work ever since 1913. He must be very much displeased with me. He showed it a little when he wrote in letters that he was "going back to nature" and practically ordered me to do the same, feeling himself to be a docent and me a follower. A few years ago he had a falling out with Kuhn. I think they made it up. He must be peeved at me. Davies is a strong character and has always seemed to handle the Pach temperament.

How could Walter change his mind about my work and ignore me as a painter, make me only a "young architect?"

1940

MAR 16 Winter is ending and only six paintings have been brought to a satisfactory finish. More have been started and so far unspoiled. Let them rest. A good design can never be destroyed.

DEC 15 Coming in to a warm room after 8 hours in tree tops (temp. 5 degrees), I line up the paintings of the last dozen months. The display, to me, is thrilling. I can see what I can be doing when I get some relief. With the results of farming in the last six years I can see a break in the financial clouds that promises a clearing. All mortgages were paid up in '36. No debts are outstanding. A few gambles on the N.Y.S.E. have been successful. Bank cashier tells me if I need money all I have to do is sign my name.

Gerard is not likely to beome a farmer. He is contemplating enlisting in the Air force. Hope is established as a teacher. Carolyn has given up college for a while and is supporting herself working in Lansing.

Old age is a long way off yet!

D

APPENDIX 2

Transcription of Letters from Walter Pach to Manierre Dawson

Association of American Painters and Scultpors, Inc.
122 East Twenty-fifth Street, New York City

Arthur B. Davies, President
Elmer L. Macrae, Treasurer
John Mowbray-Clarke, Vice President
Walt Kuhn, Secretary

Telephone, Madison Square 7628
1135 Park Avenue
New York June 17th 1913

Dear Mr. Dawson,

With the most (it has been too congenial to call it worst) of the exhibition work behind me I am getting around to my own very gradually and am catching up a bit on my arrears of correspondence. So here goes,—mainly to get you to write me, for I am ever so interested to know if the questions you were pondering when I last saw you have found an answer yet. Speaking of that time in Chicago, there is a man named Von Frantzius (spelling not certain) whom you might do well to locate. He is a broker, very well-to-do, I believe, and an art (?) collector. If you don't trace him through those details, Mr. Giddings of the Institute will tell you at once where he is. But perhaps the reason for my not writing you of him at once will deter you from wanting to know of him. The reason for speaking of him at all is that he said he would give $200 for your Duchamp. But he hates the Cubists and just wanted the picture "as a joke, to show his friends." I was so sure that you would want nothing to do with him that I did not write about him specially and put it off till I should write you a general friendly letter which I expected to do sooner. Still it is best that you should know of Von Frantzius (who is not without interest, as an individual—a hard-headed but thick-skulled German, rather common, obstinate, but sort of vigorous). It might be a way of realizing on your purchase quickly (if he hasn't changed at that never-to-be-reached, I-hope, epoch).

Well, the picture looked very well in Boston and I got to like it better and better.[1] Once in my endlessly-applied for explanations, I made up a romantic libretto for it. I said that (if they had to have a subject for it) they should take it as inspired by some experience that would be written about by a poet as a person coming out of the darkness into one's life and being very strong and important there for a time and then going slowly back again. That doesn't seem even pretty as I write it, but I believe I had enthusiasm enough as I stood before the pictures to carry quite a few people over the line. I got trickier and trickier; one mean stunt I worked several times was to ask people what they thought of those lines at the end of Twelfth Night (not telling them what it was). "When that I was a little, little boy" etc. and when they said it was just nonsense, I would say that Shakespeare wrote it and show them that "unreasonable things" like this work and the Cubists' could be good. I met some fine people in Boston, with many thousand rotters and gapers of course, but New York was the only place for sales.

I started this letter before lunch; just afterward the post-man rang and as I went down stairs I thought it would be just the way things sometimes happen if I got a letter from you. When I saw the post-mark I should have been tremendously surprised if it hadn't been from you—and it was, and I was ever so glad to get it. Now that you have answered my questions about externals and also now that you see I wasn't forgetting to write, I hope you'll feel sometime like writing about the other matters you had in mind. I shall be powerfully interested in the art-ideas you speak of and will show myself a fair correspondent—though sometimes I let a certain (?) amount of time elapse between letters. I guess it won't be too long though for I shall want to say what I think of the matter and probably get a reply from you soon. I certainly do wish you all kinds of luck with the bank decorating.[2] It will be great to have something to do for a particular place and I am sure you will make a success of it. While I don't know the conditions of your standing with those people, I have found that a French proverb one of the my old professors used to tell me, "Il faut se valoir," has often stood me in good stead. I don't believe in giving the idea that one is less anxious for a job than one is, but if you can let them know that it is of importance to them (financially or artistically) to have you do the work, you can make better terms—either for money or for freedom in carrying out your ideas.

I am skipping days now in going down to our office and working to close the business of the exhibition, but up to last week I was at it pretty steadily and what time I have had for myself I have more or less frittered away (if I may call friendly visits, letter-writing, sightseeing and resting up that). I have quite a bunch of literary work to do now and while on that shall look around for futures and so decide whether I'm to stay in this country or do back to Paris. It isn't an easy question. I feel that Paris is incomparable for pulling one along,—but I might do well anyhow to stay here a while and get to painting at once, and solidify myself financially. I think I should be about decided in a month, though perhaps it would take till the fall to make my plans. I'll let you know naturally, when they are formed.

Please give my kindest good wishes to your family. Last night I went for the first time to play violin with a friend who accompanies, and I took along my batch of little Italian songs, it was good to hear them again, even played, but it would have been better if there had been some one like your father to sing them.

Now I must get at my article, so good-bye.

Yours cordially
Walter Pach

1135 Park Avenue, New York,
Dec. 10th 1913

Dear friend Dawson,

I have your two letters with the good news that you will show with us.[3] We are all showing three things (or more where they are very small) so send on three to Arthur B. Davies, c/o The Artists' Packing & Shipping Co., 139 West 54th St. N.Y. They should be here by the 31st of December. (If there were more time I'd let you know but I think there won't be). If you got a picture later on that you wanted to substitute for one of these at a subsequent exhibition it could be done. We'll have a number of such cases, everyone is moving on so much. I want to give you Davies' address in case I were called away, but please keep it altogether for yourself as he does not like to have it in too many people's hands—"bores" are so likely to get hold of you and encroach on your time,—337 East 57th St.

Pittsburgh is having a fine time with the show. The papers are sort of impressed though they don't understand much. Send your things as soon as you like, I'm awfully anxious to see them.

Yours cordially,
Walter Pach

13 East 14th St.
New York, February 4th 1919

Dear friend Dawson,

For a long time I have [been] thinking that I must not lose sight of you entirely, and just of late an incident occurred that brought back to my mind my resolution to write. I will come to that phase of my letter at once and then go on to the personal side.

The friend in the west who bought Duchamp's "Nude descending a Staircase" needed to lay hands on some money (I imagine he must have needed it pretty much) and wrote to ask if I could sell the picture for him. There are only a few people today who would but it, but as I know several of them at least, I was able to send him his check in a few days, with only the one regret that I was not able to keep the picture myself. Now I do not think of you as wanting to dispose of your Duchamp, but if things ever turn out so that you did want to, I wish you would write me of it. In this case of last week, I did not expect or want any commission, and as the former owner of the picture is a very good friend of mine, I do not think it has occurred to him to offer me one,—I hope it does not. But, I was anxious to see the picture in good hands and so was glad that he addressed himself to me. I think of Duchamp's work as something very important, more so even than I did in 1913 and I should hate to see any examples of it in the hands of people who would bury it in a dead place where no-one got any pleasure or benefit from it. (One or two persons would keep a place out of that category, so you will not think I am speaking of Ludington).[4] So there,—I do not imagine, as I said, that you have any idea of parting with the picture, but I wanted to give you this as a memorandum in case the question ever arose with you.

Well, how are you? The last I heard was of your settling down to the joys of family life in the country and had not yet gotten around to working out the pictures I remember writing you for. Have you done so since, or are the "things" finding other outlets? They must be somewhere, even if it is just tumbling around in your mind.

I certainly have a lot of wheels going in my head. Sometimes I think they are a commonplace lot, just revolving along the old dull lines and that even the names people gave them some years ago are not very fresh anymore. Other times I can think (praise goodness!) that I am getting on, in however slow a way, and that what I have done is solid and can be built on in the years ahead of me. The devilish job is still to get those years free of the material encumbrances. This winter has been the worst in that respect, for ten years. The job of earning a living [is] taking so much of my time that I have hardly had any chance to paint. I don't exactly see where relief is to come from but somehow I hope that things are not going to be as tough again. Right after peace came, people began to buy a few pictures again.

The wife and boy are well and we are all the best kind of friends. Master Raymond is now four and is lively, inquisitive and generally interesting. The wife holds out well, despite the bumps of artist-life and is a good chum.

I hope all your family are well and that some day you may be able to look in on us. Do write soon.

Yours very sincerely,
Walter Pach.

The Stratford Hotel
Michigan Ave. and Jackson Blvd.
Chicago

April 30, 1922

Dear Dawson,

I am out here through a curious chain of circumstances—not worth taking time to tell.

What I want to write you—at once—is that through the kindness of your brother Mitchell, I was able to see your work last night—at his house and your father's. I was delighted with it. After that pale and gloomy letter I wrote you from New York you can see that I am not a "complimenteur" as Cézanne called them.[5] No, it was a big pleasure to see that work entirely irrespective of who did it. I do not take back what I said of the Independent picture, I just think it was almost the least successful choice you could have made,—nine-tenths of your work pleased me more, including (very decidedly) the other picture on this theme that you did. Yet I see why you might incline to this as theoretically the most advanced of your work. I still feel it as unsubstantial and the same quality ran through a number (by no means all) of the works I saw last night.

To get done with the things in this vein: I had been holding on to your picture to show Duchamp[6]—he came down, finally, a night or two before I left, saw his own picture for the first time in nearly ten years, studied it with great attention and seemingly with satisfaction and wrote its proper name, "Jeune Homme triste dans un Train," on the back.[7] He was much interested in your picture but said it has not gone far enough, that there was not enough there for a final opinion etc. Like myself, he hesitated how much he could pay.

I am confident he would have been as different as I when I saw your things last night, had he been there. There is the right inspirational quality, the right aloofness from dead matter, fine color, fine line, a personal note that rises above all reminiscences, a few times completeness (as in a green picture with two trees, a brown abstract picture and especially in a wood interior (see sketch) of very finely proportioned and controlled masses (foreground brown-red, I think).

I am glad to have come to Chicago if only for seeing those works. (I did enjoy being with your brother and sister-in-law so much, also.)

Your brother told me of the way you had dashed off that bunch of work and I am sure it was what you needed to do at the time. It is dangerous for me to say anything of the other way of working: to go over and over a canvas till it has reached saturation, because that is the way I have been trying to do in recent years and I may so easily be speaking of my own needs under the illusion that I am discussing yours. Still I will risk saying I think you can get something—sometime—by that method even if it is not what you want to do now. I must mention the pleasure I had in a drawing of two heads bending over. I shall return your painting when I get back to New York. I left unexpectedly and had no time, after Duchamp was there, to have the picture boxed and shipped. I wish I could go home by way of Ludington but fear I must not: I have been away now much longer than I expected, must stay at least till Thursday and the work that's waiting for me in New York is sinful to think of.

With good wishes,
Yours cordially
Walter Pach

Once more,—I do not attach undue importance to my opinion of people's work. I just thought that being alone as you are it might be of some interest to you, whatever its value.

Pennsylvania Railroad
En Route

New address: 48 West 56 St.
New York, January 11, 1927

Dear friend Dawson,

Perhaps your brother has let you know sometimes of my visits to Chicago, but this time I have had one that included a meeting with your mother and father—for the first time in fourteen years—so I want to write you a word about it myself. The word is mainly that I found them astonishingly like my memory of them in 1913. And I do remember that evening at your house well—and with the greatest pleasure. Today I spoke for the No Jury Society and your mother paid me the compliment of attending the lecture—which was kind of her. I wish you could have been in town. I don't know how hard it may be for you to get to Chicago, but for the next ten days or so Marcel Duchamp will be there. He is running the Brancusi show at the Arts Club, and being run after by all sorts of people. I had him out at your brother's house for a short visit which I hope will lead to a better acquaintance.[8] Marcel is a rare person; I can not reconcile myself to his abstaining from painting, especially as his mind remains so clear and strong.

And what of yourself? It is long since I have had news of you. Is there any daylight ahead in the matter of your getting off the farm? Perhaps you don't call that daylight but I am a more confirmed big-town man than ever and I could not imagine myself in the country for so long. Are you anywhere near Ann Arbor? A friend of mine is lecturing there for two or three weeks. He is Lewis Mumford, author of "Sticks and Stones" (American architecture, a real fine book) and just lately "The Golden Day," (American thought and literature—a corking book). If you could meet him (and he would be delighted to see you) you would meet one of the most brilliant and likeable men I know.

I get more time to paint than formerly and have made progress. Interruptions still cut in badly enough, to be sure. Last summer I ran New York University's summer school at the Louvre. That gave me a couple of months in Paris and the sight of lots of art, ancient and modern, but no painting for me. They want me to do it again this summer and I may, but I'd really prefer to stay in my nice studio and paint steadily. The boy goes to camp in the summer now, he is just twelve and growing up nicely. The wife gets to be a better pal than ever. And we go on buying pictures when we can, which is not very often. But we got a Matisse last summer that is a big thing: he grows; his last work is tremendous.

I have always had a remainder of doubt in my mind about not letting you give me a picture that time. I saw one at your brother's that I did not know—an old one, that was very fine.

Do let me hear from you one day. With many good wishes to yourself and your family, I am

Yours cordially,
Walter Pach

Notes

1. Pach is referring to the Marcel Duchamp painting that Dawson bought from the Armory Show in Chicago. The painting traveled with the exhibition to Boston before he took possession.

2. Dawson had been contacted by C.G. Wing, President of the Ludington State Bank, Ludington, Michigan, and a college friend of Dawson's father about painting a mural in the lobby of the new bank building then being planned. Dawson exchanged letters with Wing through 1913 and 1914, but the project was never realized.

3. Through a letter from Pach, Davies had invited Dawson to participate in an exhibition he was organizing for the Montross Gallery, New York. Dawson sent two paintings and a charcoal drawing.

4. Dawson's Duchamp painting hung in his father's house in Chicago from mid-1913 until he was settled in his own house on his farm in 1915. At the writing of this letter, the Duchamp and the Amadéo de Souza Cardoso which Dawson also bought from the Armory show, were hanging in his farmhouse near Ludington, Michigan.

5. Dawson apparently did not save "that pale and gloomy letter" to which Pach refers, however, he did record in his journal that "Walter can't quite get the stark simplicity of my picture but does say 'it has the indefinable air of being the work of an artist.'" Dawson, journal, March 29, 1922.

6. Here Pach is referring to Dawson's submission to the Society of Independent Artists exhibition.

7. Pach had repeatedly hinted that he wanted to buy Dawson's Duchamp. In January 1922 he made an offer which Dawson accepted. He sent the painting to Pach in March with his submission to the Society of Independent Artists exhibition. Duchamp's inscription of "Jeune Homme triste dans un Train" and his signature survive on the back of the painting in the Peggy Guggenheim Collection, Venice. Angelica Zander Rudenstein, *Peggy Guggenheim Collection, Venice.* (New York: Harry N. Abrams, Inc. Publishers, 1985) pp. 259–260.

8. Dawson's brother Mitchell and Marcel Duchamp did exchange letters at least once after Pach introduced them. A letter dated February 15, 1927 from Duchamp to Mitchell Dawson in the Mitchell Dawson Papers, Newberry Library, Chicago.

SELECTED BIBILOGRAPHY

ARCHIVAL MATERIAL

Dawson, George E. *Autobiography of George E. Dawson.* Privately printed, Peter Lockwood Collection, Arlington, Tex., n.d.

———. *The Dawson Family.* Privately printed, Peter Lockwood Collection, Arlington, Tex., 1932.

Dawson, George E. and Eva (Manierre) Dawson. *The Manierre Family.* Privately printed, Peter Lockwood Collection, Arlington, Tex., n.d.

Dawson, Manierre. Journal, 1908–1940. Manierre Dawson Papers, Archives of American Art, Smithsonian Institution, Washington, D.C.

———.Record of Painting and Sculpture. Manierre Dawson Papers, Archives of American Art, Smithsonian Institution, Washington, D.C.

———. Correspondence with Robert Schoelkopf. Robert Schoelkopf Papers, Archives of American Art, Smithsonian Institution, Washington, D.C.

———. Correspondence with Tracy Atkinson. Milwaukee Art Museum, Milwaukee, Wis.

———. Correspondence with Karl Nickel. John and Mable Ringling Museum of Art, Sarasota, Fla.

———. Correspondence with E. Robert Hunter. Norton Museum of Art, West Palm Beach, Fla.

Manierre, George Jr. Manierre Family Scrapbook. Chicago Historical Society Collection, Chicago.

Manierre, Edward. "Old Days in Chicago: Stories from Edward Manierre." Typescript, Chicago Historical Society Collection, Chicago, n.d.

Pach, Walter, Dudley Crafts Watson, Jerome Blum, C.G.Wing, and Hi Simmons. Correspondence with Manierre Dawson. Manierre Dawson Papers, Archives of American Art, Smithsonian Institution, Washington, D.C.

PUBLICATIONS ABOUT THE ARTIST

Bessire, Mark H., and Mary Jo Peer. *Manierre Dawson: Early Abstractionist.* New York: Whitney Museum of American Art, 1988.

Davidson, Abraham. "Two from the Second Decade: Manierre Dawson and John Covert," *Art in America* 63, no. 5 (September–October 1975): 50–55.

Gedo, Mary Mathews. *Manierre Dawson: A Retrospective Exhibition of Paintings.* Chicago: Museum of Contemporary Art, 1976.

———. "Manierre Dawson: The Prophet in His Own Country." *American Art Review* 4, no. 3 (December 1977): 65–76, 121–125.

———. "Modernizing the Masters: Manierre Dawson's Cubist Transliterations." *Arts Magazine* 55, no. 8 (April 1981): 135–45.

———. *Manierre Dawson: Paintings, 1910–1914.* New York: Robert Schoelkopf Gallery, Ltd., 1981.

———. "The Secret Idol: Manierre Dawson and Pablo Picasso." *Arts Magazine* 56, no. 4 (December 1981): 116–24.

Hey, Kenneth R. "Manierre Dawson: A Fix on the Phantoms of the Imagination." *Archives of American Art Journal* 14, no. 4 (1974): 7–12.

Kramer, Hilton. "Art: Manierre Dawson, a Kandinsky." Review of exhibition at Schoelkopf Gallery. *New York Times,* April 10, 1981, 19.

Manierre Dawson. Sarasota, Fla: Sarasota Art Association, 1975.

Nickel, Karl. *Manierre Dawson: Paintings 1909–1913.* Sarasota, Fla.: John and Mable Ringling Museum of Art, 1967.

———. *Manierre Dawson: Painting 1909–1913.* New York: Robert Schoelkopf Gallery Ltd., 1969.

Ploog, Randy J. "Manierre Dawson: A Chicago Pioneer of Abstract Painting." Ph.D. diss., Pennsylvania State University, 1996.

———. "The Chicago Sources of Manierre Dawson's First Abstract Paintings." *Block Points 3* (Evanston, Ill.: Block Museum, Northwestern University, 1999).

Powell, Earl A. III. "Manierre Dawson's 'Woman in Brown.'" *Arts Magazine* 51, no. 1 (September 1976): 76–77.

Retrospective: Paintings by Manierre Dawson. Grand Rapids, Mich.: Grand Rapids Art Museum, 1966.

GENERAL REFERENCES

Agee, William C. *Modern American Painting 1910–1940: Toward a New Perspective.* Houston, Tex.: The Museum of Fine Arts, 1977.

Avant-Garde Painting and Sculpture in America, 1910–1925. Wilmington, Del.: Delaware Art Museum, 1975.

Brown, Milton W. *The Story of the Armory Show.* New York: Abbeville Press, 1988.

Coyle, Laura. "Amadeo and America." *At the Edge: A Portuguese Futurist—Amadeo de Souza Cardoso.* Lisbon: Office of International Relations, Ministry of Culture, 1999.

Davidson, Abraham A. *Early American Modernist Painting, 1910–1935.* New York: Harper and Row, 1981.

The Emergence of Modernism in Illinois, 1914–1940. Springfield, Ill.: Illinois State Museum, 1976.

Exhibition of Paintings and Sculptures. New York: Montross Gallery, 1914.

Gerdts, William H. *Art Across America: Two Centuries of Regional Painting in America, 1710–1920,* vol. 2. New York: Abbeville Press, 1990.

———. *The Color of Modernism: The American Fauves.* New York: Hollis Taggart Galleries, 1997.

Haskell, Barbara. *The American Century: Art & Culture, 1900–1950.* New York: Whitney Museum of American Art, in association with W. W. Norton & Company, 1999.

Hey, Kenneth R. "Five Artists and the Chicago Modernist Movement, 1909–1928." Ph.D. diss., Emory University, 1973.

McCarthy, Laurette E. "The Modernists on Tour: A New Look at a Historic Show." *Archive of American Art Journal* 37, nos. 3 and 4 (1997): 2–16.

Levin, Gail, and Marianne Lorenz, eds. *Theme and Improvisation: Kandinsky and the American Avant-Garde.* Dayton, Oh.: Dayton Art Institute, 1992.

Mellon, James R. *Charmed Circle: Gertrude Stein and Company.* New York: Avon Books, 1974.

Milwaukee Art Society. *Exhibition of Paintings and Sculptures in "The Modern Spirit."* Milwaukee, Wis.: Milwaukee Art Society, 1914.

Pach, Walter. *Queer Thing, Painting: Forty Years in the World of Art.* New York and London: Harper and Brothers Publishers, 1938.

Ploog, Randy J. "Yesterday's City: Critiquing Cubism." *Chicago History: The Magazine of the Chicago Historical Society* 23, no. 2 (fall 1994): 58–72.

Prince, Sue Ann, ed. *The Old Guard and the Avant-Garde: Modernism in Chicago, 1910–1940.* Chicago and London: University of Chicago Press, 1990.

Rand, Harry. "Gorky's Waterfalls (1943)." *Artnews* 96, no. 10 (November 1997): 118–122.

Recent Acquisitions. Springfield, Ill.: Illinois State Museum, 1981.

Rudensteine, Angelica Zander. *Peggy Guggenheim Collection, Venice.* New York: Harry N. Abrams, Inc., 1985.

Sheon, Aaron. "1913: Forgotten Cubist Exhibitions in America." *Arts Magazine* 57, no. 7 (March 1983): 93–107.

Watson, Dudley Crafts. "Recent Notable Exhibitions." *The Art Bulletin* (Milwaukee Art Institute) 24 (February 1923): 2.

DR. HENRY ADAMS a noted scholar of Thomas Hart Benton, currently serves as Curator of American Art at the Cleveland Museum of Art and Professor of American Art at Case Western Reserve University. He has published over a hundred articles in scholarly and popular journals, and has served as a curator at the Carnegie Museum of Art in Pittsburgh, Pennsylvania; the Nelson-Atkins Museum of Art in Kansas City, Missouri; and the Cummer Museum of Art in Jacksonville, Florida.

DR. RANDY J. PLOOG who wrote his doctoral dissertation on Manierre Dawson, is the Associate Director of the Institute for the Arts and Humanistic Studies at Pennsylvania State University. He has served as Curator of American and Contemporary Art at the Palmer Art Museum in University Park, Pennsylvania, and has contributed articles to many art-related publications.

HOLLIS TAGGART GALLERIES

48 East 73rd Street New York City 10021 Tel 212 628 4000 Fax 212 717 4119

Web site and Email: www.HollisTaggart.com Monday to Friday 10 to 5, Saturday 11 to 5